Introducing Distributed Application Runtime (Dapr)

Simplifying Microservices Applications Development Through Proven and Reusable Patterns and Practices

Radoslav Gatev

Foreword by Yaron Schneider,
Principal Software Engineer and Dapr co-founder, Microsoft

Apress®

Introducing Distributed Application Runtime (Dapr): Simplifying Microservices
Applications Development Through Proven and Reusable Patterns and Practices

Radoslav Gatev
Gorna Oryahovitsa, Bulgaria

ISBN-13 (pbk): 978-1-4842-6997-8   ISBN-13 (electronic): 978-1-4842-6998-5
https://doi.org/10.1007/978-1-4842-6998-5

Managing Director, Apress Media LLC: Welmoed Spahr
Acquisitions Editor: Joan Murray
Development Editor: Laura Berendson
Coordinating Editor: Jill Balzano

Cover image designed by Freepik (www.freepik.com)

Distributed to the book trade worldwide by Springer Science+Business Media LLC, 1 New York Plaza, Suite 4600, New York, NY 10004. Phone 1-800-SPRINGER, fax (201) 348-4505, e-mail orders-ny@springer-sbm.com, or visit www.springeronline.com. Apress Media, LLC is a California LLC and the sole member (owner) is Springer Science + Business Media Finance Inc (SSBM Finance Inc). SSBM Finance Inc is a **Delaware** corporation.

For information on translations, please e-mail booktranslations@springernature.com; for reprint, paperback, or audio rights, please e-mail bookpermissions@springernature.com.

Apress titles may be purchased in bulk for academic, corporate, or promotional use. eBook versions and licenses are also available for most titles. For more information, reference our Print and eBook Bulk Sales web page at http://www.apress.com/bulk-sales.

Any source code or other supplementary material referenced by the author in this book is available to readers on GitHub via the book's product page, located at www.apress.com/9781484269978. For more detailed information, please visit http://www.apress.com/source-code.

Printed on acid-free paper

To my girlfriend Desislava who supports me unconditionally.

Table of Contents

About the Author

Radoslav Gatev is a software architect and consultant who specializes in designing and building complex and vast solutions in Microsoft Azure. He helps companies all over the world, ranging from startups to big enterprises, to have highly performant and resilient applications that utilize the cloud in the best and most efficient way possible. Radoslav has been awarded a Microsoft Most Valuable Professional (MVP) for Microsoft Azure for his ongoing contributions to the community in this area. He strives for excellence and enjoyment when working on the bleeding edge of technology and is excited to work with Dapr. He frequently speaks and presents at various conferences and participates in organizing multiple technical conferences in Bulgaria.

About the Technical Reviewer

As a freelance Microsoft technologies expert, **Kris van der Mast** helps his clients to reach their goals. Actively involved in the global community, he is a Microsoft MVP since 2007 for ASP.NET and since 2016 for two disciplines: Azure and Visual Studio and Development Technologies. Kris is also a Microsoft ASP Insider, Microsoft Azure Advisor, aOS ambassador, and Belgian Microsoft Extended Experts Team (MEET) member. In the Belgian community, Kris is active as a board member of the Belgian Azure User Group (AZUG) and is Chairman of the Belgian User Group (BUG) Initiative. Since he started with .NET back in 2002, he's also been active on the ASP.NET forums where he is also a moderator. His personal site can be found at www.krisvandermast.com. Kris is a public (inter) national speaker and is a co-organizer of the CloudBrew conference.

Personal note:

While doing a book review, I also like to learn new things on the go. With this book I sure did. I hope you will enjoy reading it at least as much as I did.

Foreword

In the year leading up to the first release of Dapr as an open source project in October 2019, Haishi Bai (my partner in co-founding Dapr) and I observed just how much the cloud-native space had matured. It had grown to provide ops and infrastructure teams with first-class tools to run their workloads either on premises or in the cloud.

With the rise of Kubernetes (K8s), an entire ecosystem of platforms has sprung up to provide the missing pieces for network security, traffic routing, monitoring, volume management, and more.

Yet, something was missing.

The mission statement to make infrastructure "boring" was being realized, but for developers, many if not all of the age-old challenges around distributed computing continued to exist in cloud-native platforms, especially in microservice workloads where complexity grows with each service added.

This is where Dapr comes in. First and foremost a developer-facing tool, Dapr focuses on solving distributed systems challenges for cloud-native developers. But just like any new technology, it's critical to be able to understand its uses, features, and capabilities.

This book by Radoslav Gatev is the authoritative, technical, hands-on resource you need to learn Dapr from the ground up. Up to date with version 1.0 of Dapr, this book gives you all you need to know about the Dapr building blocks and APIs (Application Programming Interfaces), when and how to use them, and includes samples in multiple languages to get you started quickly. In addition to the Dapr APIs, you'll also find important information about how to debug Dapr-enabled applications, which is critical to running Dapr in production.

Radoslav has extensive, in-depth knowledge of Dapr and is an active Dapr contributor, participating in the Dapr community and helping others learn to use it as well. He makes the project better by working with maintainers to report issues and contribute content.

You really can't go wrong with this book, and I highly recommend it to anyone who wants to start developing applications with Dapr.

Yaron Schneider

Principal Software Engineer and Dapr Co-founder, Microsoft

Acknowledgments

In every venture uncommon to a self, there should be a great catalyst. I would like to thank Apress and especially Joan Murray, Jill Balzano, Laura Berendson, Welmoed Spahr, and everyone else involved in the publishing of this book. I had been thinking about writing a book for quite some time, and I am grateful that Joan reached out to me. At that moment I had a few conferences canceled, a few professional opportunities lost because of the risks and the great uncertainty at the start of COVID-19. Fast-forward a year from then, the book has been finished, and I am writing this. A year of lockdowns spent in writing is a good year, after all.

Additionally, I would like to thank Mark Russinovich for being such an inspiration and knowledge source for me. Sometimes, it takes just a tweet to change the life of a person. He retweeted a blog post of mine about Dapr. It gained a lot of attention, and to a large extent, because of that, *Introducing Distributed Application Runtime (Dapr)* is now a reality. I would like to thank Yaron Schneider and all Dapr maintainers who are always friendly and supportive. They helped a lot by answering some of the questions I've had in the process.

I would also like to thank Kris van der Mast, the technical reviewer, for the excellent feedback and suggestions that added immense value to this book.

I would like to thank Mihail Mateev who gave me the opportunity to do my first public session a couple of years ago. Since then, we have been collaborating with a lot of other folks to make some of the biggest conferences in Bulgaria possible. Of course, thanks to the community that still finds them interesting, and from the fascinating discussions, they sparkle. I would like to thank Martin Tatar, Cristina González Herrero, and Irene Otero for their great help and continuous support to us, the Microsoft Most Valuable Professionals.

I would like to thank Dimitar Mazhlekov with whom we have been friends, teammates, business partners, and tech junkies. We have walked a long way and learned a lot together.

I would like to thank all my teachers, professors, and mentors who supported me a lot throughout the years. To find a good teacher is a matter of luck. And with you all, I am the lucky person for being your student.

ACKNOWLEDGMENTS

I would like to express my gratitude for being able to work with organizations around the globe that gave me exposure to their unique and intriguing challenges that helped me gain so much knowledge and experience. Thanks to all the team members I met there and for what I was able to learn from every one of them.

And last but not least, to my girlfriend Desislava, my parents, extended family, and friends, thank you for the endless support throughout the years! Thank you for keeping me sane and forgiving my absence when I get to work on something challenging.

Introduction

Being able to work on various projects, one should be able to identify the common set of issues every project faces. It doesn't mean you can always apply the same solution over and over again, but it puts a good structure. I was very lucky that early in my career, I was pointed to the proper things to learn. I have already been using object-oriented programming (OOP) for some time, but I was stunned when I read the book *Design Patterns: Elements of Reusable Object-Oriented Software* by Gamma, Helm, Johnson, and Vlissides for the first time. It gave me the answers to some of the questions I'd been asking myself. From there on, I am a strong believer that patterns do not only serve as reusable solutions to common problems, they become a common lingo and teach you how to think in an abstract way. Being able to work at a conceptual level, instead of focusing too much on the details, I believe made me a better professional.

I heard of Distributed Application Runtime (Dapr) for the first time when it was announced at Microsoft Ignite 2019, Microsoft's annual conference for developers and IT professionals. At first, the idea of it resonated within me but I didn't completely understand it, and so I decided to start playing with it. In September 2020, a transition to an open governance model was announced to ensure that the project is open and vendor neutral. Fast-forward to February 2021 when Dapr v1.0 was released. Now that Dapr is stable and production-ready, it is also in the process of being donated to the Cloud Native Computing Foundation (CNCF) as an Incubation project. By the time you read this, it may be finalized.

Dapr greatly simplifies the development of Microservices applications. It works with any language and any platform. You can containerize your applications or not, you can use Kubernetes or not, you can deploy to the cloud or not. You can sense the freedom here. From a development perspective, Dapr offers a number of capabilities grouped and packaged as building blocks. Let's face it. You will have to use some services that are external to the application you are aiming to build. It is very normal to not try to reinvent the wheel and build everything from scratch. By using the building blocks provided by Dapr, you use those external services without thinking about any SDKs or specific concepts imposed by the external service you are trying to integrate with. You just have to know how to work with the building block. This simplifies the operations you want to execute on the target external services, and Dapr serves as the common denominator. That's why you can swap one technology with another in the scope of the building block, that is, reconfiguring Dapr from persisting state to, say, Redis to MySQL, for example.

Some believe Dapr is the service mesh but done right. The reason for that is that service meshes rely on the sidecar architecture as Dapr does. However, service meshes are for network infrastructure, while Dapr provides reusable patterns that are easy to apply and repeatable. In the future, I expect building blocks to expand in functionality and maybe new building blocks to come to Dapr. With that, the reach to potential external services will become so wide. For greenfield projects, this will mean that Dapr can be put on the foundational level of decisions. Once you have it, you can, later on, decide what specific message broker or what specific persistence medium to use for state storage, for example. This level of freedom unlocks many opportunities.

Introducing Distributed Application Runtime (Dapr) aims to be your guide to learning Dapr and using it for the first time. Some previous experience building distributed systems will be helpful but is by no means required. The book is divided into three parts. In the first part before diving into Dapr, a chapter is devoted to set the ground for the basic concepts of Microservices applications. The following chapter introduces Dapr: how it works and how to initialize and run it locally. The next chapter covers the basics of containers and Kubernetes. Then all that knowledge is combined in order to explore how Dapr works inside Kubernetes. The part wraps up by exploring the various options to develop and debug Dapr applications, by leveraging the proper Visual Studio code extensions – both locally and inside Kubernetes.

The second part of the book has a chapter devoted to each building block that explores it in detail. The building blocks are:

- Service Invocation

- Publish and Subscribe

- State Management

- Resource Bindings

- The Actor model

- Secrets

- Observability

The final part of the book is about integrating Dapr with other technologies. The first chapter outlines what middleware can be plugged into the request pipeline of Dapr. Some of the middleware enable using protocols like the OAuth2 Client Credentials and Authentication Code grants and OpenID Connect with various Identity Providers that support them. The examples in the chapter use Azure Active Directory. The following chapter discusses how to use Dapr with ASP.NET Core by leveraging the useful attributes that come from the Dapr .NET SDK. The last two chapters cover how to combine Dapr with the runtimes of Azure Functions and Azure Logic Apps.

Code samples accompany almost every chapter of the book. Most of them are implemented in C#, but there are a few of them in Node.js, to emphasize the multiple-language approach to microservices. You can find them at `https://github.com/Apress/introducing-dapr`. You will need to have .NET and Node.js installed. Some of the tips and tricks in the book are applicable only to Visual Studio Code (e.g., the several extensions that are covered in Chapter 5: Debugging Dapr Applications), but you can also use any code editor or IDE like Visual Studio. For some of the examples, you will also need Docker on your machine and any Kubernetes cluster – either locally, as part of Docker Desktop, or somewhere in the cloud.

I hope you enjoy the book. Good luck on your learning journey. Let's start Daprizing! I am happy to connect with you on social media:

LinkedIn: `www.linkedin.com/in/radoslavgatev/`

Twitter: `https://twitter.com/RadoslavGatev`

Feel free to also check my blog: `www.gatevnotes.com`.

PART I

Getting Started

CHAPTER 1

Introduction to Microservices

Digitalization drives businesses in such a direction that every system should be resilient and available all the time. In order to achieve that, you have to make certain decisions about the application architecture. In this chapter, you will learn how systems evolved from calculation machines built to serve a specific purpose to general-purpose computers. Making the same parallel but on the software side, we will discuss what Monolithic applications are along with their pros and cons. Then, we will go through the need of having distributed applications dispersed across a network of computers. You will also learn about the Microservices architecture as a popular way for building distributed applications – how to design such applications, what challenges the Microservices architecture brings, and some of the applicable patterns that are often used.

A Brief History of System Design

It's always good to take a look back at history to understand how the concepts have evolved over time making almost every innovation by building on the existing knowledge and experience. There has been a long way for computers until you could walk with a computing device in the pocket or on the wrist.

The first computing devices were entirely mechanical,[1] operating with components like levers, belts, gears, and so on to perform their logic. That's a lot of moving parts that

---

[1]The first mechanical computer is considered to be the Difference Engine that was designed by Charles Babbage in the 1820s for calculating and tabulating the values of polynomial functions. Later on, he devised another machine called the Analytical Engine that aimed to perform general-purpose computation. The concepts it was to employ can be found in modern computers, although it was designed to be entirely mechanical.

© Radoslav Gatev 2021
R. Gatev, *Introducing Distributed Application Runtime (Dapr)*, https://doi.org/10.1007/978-1-4842-6998-5_1

3

take a lot of space. Apart from the slowness of their operation, each of them was a point of failure on its own. But over time, the mechanical parts started getting replaced by their electric counterparts.

Hardware Progress

To perform some logic, you need some way of representing state – like 1 and 0 in the modern binary computers. Likewise, the relay was identified as a viable component that was widely known and available to be utilized for performing the "on" and "off" switching. But still, relays were rather slow as they had a moving mechanical part – an electromagnet opens or closes a metal contact between two conductors. Then *vacuum tubes* gained traction as a way of switching. They didn't have any moving parts; however, they were still big, expensive, and nonefficient. Then they got replaced by *transistors*. But imagine what is soldering thousands of discrete transistors in a complex circuit! There will be faulty wirings that are hard to discover. Later on, the need for soldering discrete transistors was avoided with *integrated circuits* where thousands of tiny transistors were placed on small chips. This ultimately led the way to modern *microprocessor* technology. These evolutionary steps were restricted by the speed, size, and cost of a single bit.

Early computers used to be expensive and could easily fill an entire room. Because they weighed a lot, they were usually moved around using forklifts and transported via cargo airplanes. Announced in 1956, IBM 305 RAMAC was the first computer to use a random-access disk drive – the IBM 350 Disk Storage Unit that incorporated 50 24-inch-diameter rotating disks that could store 5 million 6-bit characters or the equivalent of whopping 3.75 MB of data. This is the ancestor of every hard drive produced ever since.

That's how typically technology evolves. Advances of knowledge are being used to build new things on top of the old knowledge base. Every decision at a time is restricted by various boundaries we face – physical limits, cost, speed, size, purpose, and so on. If you think about the purpose of the early computers, in the beginning, they were devised with a sole purpose – from solving polynomial functions to cracking secret codes ciphered by machines such as the German Enigma machine. There was a long way until we could use general-purpose computers that are highly programmable.

Without making any generalizations, it will be highly inconvenient to build anything. You have to manage all of the moving parts right from the beginning, which is a lot of effort. For example, you had to either be a genius or be among one of the inventors to be able to use the computer in the 1950s. With the introduction of personal computers, it started to get easier. The same applies to software development.

Software Progress

While hardware tried to address the physical aspects of computer systems, kind of the same evolution happened with software. The early programs were highly dependent on the architecture of the computer executing them.

Applications Development

When writing low-level code, you have to think about everything – machine instructions and what registers to use and how. With the advances of modern compilers, we have a comfortable abstraction to express just what the program should do without thinking about what instructions will be executed by the *Central Processing Unit* (CPU).

Programs used to be a self-sustainable piece of code without any external dependencies. *Object-oriented programming* is a paradigm that essentially gave us yet another powerful abstraction. By utilizing the power of interfaces, we can reuse a lot of code. Every piece of code that we use out of the box has an interface (or a contract that it serves). Software libraries emerged, and they became the building blocks of modern software. Let's face it: system software, server software, frameworks, utilities, and all kinds of application software are all built using well-known and widely used libraries and components.

Some programs are still dependent on some operating system features or third-party components that were installed on the developer's machine. And the typical case is that the program you just downloaded does not run on your machine. "But it works on my machine," they would say.

A few years ago, containers started to gain more and more popularity. Containers are the solution to make your code easily transferable across machines and environments by packaging all application code along with all of its dependencies. By doing this, you are effectively isolating the host machines and their current state from your code.

Infrastructure and Scalability

In the past, programs were running on a single machine and were used only on that same machine. This was until computers could be connected to networks where they could talk to each other. The machine that hosts applications is called a server, and the other machines that use the applications are called clients.

Over time what happened with some applications is that the number of clients started to outgrow the capacity of the servers. To accommodate the ever-increasing load resulted in adding more resources to each server, the so-called *vertical scaling*. The application code is still the same but running on a beefier machine with a lot more processing power and memory. At some point, the technological limits will be reached, or it will become too expensive to continue adding power to a single machine. And in case something happens with this machine, your application will become inaccessible for all clients. The number of options to alleviate the issue was pretty much exhausted.

Then it became obvious that the applications should be distributed across different servers. There are more instances of your applications running across a set of machines instead of relying on a single big machine. The incoming load is typically distributed across all machines. That's called *horizontal scaling*.

To be able to achieve horizontal scaling, you have to make sure that every instance of the application doesn't hold any internal state, that is, your application is *stateless*. This is needed because each application replica should be able to respond to any request. As you replicate software across more instances, you are starting to treat your servers more like cattle as opposed to much-loved pets. You don't really care even if you lose an entire server if you have a couple of others that are still healthy and taking traffic. Of course, as with any decision, this comes with certain trade-offs.

Even if you achieve some level of scalability, it doesn't mean that your application is prepared to withstand future requirements. Not only traffic can grow but also the application functionality evolves and extends. Respectively with functionality, team size is also a subject of change.

In the next sections of this chapter, I will walk you through the two popular architectural styles for building an application – the Monolithic and the Microservices architecture. It doesn't make sense to explain one without mentioning the other because they have rather contradictory principles.

Monolithic Architecture

According to the Merriam-Webster dictionary, the definition of the word monolith is "a single great stone often in the form of an obelisk or column" or "a massive structure." Taking the broad meaning of a *massive structure*, a Monolithic application is built as a single unit. This single unit contains all your application logic. Internally, this Monolithic application can consist of different layers. One of the layers could be the presentation layer, which deals with the user interface of the application; another layer can hold some business logic; a third layer can be used for accessing the database. But it doesn't mean that those layers cannot be separated from one another in terms of a codebase. For example, the business logic layer can spread across numerous small modules, each of them implementing just a small part of the overall functionality. This generally improves the quality of the code; however, those modules are still living in the same layer of the application.

Figure 1-1 shows what typically happens when a user invokes Function A in a Monolithic application. Function A passes the control to Function B, which depends on Functions C and D (which depends on Function E), and when they return a result, Function B will be able to pass the result to the user. Although the functionality is separated into discrete functions, which are likely placed in separate class libraries, they are all sharing common resources like the database and are running inside the same process on the same machine.

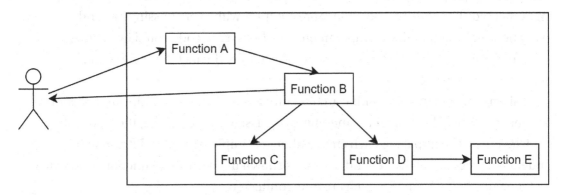

Figure 1-1. *Functions inside a Monolithic application*

Benefits of the Monolithic Architecture

However, "monolith" can be used as defamation nowadays for an application that doesn't follow modern trends that can result in a lot of prolonged discussions. At this point, we have to acknowledge that there are still loads of Monolithic applications out there that are business-critical. Developing monoliths has some benefits as well.

The first thing probably is the simplicity that comes with Monolithic applications. If you think about it, *Integrated Development Environments (IDEs)* and application frameworks are driving you in this direction. It's very easy to create a new web project and implement its models, views, and controllers. You click the Run button of your IDE and voilà, it is up and running on your machine. Everything can be debugged end to end. It feels really natural and fast. The deployment is also easy – package the application and move it to the server that will host it. Done.

Later on, several other developers can join you and work on this application. And you probably won't have serious conflicts for most of the things you are implementing, as long as the application is not very big and you are just a handful of people.

When your server starts facing pressure from traffic growth, you can probably replicate the application to multiple servers and put a load balancer in front. This way each replica will receive a portion of all requests, and it won't get overwhelmed. This approach is the so-called *horizontal scaling*.

Drawbacks of the Monolithic Architecture

However, as time goes by, your application will have more and more functionality implemented. The code will become more complex with every passing day and every new requirement that is implemented. Although the code could have been separated into different modules, it is very easy to miss the fact there are so many cross-dependencies in place.

This means that the Monolithic architecture is easy in the beginning and becomes trickier over time. The more team members you assign to the project, the slower they work together. The impact of each change that gets implemented is difficult to be understood because of the dependencies. As shown in Figure 1-1, Function A depends on Functions B, C, D, and E, which are interconnected.

Imagine there is a serious performance issue in Function B that makes your CPU and memory go crazy high. This will likely bring down the whole process that is hosting it. But wait. We have several other instances, right? Well, the same piece of code is running in all the replicas, so it means that you are also replicating all performance issues and bugs. Although the issue comes from a tiny function that lives in a small module of your application, it impacts the availability of your whole application.

Let's say that your team fixed the issue in Function B. You cannot just deploy the changes made on Function B. Instead, you will have to package the whole application, deploy it, and wait for it to warm up and start serving again.

What if at some point in time you identify that most of the load in the application goes to a particular feature that the majority of clients use? You start wondering how to scale out only the pieces of functionality in question to achieve a fine-grained density with the hardware you have at hand.

Or maybe you want to start implementing new features with some new technology that makes sense for the application you have and some of the team members are knowledgeable about it. Let's say it's a different framework in a different language than the ones you have based your Monolithic application on. Unfortunately, utilizing such technology won't be possible as you are locked in a certain execution model that spans the whole application. And generally speaking, attempts for mixing various technologies that bring different concepts don't end well in the long term.

It's a monolith. You cannot easily dismantle it as its components are *tightly coupled.* If you waited too long, it might be that your application is a homogeneous mixture of functions. Let's see what is the case with the popular Microservices architecture.

Microservices Architecture

The Microservices architecture is an architectural pattern for building distributed systems in such a way that they are comprised of different *loosely coupled* components called services that run in different processes and are independently deployed.

Figure 1-2 shows how the Monolithic application you saw earlier in Figure 1-1 can be shaped in the Microservices world. Each of the functions has its own service. The services can be independently deployed and distributed across different machines. But still, they are part of the same application and work as a whole. The services communicate with each other by using a clearly defined *Application Programming Interface* (API) via protocols such as HTTP, gRPC, AMQP, and others.

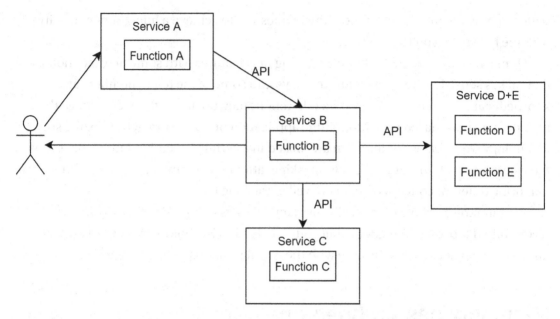

Figure 1-2. *The Monolithic application translated into a Microservices application*

For the sake of the example, I have oversimplified the process of converting a Monolithic application to one based on the Microservices architecture. It's not a straight two-step process. It takes careful analysis and thorough design beforehand.

Designing Microservices

Now that you know that an application should be split into multiple pieces, how do you define how big those pieces are? There are various approaches to tackle this. But designing microservices is pretty much a piece of art. You can start by understanding how the business that you are digitalizing works and what are its processes and rules. And then identify what are the *business capabilities* that the application should provide. You can probably group them into several categories and identify the main objects.

Alternatively, you can use some of the tactics from *Domain-Driven Design*. You can decompose the main domain into subdomains and identify the *Bounded Contexts* we have. This is a strategy to split a large problem into a set of small pieces with clear relationships. Instead of defining a large ubiquitous model that will end up representing a lot of perspectives, the Bounded Contexts enable you to project small parts of the whole domain from different lenses. Having outlined the Bounded Contexts and the models, it's easier to start thinking about the functionality of the service. Let me give you an example. Let's say we are designing an online store. We may have a Cart microservice, a Payment microservice, and a Shipment microservice, among others. When a customer purchases an item from the store, the underlying work will be performed by those microservices. But each service sees the customer from a different perspective. The Cart microservice sees the user as a Customer who added some product into the cart. Customer is the entity representing the user in the context of managing a cart. To the Payment service, the user is a Payer who uses a specific payment method to remit the money. From the perspective of the Shipment service, the user is an entity named Receiver that contains the user's address. All three entities share the same identifier of a user but have different attributes depending on the problem being addressed.

The goal of identifying the boundaries of a service is not just to make it as small as possible. In the example in Figure 1-2, Function D and Function E are placed in the same microservice as their functions belong to the same business capability. You should not aim to create a microservice for the smallest piece of functionality. But ideally, a microservice should comply with the *Single-Responsibility Principle*.

The first design of your microservices won't stay forever. As the business evolves, you will likely do some refactoring to refine the size and granularity of the services. Getting back to the example with the online store, if you find yourself constantly merging the information about the user from Payment and Shipment services, for example, Payment calls the Shipment service upon every operation, there is a huge chance those two should be merged into one service.

Each service is responsible for storing its data in some persistence layer. Depending on the nature of data, it can be persisted in various types of databases. Some of the data can be cached to offload the performance hit on the services and their respective databases. The potential of using different technologies in each service depending on the case is enormous. In contrast to monoliths, you can choose whatever programming languages, frameworks, or databases that fit best the problem you are solving or the expertise of the team.

Benefits

The drawbacks of Monolithic applications, in general, are addressed by the Microservices architecture.

The main benefit of microservices is coming from the fact services run in different processes. Each service is a standalone unit of deployment that is isolated from any other parts of the application. If the load on this service starts to increase, then you can scale it out on its own. In this way, you can achieve a better density by scaling only what needs to be scaled.

This process isolation results in fault isolation. Let's assume that there is a memory leak in Function A in Service A. Service A won't be stable, but fortunately it will fail on its own. Since it is separated from other services, it won't bring the whole application down. Of course, it depends on how services are interconnected and what type of communication is chosen – *asynchronous* or *synchronous*. If there is a huge chain of synchronous requests across services, a failure in just one of them can affect a bigger part of the application. Once the issue with Service A is resolved, it will be deployed on its own while other services keep running. This is also a benefit that applies to the deployment workflow of the entire application – small parts are getting rolled out as opposed to the whole application at once. The deployment can be coordinated only within the team that is responsible for this microservice.

When I covered the topics related to the design of microservices, I mentioned that there were several ways to decompose the domain and manage the granularity of the services. One alternative way of addressing the problem from the people collaboration perspective is using the effect of Conway's law[2]:

> *Any organization that designs a system will inevitably produce a design whose structure is a copy of the organization's communication structure.*

From an architecture perspective, this observation means whatever the communication style is inside the team, the software will reflect it. Flat teams that work from the same location and have high cohesion between members tend to produce more tightly coupled systems as opposed to distributed teams around the world. The more you communicate with someone, the better chance you will interlace with their code and create unneeded dependencies.

A different approach can be taken when an application based on the Microservices architecture needs to be developed. If you apply Conway's law in the opposite direction, you will start with the people and the organizational structure first. Therefore, a team to develop a particular service or a group of services can be formed. This team will own the entire group of services end to end from design to deployment and management.

---

[2]Conway, Melvin E., How Do Committees Invent?, *Datamation* magazine, April 1968

The team will be organized around the capabilities that a service addresses as opposed to being cross-functional and spanning across the entire application. And in general, that's what makes people happier because they fully own something and they don't have to switch the context as much.

If a single team owns a particular service, this gives the freedom to decide what technology fits best the problem you are trying to solve. There is more room for doing controlled experiments and attempts to utilize the latest technologies. For example, one service can be based on Node.js and MongoDB, and another is implemented in ASP.NET Core and SQL Server. Or maybe for the future, you have decided to move to Python as the main programming language because why not? You can gradually start reimplementing on a service-by-service basis and measure how each of them performs on the new stack. Or you may decide that one service should take advantage of the *event-driven architecture* while another needs to be a scheduled job running every once in a while. You are free to use whatever programming model, framework, and language you want.

The Microservices architecture may give you a better approach for building a bigger application that scales well enough. But it doesn't come for free though.

Downsides

The distributed nature of microservices brings a lot of complexity from the get-go.

Starting with the design, you need to decide where to put the boundaries and how to control the scope of the services. Then you have to figure out what to use for interservice communication. Does it make sense to have direct communication between services, or would that create a long chain of requests and cause problems? Or should you only rely on asynchronous communication via a message broker?

Moving to the development, developers are working just on a subset of all services. They usually don't know in greater detail how every other microservice works. This can be both viewed as a benefit and a drawback. It may turn out that some complex interaction between services doesn't work as expected, so you have to collaborate with other teams to be able to understand it and troubleshoot it. Traditional IDEs are working well with Monolithic applications built around a single technology stack. You have to find a way to debug end-to-end scenarios that span multiple services implemented with multiple technologies.

A good strategy is needed to deploy services across machines – how to distribute the load between replicas, how to manage uptime, and how to monitor them in a way that you can tell how the application works as a whole. Deploying and operating such applications with bare hands across servers is a very difficult task. It will require a lot of effort and a lot of people. Depending on what goes wrong, the person will have to know what specific action to take. Without knowing how each of those services is implemented, taking the right action will be almost impossible. Ideally, builds and deployments should be fully automated, as coined by the DevOps principles and practices. I am obligated to mention that Monolithic applications could also benefit from this; however, for microservices, it is a must. Managing the load across servers can be handled by orchestration and scheduling tools.

If you are used to working with relational databases, you would expect to use ACID (Atomicity, Consistency, Isolation, Durability) transactions for the data stored by the application. Each service holds just its own set of data, so it means that data is partitioned and doesn't necessarily use the same technology. So we lose the capability to perform atomic transactions across the entirety of data. Patterns like *Saga* exist for executing distributed transactions across different systems, but generally, the *eventual consistency* should be embraced. Eventual consistency means that if you update a data item, the returned value upon reading will emerge with time to the last updated value. This means that all replicas at some point in time will know the last value of this item, but before that, it may return some previously stored value.

As the business evolves, the Microservices application behind it does so. At some point, you will have to change the way your application works. I am talking about changes across plenty of services.

What do we know when things become complex? Change technology, add some abstraction, employ some proven patterns, and change course so it becomes easier, right?

Abstract Infrastructure

A Microservices application is a set of tens to thousands of services. So you typically provision N number of servers (either bare-metal or virtualized) that will host your application and all its services. You have to find a way to place an instance of each service on those servers.

Let's say you somehow managed to have your services running inside those machines. One of them may utilize the CPU to the maximum level. A service may have a dependency that conflicts with the version of the same dependency used in another service. Because you cannot achieve good isolation between those services when they run directly on the same host machine, you will have to allocate a separate machine just to run a particular service. That's not so efficient as you will need to have an operating system (OS) installed on every machine. It takes space, and it's the case of hardware not being optimally utilized. Furthermore, you have to find a way to move services to a new server when they fail. It's not impossible to have a Microservices application running in the above-mentioned setup, but it will be a very labor-intensive effort if you manage to do it right. Most likely you will have to build some automation to keep your sanity. Let's see how to address those concerns.

Containers are a packaging mechanism relying on virtualization at the OS level. So when you package your service as a container image, it will hold your compiled code along with all its dependencies such as runtimes and libraries. It's a sandbox environment for running a service in an isolated way from all other services. Instead of virtualizing at the hardware level by using a hypervisor to spin up more *Virtual Machines (VMs)* in a single physical machine, multiple containers can share the same OS kernel. That is what makes them start much faster and use fewer resources as you don't have to install a guest OS for each container as is the case with traditional VM-based deployments. Containers can even be limited to how much memory and CPU to use. So you don't have to worry about resource contention. One of the first and most popular container platforms is *Docker*. Since Docker played a big part in establishing what containers are today, Docker means different things to different people. You will learn more about Docker in Chapter 3: Getting Up to Speed with Kubernetes.

The applications or services are packaged into a common format called a container image. Images run as containers on a container runtime, for example, the Docker Engine. Once you install the Docker Engine, you can execute any Docker image. But please remember that the Microservices applications consist of a set of distributed services. How do you distribute service containers across nodes? That is still a challenge!

You need some type of a *cluster management* system that runs across all nodes and knows how to manage the lifecycle of those containers. For solutions that are based on containers, you will hear about them as *container orchestrators*. If you assume the containerized services are the musicians playing in an orchestra, the conductor is the container orchestrator that stands in front of them and guides them altogether. It knows how many nodes you have at hand and how to distribute the workload across them. It also continually monitors all containers and nodes and knows how to move containers across nodes to provide better utilization of resources as well as reacting to unexpected things – as both containers and nodes hosting them do go down. Choosing to base your application on proven containerization technologies and orchestrators makes things simpler as you stick to their proven concepts. One of the most popular container orchestrators is *Kubernetes,* which together with *Docker* is the *de facto standard* nowadays. I will cover both in more detail in Chapter 3: Getting Up to Speed with Kubernetes.

Some Useful Patterns

Patterns are proven solutions for common problems. There are many patterns that can help to address the challenges brought by the Microservices architecture. Let's take a brief look at some of the most commonly used.

API Gateway

Let's assume that you have designed and implemented your applications using the Microservices architecture. You should have a suite of independently running services, and each of them exposes some kind of API and knows how to communicate with other services.

Typical users want to use a mobile application, a web application, or maybe a combination of them to expose different parts of the business to people with different roles. Back to the example with the online store, besides having the web and mobile applications for consumers, we can have apps that the store employees use – one for managing the products catalog, another for pricing, and one for managing the inventory. Each user interaction happening in the UI of those clients will have to execute certain operations that are performed by particular services. But if you are developing those client applications – mobile, web, and so on – how do you know which particular services to call, what particular endpoint to use, and in what order?

Client code will become very complex because of the following issues:

- Calling particular services means that clients know too much about the way the services are decomposed internally. If some services get refactored (either split to multiple or merged into one), those changes should be also made on each client application as well.

- Client applications should handle transient failures on their own and retry operations.

- Multiple network roundtrips between the client application and multiple services generate a big overhead.

It also makes it difficult for the implementation of those public-facing services, as each of them should deal with the following concerns:

- SSL

- Authentication and authorization

- Rate limiting

- Caching

- Supporting a protocol that is handy for client applications to use

API Gateway is a communication pattern that introduces a service that sits between clients and services to proxy traffic between them. It also serves as an abstraction layer as clients don't know which specific service was invoked as part of some operation. Since it's the central entry point that the client application uses to access the underlying services, it can perform some additional functions like *caching* and *logging*, as shown in Figure 1-3. It also provides a suitable way for clients to connect to underlying services as they may not always natively support friendly protocols like *HTTP* and *gRPC*.

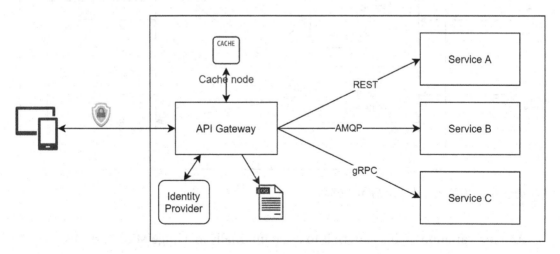

Figure 1-3. *API Gateway*

API Gateway can bring simplification in three main aspects:

- Routing – API Gateway can be a simple reverse proxy that connects clients to back-end services.

- Aggregation – A single request to API Gateway can aggregate data from several services. It has to dispatch requests to those services and then aggregate their outputs into a single result.

- Offloading – Rather than implementing the following for each service, API Gateway can take care of many of the following concerns – authentication, authorization, caching, compression, SSL termination, rate limiting, and logging.

If you find that each client needs a totally different set of data, it may make sense to utilize a variation of API Gateway, called *Backends for Frontends*. Typically, mobile applications display way less information and support a smaller set of functionality compared to web applications. There's an option to provide a client-specific API Gateway as shown in Figure 1-4.

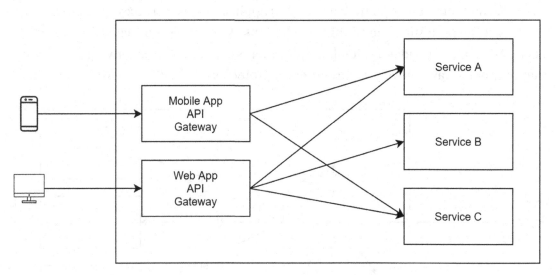

Figure 1-4. *Backends for Frontends*

Another variation of this pattern is to use it internally in a huge Microservices application to provide a single entry point to a given domain. Imagine how hard it would be to identify the particular service you want to call if your application contains hundreds or thousands of services. So you can take a step further and put several services from a domain behind an API Gateway.

Saga

Saga is a pattern for managing data consistency across services. In the Microservices world, data is split across multiple services because each service typically manages its own data. Therefore, there is no way to execute transactions over a larger set of data. The Saga pattern takes a different approach – distributed transaction happens as a sequence of smaller local transactions each executing in sequential order and taking place on a particular service. Once the service is done processing the transaction, it should report that the operation has successfully finished so that the next services can take over and execute their work. In case a local transaction fails, the previous services that have successfully performed their part have to undo the work by executing compensating transactions.

There are two approaches to implement the Saga pattern – *orchestration* and *choreography*.

Orchestration

Saga can be implemented with a central controller called orchestrator as displayed in Figure 1-5.

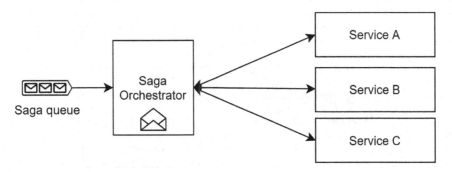

Figure 1-5. *Saga with orchestration*

A service publishes a message in the Saga queue. This message contains all of the details of the Saga that needs to be executed across different services. Once the Saga orchestrator receives a message from the queue, it knows which services to call and in what order. Since it controls the order of the whole Saga, some of the operations can be executed in parallel, and the risky operations can be left for the end of the Saga as their retry would likely be a more expensive operation. Risky operations are those that should not or cannot be reversed. For example, the Saga orchestrator from Figure 1-5 calls the services in alphabetical order: Service A is called and executes successfully. Then the orchestrator invokes Service B but it happens to fail, so it has to initiate the undo action on Service A as it was previously executed successfully. Service C would have been called only if Service B succeeded.

However, the Saga orchestrator happens to be a point of failure on its own. What happens if the Saga orchestrator goes down while it is in the middle of a transaction? This is the reason that Sagas are flowing through a message queue because it provides *fault tolerance*. If the Saga orchestrator goes down, the message will return in the queue. A new instance of the Saga orchestrator can get it and start the transaction from the beginning. Therefore, operations happening on each service must be *idempotent* because they can be retried multiple times.

A potential drawback of this approach is that the Saga orchestrator should be designed, implemented, and maintained. It becomes a part of the application and introduces coupling as it calls specific services in a specific order.

Choreography

Instead of depending on a central orchestrator, services can talk with each other via a message broker as shown in Figure 1-6.

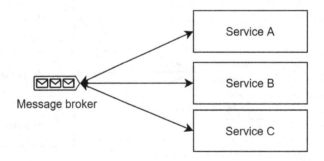

Figure 1-6. *The choreography approach for implementing Saga*

A service publishes a message to a particular queue designated for one event type. Then this message gets processed by one or many services that are subscribed to this type of message. Having performed the operation, each of the subscribing services is responsible to emit a message with the outcome in the same or a different queue. In the case of success, new services are picking up the message and continuing the Saga; in the case of failure, preceding services can undo the actions.

By using the choreography approach, services remain loosely coupled. However, it may be very difficult to trace the execution of the entire Saga as it involves multiple services. The role of the orchestrator is implicitly transferred to the services because each of them is responsible for managing the resiliency of their operation as well as the necessity to publish the result of their action (successful or not) so that other services can execute their part accordingly.

Sidecar

There are some cases where certain applications cannot be modified. Imagine an application that is provided by another company. Or maybe there is an application that is built with some old technology that is not supported now so it's not reasonable to try extending it. Or in other cases, some common functionality that is used across many services needs to be provided in a reusable way. The sidecar pattern helps to have this functionality in a language- and framework-agnostic way by relying only on intraprocess communication.

As shown in Figure 1-7, the application and the sidecar run side by side on the same host where each of them runs in its own process or container.

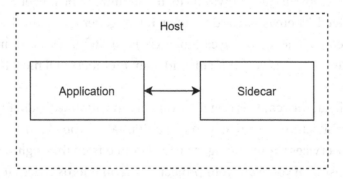

Figure 1-7. *The sidecar pattern*

The pattern is named after the sidecar motorcycle. In the same way, the sidecar is attached to another application and provides some supporting features. Those could be, for example, logging, monitoring, configuration management, health checking, and so on.

Both the sidecar and the application share the same resources on the host, for example, storage and network.

Let me walk you through a real example where the sidecar pattern can prove to be useful. Consider that you have an old application that works over HTTP. At some point, a requirement to switch it over to using HTTPS comes by. So one of the approaches would be to reconfigure the application to work with HTTPS. But imagine that for some reason you cannot change its code – for example, you cannot compile the source code of this application. Furthermore, you cannot change the way it is hosted. A possible solution that requires no changes on the application itself would be to deploy the *NGINX proxy* as a sidecar and expose it externally. It will receive the incoming TLS connections and pass the unencrypted requests to the application via *HTTP*.

Adopting Microservices

Whenever something new pops up on our technology radar, we as developers always wonder whether to move on the bleeding edge and adopt the modern technology or approach. The reality is that technology is developed to serve a *purpose*. In the case of microservices, your applications will mostly benefit from improved scalability and resiliency. There are also some organizational benefits. Big organizations are enabled to utilize more people by splitting them into many smaller teams that do not overlap so much as they own a single service or a group of services. When it comes to size, according to the two-pizza rule, individual teams should not be bigger than what two large pizzas can feed. There is no hard number, but in general, a team should consist of fewer than ten people. The team size cannot increase indefinitely as communication with more than ten people is very difficult and team members will most likely have many conflicts in code.

Sounds good, but the reality is that not every organization will benefit from the Microservices architecture as it creates some additional overhead right from the beginning. Microservices should be rigorously designed from the beginning as this is a foundational decision. If you want your project based on microservices to be successful, you have to fully embrace the DevOps culture and practices. When people hear DevOps, they are usually triggered by the tools for *Continuous Integration* and *Continuous Deployment*. But holistically, DevOps is the convergence of people, processes, and tools throughout the entire lifecycle of the software. The result of that is that there is less complexity to be handled on case-by-case scenarios and almost everything is automated, which naturally leads to fewer failures and faster release cadence. And in case of failure, the system can recover quicker. So the Microservices architecture can turn out to be a lot of effort, in the beginning, for an organization aiming to adopt it.

Most applications that are now based on the Microservices architecture were once a large monolith. And that's the direction that most startup companies follow when starting a new project. They usually don't have the financial strength to support a bigger team even though they may anticipate a big growth of users and load in the future. Most startup companies start small – building their applications as monoliths because they are simple to get started. As they evolve and grow, some capabilities of the monolith can be isolated into discrete services until the whole application is refactored to microservices and there is no trace of the monolith.

Summary

In this chapter, you learned how system evolution happens with small steps both from a hardware and software perspective. I outlined what Monolithic applications are along with their benefits and downsides. Then we transitioned to distributed applications by explaining the Microservices architecture, which addresses a lot of the downsides monoliths have. However, the Microservices architecture brings some challenges as well. Being introduced to some of the important patterns and technologies, by now you have an idea of how to overcome those challenges.

In the next chapter, I will introduce you to Distributed Application Runtime (Dapr) and show you how you can benefit from it for the applications development of distributed applications.

CHAPTER 2

Introduction to Dapr

In this chapter, you are going to learn about the value of Dapr and how it can help you to build distributed applications. It adds value by providing building blocks that depend on pluggable components. After initializing Dapr in Self-hosted mode, a simple distributed Hello World application will be created once Dapr is initialized locally.

What Is Dapr?

Distributed Application Runtime (Dapr) is an open source project initiated by Microsoft. It was announced at Microsoft Ignite 2019, Microsoft's annual trade show for IT workers, and since then it has been gaining a lot of interest and support from the community. Dapr achieved stability and thus reached production readiness with its 1.0 release in February 2021. As of March 2021, Dapr is in the process of being donated to the Cloud Native Computing Foundation (CNCF) as an Incubation project. There are more and more companies adopting Dapr.

According to the official website, Dapr is the following:

> *Dapr is a portable, event-driven runtime that makes it easy for developers to build resilient, microservice stateless and stateful applications that run on the cloud and edge and embraces the diversity of languages and developer frameworks.*

> —dapr.io

For our learning purposes, Dapr is a runtime that provides useful functionality that spans programming languages, frameworks, diverse application types, and hosting environments and supports a lot of use cases across different environments – cloud, on-premises, and the edge. But first, let's take a step back and think about how a single service is usually designed and developed. First of all, you should choose what *programming model* you want to base the development of the service on depending on

© Radoslav Gatev 2021
R. Gatev, *Introducing Distributed Application Runtime (Dapr)*, https://doi.org/10.1007/978-1-4842-6998-5_2

the type of problem it solves. Should it be an API based on the request/response model or an event-driven service for long-running tasks, or maybe should it be based on the *Actor model*? You have to pick a technology that fits the programming needs. If you are building a traditional Web API, you can choose from a variety of web frameworks – ASP. NET Core, Flask, Express.js, and so on. If you want to implement something based on the Actor model, some of the options are Akka and Service Fabric Reliable Actors, for example. They all are going to help you implement the service you want; however, each of them carries its own concepts, opinions, and programming model. Usually, combining different concepts coming from several frameworks and libraries does not end well. Application frameworks are built to guide you along the way and to protect you from making common mistakes. And that's why they are trying to enforce their rules so strictly. For example, controllers, routes, and middleware in ASP.NET Core and Express serve the same conceptual purpose; but they are implemented in a slightly different way for both frameworks.

Following the same analogy, if you want to integrate with an external service to persist some information, for example, Redis, you have to identify a library (in the form of a NuGet package or NPM package, among others) that allows you to interface with Redis in your programming language of choice. Then you must figure out how it fits within the lifecycle of the framework you use for the application. Those common concerns will be present across all services of the Microservices application that you implement, and they have to be handled on a case-by-case basis for one service at a time. Thinking about it in more general terms, it feels like the same-functioning boilerplate code is piling up in different services most likely implemented in different ways on each occasion.

How Was Complex Made Simple?

Dapr takes an ingenious approach by addressing common needs in a very uniform way. To understand my point, let's say you are in a country where people speak a language that you don't know. What are you going to do? If you can't use a dictionary, you are probably going to try using some nonverbal communication with some gestures and body language. And depending on the culture, you may succeed.

The same is with applications – you abstract away what you don't want to know. But since there isn't a good way to abstract all languages and frameworks, you go one level higher and work with the communication protocol they use. If your services can talk

HTTP or gRPC, they can talk to Dapr as well! Although Dapr provides several Software Development Kits (SDKs) for some of the popular languages, whether to use an SDK or not at all is up to you. You will learn more about the SDKs later in the chapter.

Out-of-the-Box Patterns

Let's navigate our way to the value proposition of Dapr. Dapr packages several useful patterns that come out of the box that allow you to achieve a certain outcome. To name a few functions, it can be calling another service, persisting some state, or utilizing Publish and Subscribe. The value-added patterns are called *building blocks*. Depending on how you combine the Dapr building blocks, you can achieve different things. The building blocks can be used as a stable foundation because each of them provides a set of capabilities that otherwise you have to implement from the ground up taking into account the concepts of the framework that you use, or you can bring in an external library and integrate it. If you are building a house, you are better off buying the bricks instead of figuring out how to produce them yourself. Then you just have to know how to lay the bricks (the Dapr building blocks).

For example, there is a *Service Invocation* building block that features service discovery and communication with other services. You call *Dapr* via its API, and it locates and invokes the target service for you and relays the result back. It's pretty much like a reverse proxy. You will learn more about this building block in Chapter 6: Service Invocation.

There is another building block, State Management. You want your service to store some state, but instead of dealing with the specifics of communication with a particular service capable of persisting the state, you let Dapr do that for you. You just send some state data to Dapr, and it knows how to communicate with the state store. Then when you want to access the state, Dapr knows how to gather it from the underlying state store. You will learn more about this building block in Chapter 8: State Management.

To elaborate more on the previous example, the fact that you outsource the work to Dapr makes your application loosely coupled to the service you use for persisting the state and gives you the freedom to switch technologies of the same type effortlessly. For example, during development, you may use a Redis store deployed locally for persisting the state. However, in production, you may decide to bind the State Management building block to Cosmos DB or any other cache, database, or service in general that is supported. And you can do this seamlessly without changing the code at all.

Instead, you just need to modify the way Dapr *state components* are configured so that Dapr is instructed to connect to another external service that will persist the state.

We will explore each of the building blocks in detail in Part 2 of the book, but very briefly they are:

- Service Invocation – Invoke other services and consume the returned result.

- Publish and Subscribe – Utilize the Publish and Subscribe model by leveraging a messaging system as a transport, for example, Redis Streams, Apache Kafka, and many others.

- State Management – Save and consume state that is persisted externally, for example, in Redis, Azure Cosmos DB, and many others.

- Bindings – Invoke external applications to gather some data or trigger an action or let external applications invoke your services. It supports a wide palette of integrations. Some integrations are done in a generic way by using protocols like HTTP, SMTP, and MQTT, while others are implemented for interfacing with certain Software as a Service (SaaS) applications like SendGrid, Twilio, or even social networks like Twitter.

- The Actor model – Leverage the Actor model provided by Dapr.

- Secrets – Gain secure access to secrets by leveraging Kubernetes Secrets, Azure Key Vault, and many others.

- Observability – Know what is happening across all your services.

Dapr Components

Building blocks are the reusable pieces of functionality coming from the API of Dapr, but internally they use one or multiple Dapr components that define how they are going to work – for example, what connection information to use when connecting to an external system like Redis. Components are the actual implementation of the building block capability to talk to external services. They just implement a common interface depending on the component type (state, pubsub, etc.), and that's the reason they are pluggable and easily substituted. You can change the underlying implementation of some of the building blocks and switch to using another service by changing the underlying components that will service the request coming from the building block. I know this can be somewhat confusing, and to simplify a bit, we can assume that the building blocks are the generic functional pieces and their exact behavior is configured by the respective components.

The components of a certain type share a similar configuration file that is often called manifest. To be exact, a Dapr component is defined as a CustomResourceDefinition (CRD), but that is probably too much information for now as we are going to explore this in greater detail in Chapter 4: Running Dapr in Kubernetes Mode. For now, here is the generalized format of a component manifest defined in YAML:

```
apiVersion: dapr.io/v1alpha1
kind: Component
metadata:
  name: <COMPONENT-NAME>
spec:
  type: <COMPONENT-TYPE>
  version: v1
  initTimeout: <TIMEOUT-DURATION>
  ignoreErrors: <BOOLEAN>
  metadata:
  - name: <METADATA-KEY>
    value: <METADATA-VALUE>
  - name: <METADATA-KEY>
    value: <METADATA-VALUE>
```

In this case, the value of the `metadata.name` field is the custom-defined name of the state component. Naming a component is entirely up to you, and later on you will be able to reference this component by name. That's the reason a building block can work with multiple components. For example, when you want to store something in a particular state store, you refer to it by specifying the name of the state component when you call the State Management building block.

The scalar value in `spec.type` points to the particular component implementation. The type names of the components are prefixed with the building block for which they serve a purpose. For example, if you want a state component, for a type, you can specify `state.redis` to use Redis as a state store. Or it can be `state.azure.cosmosdb` for Azure

Cosmos DB. Depending on the chosen component type, the `spec.metadata` section will contain a list of the specific connection properties provided as key-value pairs. For example, the Redis state component needs just `redisHost` and `redisPassword` to be provided. Similarly, the Cosmos DB state component accepts the URL of the Cosmos DB account endpoint, `masterKey`, `database`, and a `collection`. In other words, the metadata section contains all properties needed to establish a connection or to modify the behavior of a component. You are going to learn more about the State Management building block in Chapter 8: State Management.

Another field `spec.version` specifies the version of a given component. You can think of components as modules that implement a certain interface (that of the building block), but those components are developed under another GitHub repository that is independent of the Dapr runtime – `https://github.com/dapr/components-contrib`. As of Dapr 1.0, most of the components are in version 1; however, over time components will be released and versioned independently.

There are also two optional fields that control what should be the behavior when loading components, and those are `spec.initTimeout` and `spec.ignoreErrors`. The former specifies how long a component is permitted to take for its initialization, and by default, this period is 30 seconds. The latter states whether or not Dapr should continue its initialization in case a component fails to load. Now that we touched on initialization, let's explore how Dapr works.

How Does Dapr Work?

You might be starting to ask yourself where those building blocks are hosted and how you can get access to them. The capabilities that Dapr provides via its building blocks come from the Dapr runtime. Both the runtime itself and the suite of components are implemented in Go under the following GitHub repository – `https://github.com/dapr/dapr`. Go is a programming language that was designed at Google. It features static typing, compilation, and high performance. There are a lot of open source projects that are based on Go – Docker and Kubernetes, among others.

The Dapr runtime has to do a lot of housekeeping stuff that you won't see from the outside. The instances of the runtime run side by side with your services following the *sidecar pattern* that we explored in Chapter 1: Introduction to Microservices.

Figure 2-1 shows how two services work with Dapr together with its sidecars, building blocks, and components. Each service has a dedicated sidecar. Each pair of service and sidecar is displayed isolated to keep things more logical, but these pairs are not necessarily isolated on a network level when they are deployed to a host. Each instance of your service knows that there is a sidecar running on a specific port should it use any of the Dapr building blocks. And in the opposite direction, each Dapr sidecar knows that it was brought up to serve a single service that is listening on a specific port. For example, the sidecar may trigger some of your service's endpoints whenever a new message comes in or something happens in an external system. Or if you want to get some data from a state store, you do so via the API hosted by this sidecar.

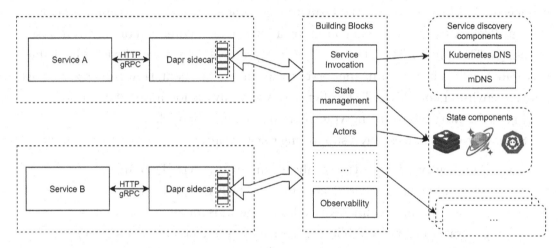

Figure 2-1. *Applications with Dapr sidecars, building blocks, and components*

Dapr sidecars contain the full set of all available building blocks and are described in greater detail in Part 2 of the book. Keep in mind that a single component type can be used by several building blocks. For example, the state components are used both in the State Management building block and in the Actors building block. To illustrate, let's look at two examples.

Let's say Service A wants to save some state. In order to do that, it invokes the State Management building block and passes the state data and the name of the state store. Then Dapr has to find a specific definition of a state component by looking for the provided name. In Figure 2-1, there are only three state components shown – Redis, Azure Cosmos DB, and etcd out of the many supported. As I already mentioned, although those components are talking with different end services to persist state, they all implement certain operations coming from the common interface defining all state components. And the State Management building block doesn't care what the internal implementation of a state component is as long as it conforms to the interface.

Alternatively, let's say Service A wants to talk to Service B; it will use the Service Invocation building block that's provided by its sidecar. Then the Service Invocation building block will query a service discovery component to find the address and port on which Service B's sidecar is running. Then Service A's sidecar will instruct Service B's sidecar to call a particular method of Service B. The result will be proxied back to Service A via the system of sidecars.

Dapr does not only bring some reusable functionality packaged as building blocks, but it also handles some cross-cutting concerns out of the box like observability – it collects tracing, logs, and metrics information generated across services and the Dapr runtime itself. Also, cross-sidecar communication can be secured out of the box by just enabling mTLS (Mutual TLS). The standard TLS protocol only proves the identity of the server to the client by providing the server certificate to the client. However, in zero-trust network environments, Mutual TLS offers a way to verify the identities of the parties staying on the two sides of an encrypted communication channel.

Several system services play a supporting role to Dapr:

- Dapr Sentry service – The certificate authority (CA) of Dapr that issues and manages certificates. mTLS heavily depends on this service. During the time while a Dapr sidecar is initializing, it generates a pair of a public and a private key and creates a Certificate Signing Request (CSR) that is then sent to the Sentry service for signing with its private key. In this way, each sidecar has its own workload certificate to use when talking to other sidecars.

- Dapr Placement service – This service helps *Dapr runtime* to keep track of how actors are being distributed across actor hosts. It is only needed whenever the Actors building block is used. The Actor model will be described in more detail in Chapter 10: The Actor Model.

Hosting Modes

So far we have explored Dapr from a conceptual perspective – what it is and what capabilities it has – and we touched on how it works behind the scenes. Now, let's get a bit closer to the more technical and practical side. Dapr can be initialized and therefore hosted in two ways (hosting modes):

- Self-hosted – Runs on the local machine as a process. This means that the Dapr runtime runs as a sidecar process alongside your service (application) process. Sometimes this is referred to as Standalone mode.

- Kubernetes – Dapr is deployed in a Kubernetes cluster. Your service is containerized, and the Dapr runtime is just a sidecar container running along with your service container. A few additional system services are needed in this mode – the Sidecar Injector service and the Operator because of the specifics in the way Kubernetes works. I will show you what this means in Chapter 4: Running Dapr in Kubernetes Mode.

Note   The Self-hosted mode has a dependency on Docker installed locally so that it can spawn containers for the Dapr system services. There is a variant of Self-hosted mode without any dependency on Docker called *Slim Self-hosted mode*. However, we won't be looking at this mode as it is not very useful for development. The reason is that it is much easy to have Docker installed locally and take containers for granted. Otherwise, with Slim Self-hosted mode, you have to deal with starting up binaries for the various system services you are going to need, for example, Dapr Sentry, Dapr Placement, and so on.

Kubernetes mode is the go-to mode for production usage that is battle-tested for performance and scalability. Self-hosted mode is a good fit for development, but it also gives you the most freedom to choose how to host your applications. For example, if Kubernetes is not a good fit for you, you may want to try hosting Dapr in Self-hosted mode with Service Fabric. But for certain things, for example, to make the Service Invocation building block work, you have to deal with the underlying platform.

Getting Started with Dapr in Self-Hosted Mode

To use Dapr, first, you need to initialize it. The easiest way to do so is to use the Dapr command-line tool. The Dapr CLI will not only help you initialize Dapr but also do the operations-related actions for Dapr in both Self-hosted and Kubernetes modes, for example, check all Dapr configurations, get logs of a Dapr sidecar, and many others.

Download Dapr

The Dapr cross-platform CLI makes it easy to initialize Dapr and run, manage, and monitor Dapr applications. Let's see how to get it on your machine:

1. Download the latest release of the Dapr CLI that is appropriate for your operating system from `https://github.com/dapr/cli/releases`:

   a. Windows: dapr_windows_amd64.zip

   b. macOS: dapr_darwin_amd64.tar.gz

   c. Linux: dapr_linux_amd64.tar.gz

   d. Linux on ARM: dapr_linux_arm.tar.gz/dapr_linux_arm64.tar.gz

2. Unpack the Dapr CLI binary.

3. Move it to a suitable location:

   a. On Windows, you can add the folder in which you placed Dapr into your PATH environment variable. Or if you are like me, instead of polluting your PATH variable with various directories, have just one directory to hold all the binaries that need to be easily accessible and add it to the PATH variable, for example, *C:\binaries*.

   b. On Linux or macOS, you should place the binary under */usr/local/bin* to make it easily accessible.

4. Open a terminal and run the following command to verify the Dapr CLI is set up:

   `dapr --version`

5. And you will see the following output:

```
CLI version: 1.0.0
Runtime version: n/a
```

As you can see, the CLI cannot resolve the Dapr runtime version because it's not initialized yet.

Initialize Dapr

Next, let's initialize Dapr locally, in the so-called Self-hosted mode, so that Dapr sidecar binaries are downloaded, a few container instances (Redis, Zipkin, Dapr Placement service) are started, and a default folder that holds all components is created.

Note   As a prerequisite, you need to have Docker installed on your machine. You can use Docker Desktop if you are on Windows or macOS, or you can install the respective package for Docker Engine that is suitable for your Linux distribution. Please note that if you use Docker Desktop on Windows, you should select its Linux containers mode. More info here: `https://docs.docker.com/engine/ install/`.

In the terminal you opened previously, run `dapr init` to initialize Dapr. By default it will download the most recent stable version of Dapr; however, you may want to initialize a specific version, in which case it accepts a `--runtime-version` flag. Wait for `dapr init` for a while to finish, and you will see the following output:

```
Making the jump to hyperspace...
Downloading binaries and setting up components...
Downloaded binaries and completed components set up.
daprd binary has been installed to C:\Users\youruser\.dapr\bin.
dapr_placement container is running.
dapr_redis container is running.
dapr_zipkin container is running.
Use `docker ps` to check running containers.
Success! Dapr is up and running. To get started, go here: https://aka.ms/
dapr-getting-started
```

Congratulations! If everything went well, Dapr should have been initialized in Self-hosted mode. Let's explore what this means.

If you navigate to *%USERPROFILE%\.dapr* on Windows or *$HOME/.dapr/bin* on Linux or macOS, you will find a couple of files and folders that Dapr set up for itself. First, in the root directory, there is a file named config.yaml. This file contains configurations, and by default, the Dapr sidecars try to load it from this path. Many things can be configured in Dapr – tracing, metrics, middleware, and others. We are going to explore all options throughout the book. The daprd binary was downloaded and placed inside the bin folder. Daprd is the binary of the *Dapr runtime* that you run as a sidecar process when Dapr is in Self-hosted mode. In the components folder, you will find the initial configuration of two components as YAML files – pubsub.yaml and statestore.yaml. Those components were preconfigured to point to the dapr_redis container, which is one of the Docker containers that were brought up as part of the `dapr init` command:

- `dapr_redis` is a container running the Redis image. When you open pubsub.yaml and statestore.yaml, you will find out both components point to this Redis container that is accessible on port 6379. This means that the Pub/Sub, State Management, and Actors building blocks will use the Redis running in a container on your machine. You might ask why I intervene with the Actors building block. The reason is that the statestore component sets a metadata field called `actorStateStore` to true, which means that the Actors building block will use this particular state store to persist the state of all actors.

- `dapr_zipkin` is a container running the popular distributed tracing system called Zipkin. It is used to collect, look up, and visualize data coming from distributed systems. If you open config.yaml that can be located in the .dapr folder, you will see the Tracing Exporter component configured to send Dapr tracing data to the Zipkin's collector endpoint running on `http://localhost:9411/api/v2/spans`.

- `dapr_placement` is a container that runs the Dapr Placement service so that you can start using the Actors building block that uses it.

If you run `docker ps`, you will see those three containers. I have simplified a bit the output of the command by removing some of the columns:

```
IMAGE               NAMES             PORTS
daprio/dapr         dapr_placement    0.0.0.0:6050->50005/tcp
openzipkin/zipkin   dapr_zipkin       0.0.0.0:9411->9411/tcp
redis               dapr_redis        0.0.0.0:6379->6379/tcp
```

Those Docker containers are very helpful when you run Dapr in Self-hosted mode because you don't have to think about running things yourself.

Initializing Dapr Without Docker   Dapr in Self-hosted mode does not have any direct dependency on Docker. The Dapr CLI just makes it easier to get up and running by spawning several containers for you. However, in case you don't want to use Docker, you can run `dapr init --slim` to initialize Dapr. Along with the daprd binary that is the core component, it will also download the Placement service but this time as a binary. Whenever you want to use the Actors building block, you have to make sure that the placement binary is running; otherwise, the Actors building block won't work. Likewise, if you want to use a building block that persists state, you will need to have one of the supported state stores running either on your machine or somewhere in the cloud.

Now that Dapr is downloaded and initialized in Self-hosted mode, let's start using it.

Run Applications with Dapr

To see how Dapr can be utilized, let's follow the tradition and implement a Hello World application that uses Dapr for communication.

Distributed Hello World Application

By its very nature of being a Distributed Application Runtime, a Hello World application in Dapr cannot simply be a one-liner program returning "Hello world." It has to be sophisticated, and so the Hello World application we are going to build will consist of three services, as shown in Figure 2-2:

- Hello service – This will return the word "hello" in strange random casings, for example, "HEllLo."

- World service – This will return the word "world" translated into various languages.

- Greeting service – This will call the other two services and return the consolidated result.

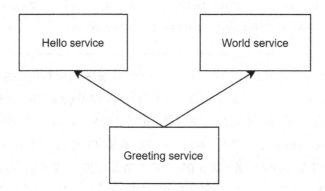

Figure 2-2. *The distributed Hello World application*

Note   As a prerequisite, Node.js has to be installed on your machine. If you don't have it installed on your machine, please go to the official website where you can download an installer that is suitable for you: `https://nodejs.org/en/download/`.

Implement the Hello Service

Now that you understand what services the distributed Hello World application consists of, let's implement them one by one, starting with the Hello service:

1. First, you will need to create a new project folder named *hello-service* and navigate into it.

2. Next, create a new file named app.js inside the project directory. This will be a simple web application built with Express.js, a popular web application framework for Node.js. The source code

is shown in Listing 2-1. It has a single HTTP GET endpoint named sayHello that iterates over the letters of hello and randomly changes their case.

Listing 2-1. The contents of hello-service/app.js

```
const express = require('express');
const app = express();

app.get('/sayHello', (_, res) => {
    let hello = '';
    for (const letter of 'hello') {
        const isUpperCase = Math.round(Math.random());
        hello += (isUpperCase) ? letter.toUpperCase() : letter;
    }
    console.log(`Sending: ${hello}`);
    res.send(hello);
});

const port = 8088;
app.listen(port, () => console.log(`Listening on port ${port}`));
```

3. Next, open a terminal in the project folder and execute npm init and follow the steps to create a package.json file. This file will hold some information about your Node.js project; you just need to follow the wizard.

4. In the same terminal, run npm install express, and it will download the Express module along with all its dependencies. Additionally, it will list Express as a *dependency* of your application in the *package.json* file. After step 4, your package.json file will look like this:

```
{
  "name": "hello-service",
  "version": "1.0.0",
  "description": "",
  "main": "app.js",
```

```
  "scripts": {
    "test": "echo \"Error: no test specified\" && exit 1"
  },
  "author": "",
  "license": "ISC",
  "dependencies": {
    "express": "^4.17.1"
  }
}
```

5. Run the application by executing node app.js. Now open http://localhost:8088/sayHello in your browser, and you should see a weird *helLO*.

6. Great, you've done it! Up until now, the Hello service was started just like most Node.js applications are usually started. Make sure to stop the execution of the previous command as it will keep using port 8088. Now let's make sure Dapr knows about our application and assigns a sidecar for its needs. As I mentioned, every application using Dapr deserves a dedicated Dapr sidecar. While you are still in the project directory, run the following command:

```
dapr run --app-id hello-service --app-port 8088 -- node app.js
```

7. This tells Dapr that the application identifier (App ID) is hello-service; it listens on port 8088 and can be started by executing the command node app.js. You will see the following output; however, I simplified it a bit by removing the redundant information to make it easier for reading:

```
Starting Dapr with id hello-service. HTTP Port: 56677. gRPC Port: 56678
== APP == Listening on port 8088

msg="starting Dapr Runtime -- version 1.0.1 -- commit 45bc40d"
msg="log level set to: info"
msg="metrics server started on :56679/"
msg="standalone mode configured"
```

```
msg="app id: hello-service"
msg="mTLS is disabled. Skipping certificate request and tls validation"
msg="local service entry announced: hello-service -> 192.168.0.103:56683"
msg="Initialized name resolution to standalone"
msg="component loaded. name: pubsub, type: pubsub.redis/"
msg="waiting for all outstanding components to be processed"
msg="component loaded. name: statestore, type: state.redis/"
msg="all outstanding components processed"
msg="enabled gRPC tracing middleware"
msg="enabled gRPC metrics middleware"
msg="API gRPC server is running on port 56678"
msg="enabled metrics http middleware"
msg="enabled tracing http middleware"
msg="http server is running on port 56677"
msg="The request body size parameter is: 4"
msg="enabled gRPC tracing middleware"
msg="enabled gRPC metrics middleware"
msg="internal gRPC server is running on port 56683"
msg="application protocol: http. waiting on port 8088.  This will block
until the app is listening on that port."
msg="application discovered on port 8088"
msg="application configuration loaded"
msg="actor runtime started. actor idle timeout: 1h0m0s. actor scan
interval: 30s"
msg="dapr initialized. Status: Running. Init Elapsed 100.7188ms"
msg="placement tables updated, version: 0"

Updating metadata for app command: node app.js
You're up and running! Both Dapr and your app logs will appear here.
```

Now let's examine the logs. As you may recall, each application has a unique ID, which in this case is hello-service. This ID will be later used for making requests to the application via the system of Dapr sidecars. According to the logs, the Dapr API that is served from the sidecar process will be accessible via HTTP on port 56677 and port 56678 for gRPC. Those port numbers are auto-generated if not explicitly set as arguments of dapr run. You can identify the logs coming from the Hello service application as they are prefixed with == **APP** == and Dapr logs follow a common format that includes the timestamp, the message, and what Dapr application generated it, among other things. You can see that Dapr does several initializations of its internal parts. The two components we explored earlier were discovered by the Dapr runtime – pubsub and statestore. This means that you can use the respective building blocks, namely, Publish and Subscribe and State Management building blocks. Furthermore, you can notice that actor runtime was also initialized. And on top of that, since the Dapr configuration file that I mentioned earlier was loaded successfully as stated by the logs, observability comes out of the box.

At this point, you may have noticed that the Dapr sidecar is running along with the Hello service. Let's open Process Explorer from Windows Sysinternals and search for *dapr.exe*. The process tree appears as shown in Figure 2-3. Notice dapr run in a PowerShell terminal. In addition, executing the Node.js application, it also launched a daprd process by passing the following arguments to it:

```
C:\Users\rados\.dapr\bin\daprd.exe --app-id hello-service --dapr-
http-port 56677 --dapr-grpc-port 56678 --log-level info --app-max-
concurrency -1 --app-protocol http --components-path C:\Users\rados\.dapr\
components --metrics-port 56679 --app-port 8088 --placement-host-address
localhost:6050 --config C:\Users\rados\.dapr\config.yaml
```

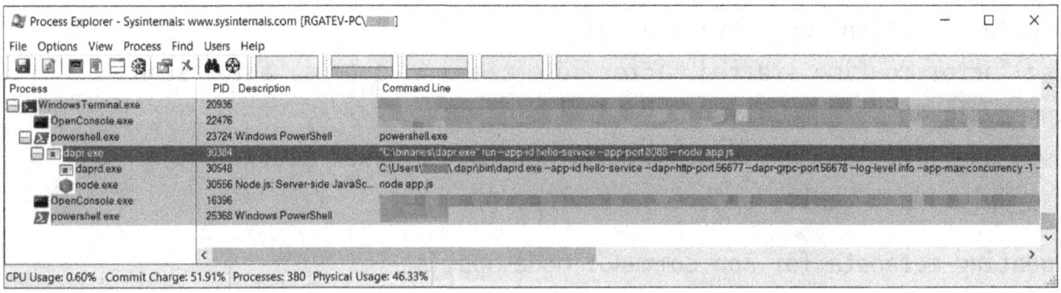

Figure 2-3. *The Dapr CLI run spawns up a daprd sidecar and starts the application*

As you can see from Figure 2-3, some of the values of those arguments passed to daprd come from the arguments passed to dapr run. Let's examine the available flags of dapr run in Table 2-1.

Table 2-1. *Command-line input of the dapr run command*

Flag	Arguments	Default	Notes
--app-id	An Application ID	Auto-generated, for example, Chillermarble-Slicer	Used for service discovery
--app-max-concurrency	The number of concurrent calls to an application that is allowed	Unlimited (-1)	
--app-ssl	N/A	This is a switch, so the default is false	Whether or not to invoke a Dapr application via HTTPS
--app-port	The application port	N/A	Used when Dapr talks to the application
--app-protocol	The protocol the application is using: HTTP or gRPC	http	Used when Dapr talks to the application
--components-path	The path where Dapr components are located	$HOME/.dapr/components or %USERPROFILE%\.dapr\components	
--config	Path to the configuration file	$HOME/.dapr/config.yaml or %USERPROFILE%\.dapr\config.yaml	
--dapr-grpc-port	The gRPC port for Dapr to listen on	Random	
--dapr-http-port	The HTTP port for Dapr to listen on	Random	
--enable-profiling	N/A	It's a switch, so the default is false	If present, enables pprof profiling via an HTTP endpoint

(continued)

Table 2-1. (*continued*)

Flag	Arguments	Default	Notes
--log-level	The log verbosity level: debug, info, warn, error, fatal, or panic	info	
--metrics-port	The port to be used to expose Dapr metrics		
--placement-host-address	The host where the Placement service resides	localhost	
--profile-port	The port for the profiler server to listen on	N/A	

You can see the list of all available flags from the Dapr CLI itself, by executing `dapr run --help`.

Note   Keep in mind that some commands in the Dapr CLI are meant to be used for Self-hosted mode and others for Kubernetes and some work with both modes. That is clearly stated in the output of `dapr --help`.

Implement the World Service

While the Hello service is running as a Dapr application, leave its terminal open, and let's implement the World service that will return the word "world" translated in a random language:

1. In a similar fashion to the previous service we developed, create a new folder named *world-service* and navigate into it.

2. Create a new file named *app.js* inside the project directory. It listens on port *8089* and has a single HTTP GET endpoint named `sayWorld` that returns translations of the word "world" in various languages, as shown in Listing 2-2.

Listing 2-2. The contents of world-service/app.js

```
const express = require('express');
const app = express();
const worldTranslations = ["world",
  "свят", "svijet", "svět", "świat", "мир", "свет", "світ", "svet", "svetu",
  "lume", "verden", "wereld", "värld", "pasaulē", "pasaulyje", "mondo",
  "monde", "mundo",
  "العالمية", "世界", "세계", "विश्व", "বিশ্ব", "โลก"];

app.get('/sayWorld', (_, res) => {
    const index = Math.floor(Math.random() * worldTranslations.length);
    const world = worldTranslations[index];
    console.log(`Sending: ${world}`);
    res.send(world);
});

const port = 8089;
app.listen(port,() => console.log(`Listening on port ${port}`));
```

3. Open a terminal in the project folder, run `npm init`, and follow the steps to create a package.json file.

4. Run `npm install express` to install Express and list it as a dependency in package.json.

5. And finally, in the terminal you opened, execute `dapr run --app-id world-service --app-port 8089 -- node app.js`. By now you should have two Dapr applications running in two terminal sessions. Both applications will be accessible on the ports they are listening on; however, that's not the way the Greeting service will be accessing them.

Implement the Greeting Service

Now that we have *Dapr-ized* two Node.js applications, it's time to implement the one that will consume and consolidate the results from the Hello service and the World service, which is the Greeting service.

1. First, let's create a new folder named *greeting-service* and navigate into it.

2. Next, create a new file named app.js inside the project directory. It listens on port 8090 and has a single HTTP GET endpoint named greet that calls the other two services and concatenates the output from them so that it returns a proper Hello world greeting, as shown in Listing 2-3.

Listing 2-3. The contents of greeting-service/app.js

```
const express = require('express');
const fetch = require('node-fetch');

const app = express();
const daprPort = process.env.DAPR_HTTP_PORT;
const invokeHello = `http://localhost:${daprPort}/v1.0/invoke/hello-
service/method/sayHello`;
const invokeWorld = `http://localhost:${daprPort}/v1.0/invoke/world-
service/method/sayWorld`;

app.get('/greet', async (_, res) => {
    hello = await fetch(invokeHello);
    world = await fetch(invokeWorld);
    const greeting = await hello.text() + ' ' + await world.text();

    console.log(`Sending: ${greeting}`);
    res.send(greeting);
});

const port = 8090;
app.listen(port, () => console.log(`Listening on port ${port}`));
```

3. In the project folder, run npm init to create a package.json file.

4. Next, run `npm install express node-fetch`. node-fetch is a module that brings the support of the Fetch API that is available in modern browsers to Node.js.

5. Then run the following command:

```
dapr run --app-id greeting-service --app-port 8090 --dapr-http-
port 3500 -- node app.js
```

This makes it a third terminal session hosting a third Dapr application.

6. When you open `http://localhost:8090/greet` in a browser, you will get something like **HELlo mondo**.

7. Lastly, open `http://localhost:9411/` and explore the distributed logs collected by *Zipkin*. As a reminder, Zipkin is one of the containers brought up when initializing Dapr in Self-hosted mode; thus, it listens on port 9411. You will be able to see the requests flowing from the Greeting service to the other two services. You will learn more about distributed tracing and Zipkin in Chapter 12: Observability: Logs, Metrics, and Traces.

As you can see from the code, the Greeting service does not know the ports the other two applications are listening on. It just references them implicitly by specifying their Dapr App IDs when calling its dapr sidecar process. Then Dapr figures out how to reach out to the respective Dapr apps.

When we called `dapr run`, we specified the HTTP port number, but this was not needed. The ports of the dapr sidecar process (the daprd binary) are injected as the environment variables `DAPR_HTTP_PORT` and `DAPR_GRPC_PORT` so that the application always knows how to access its dedicated sidecar.

Exploring the Dapr Dashboard

Keep the three Dapr applications running, as we will look at the ways you can explore what is currently running in Dapr.

If you open another terminal and run `dapr list`, it will show you all running Dapr applications along with information about their application and Dapr sidecar ports and what command was used to start them. That is a handy way to check the basic information for the currently running Dapr applications.

But if you prefer exploring it visually, you can use the Dapr Dashboard, a web application that visually shares information about the Dapr applications that are running on your machine, what Dapr components are available, and the applicable Dapr configurations, as seen in Figure 2-4. After you run `dapr dashboard`, in the output, you will find the specific port on which the Dapr Dashboard is running.

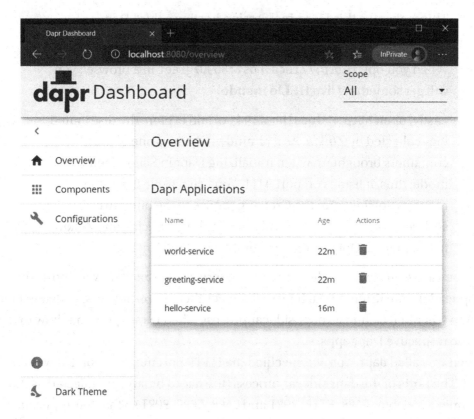

Figure 2-4. *Dapr Dashboard*

Using Dapr SDKs

As you have learned, Dapr is not tied to any specific programming language because it exposes its API via HTTP and gRPC.

However, some developers prefer relying upon language-specific SDKs that are strongly typed as opposed to making requests out in the wild. Instead of making a request to `http://localhost:${daprPort}/v1.0/invoke/hello-service/method/sayHello`, you may want to simply call the `InvokeMethodAsync` method of the `DaprClient` class passing the Dapr App ID and the name of the method. For that reason, Dapr provides several SDKs for a number of languages – C#, Java, Go, JavaScript, Python, PHP, Rust, and C++. Being written in Go, Dapr exposes its API via gRPC; therefore, its interface is specified in *Protocol Buffers (Protobuf)* format. This means it's fairly easy to generate a gRPC client stub based on the Protobuf definition for any language that doesn't have an official SDK. Actually, some Dapr SDKs are just wrapping the auto-generated client stubs and providing some language-specific improvements on top.

Summary

In this chapter, you learned the basics of Dapr and how you can benefit from it when implementing distributed applications. You were guided through the Dapr hosting modes and learned how to initialize Dapr in Self-hosted mode. You were then shown how to implement a simple yet distributed Hello World application using Node.js and Dapr and how to visually inspect your Dapr applications using the Dapr Dashboard.

Running Dapr in Kubernetes mode requires some level of knowledge of both Kubernetes and Docker, so in the next chapter, we'll explore what Kubernetes is and learn how to build Docker images that can run in it.

CHAPTER 3

Getting Up to Speed with Kubernetes

Dapr can be hosted in one of two modes – Self-hosted and Kubernetes. Self-hosted is handy for local development and gives you the freedom to host Dapr anywhere you want, but the reality is that for production workloads, you will host it in Kubernetes. So, to work with Dapr, you need to feel comfortable with Kubernetes. Kubernetes is worth a whole book. However, I will try to guide you through the basic concepts in just one chapter by covering the following topics:

- The architecture of a Kubernetes cluster

- Building Docker container images

- Running images in containers

- Container registries

- Kubernetes objects – Pods, Services, and Deployments

- Package management in Kubernetes

Kubernetes (K8s) is the leading technology for container orchestration. It is an open source project started by Google, which has had a lot of experience building and managing distributed systems. Kubernetes was inspired by the projects *Borg* and *Omega* – container management systems that enabled Google to run millions of containers in production. Along with the release of Kubernetes version 1.0 back in 2015 by Google, the project has been donated to the Cloud Native Computing Foundation (CNCF). Since then it has been adopted by companies ranging from startups to big enterprises.

© Radoslav Gatev 2021
R. Gatev, *Introducing Distributed Application Runtime (Dapr)*, https://doi.org/10.1007/978-1-4842-6998-5_3

Kubernetes: The Big Picture

Running a single container is easy, right? However, when trying to run multiple of them across different servers, things can get complex. Kubernetes provides a declarative way to specify your workloads. You specify what should be deployed and how many replicas you want, and it takes care of how to deploy it across the servers that you have available in your Kubernetes cluster. Then, it continuously monitors the whole cluster to keep your workloads just the way you specified them.

Figure 3-1 shows the architecture of a Kubernetes cluster. The cluster consists of two types of servers – K8s master nodes (also known as control plane) and worker nodes (commonly referred to as just nodes).

The components running inside the master nodes are collectively called control plane components, or just *control plane*. They are responsible for managing the worker nodes and the workloads running in them. This is the brain of the Kubernetes cluster as it takes global decisions about the cluster. For example, if a worker node goes down, the control plane recreates the same containers across the remaining worker nodes. For clusters running in production, you have to make sure the control plane is fault-tolerant and highly available. That is the reason for having an odd number of master nodes, typically three or five. The number must be odd so that it is always possible to establish a quorum if some of the master nodes go down or lose connectivity.

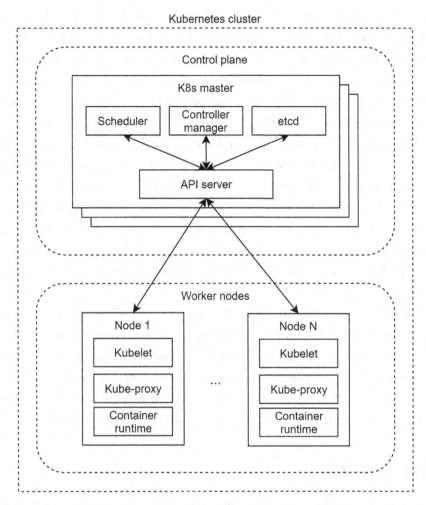

Figure 3-1. *The architecture of a Kubernetes cluster*

Control Plane Components

A central part of the Kubernetes cluster is the *API server*. It exposes an HTTP API that lets you deploy, inspect, and manage cluster resources. However, you will most likely use the Kubernetes command-line tool called *kubectl* that actually interacts directly with the API server. By calling various commands, you can explore the state of Kubernetes objects like Pods, Services, Deployments, and many others. I will explain the most important Kubernetes objects you need to know later in this chapter. For now, you should know that Pods are the smallest deployable workload unit in Kubernetes. A Pod is a collection of one or more containers that share common storage and network.

The K8s API server does not only act as the main access point from the outside but is also used internally within the cluster. As I mentioned, every object has a declarative definition that Kubernetes tries to fulfill. The API server backs up the cluster state and configuration into *etcd*. etcd is a distributed, consistent, and reliable *key-value store*.

The controller manager is responsible for reconciling the observed state with the desired state. It runs several control loops that monitor the state of the cluster via the API server and takes corrective actions when needed. There are several controller types, each of them having a separate responsibility. For example, the Node controller watches the state of the worker nodes and reacts if any of them goes down. The Replication controller makes sure that the specified number of replicas of your workloads is always fulfilled. As a sidenote, some controllers need to communicate directly with external systems in order to achieve a certain outcome on the cluster, albeit indirectly, for example, Cluster Autoscaler, which adjusts the size of a Kubernetes cluster by communicating with the APIs of a specific cloud provider.

The Scheduler watches the API server for newly created Pods that are not yet assigned to a node. Scheduling is an optimization problem where based on some constraints of the Pods, the Scheduler identifies the particular nodes eligible for taking them. A Pod can specify some restrictions and requirements. For example, a Pod may be defined in such a way to require scheduling a node with a GPU. Or you may explicitly state that two Pods of the same type should never be colocated into the same node.

Node Components

Worker nodes are the machines that run your Pods. They can be running Linux or Windows as opposed to the master nodes, which only support Linux. You can have both node types in your cluster as it gives you the flexibility to schedule workloads based on Windows containers to Windows nodes and the traditional Linux containers to Linux nodes. As shown in Figure 3-1, a worker node has three components running on it – *kubelet, kube-proxy,* and *container runtime.*

The kubelet is the agent that works closely with the control plane. Whenever a Pod gets assigned to a node, the kubelet of the node receives a definition of the Pod most often via the API server; then it ensures the containers are up and running. The kubelet also continuously monitors and collects the performance and health information for the node, pods, and containers and sends it to the control plane so that it can make informed decisions.

The kube-proxy is responsible for proxying the traffic to the nodes. A Pod has an IP address that is shared by the containers running in it. However, if you have set up multiple replicas of the same Pod, some load balancing should be happening to reach a specific Pod on a specific node. The kube-proxy handles the networking aspect of that communication, and it makes sure that the incoming traffic will reach a Pod.

As you already know, a Pod is an object that contains your application bits packaged as one or multiple containers. The container runtime is what actually runs and manages your containers. Kubernetes supports several container runtimes – containerd, CRI-O, Docker, and in general any runtime that implements the *Kubernetes Container Runtime Interface (CRI)*. The container runtime in Kubernetes is pluggable. When it comes to containers, Docker comes out as the most popular choice; however, it was not devised to be used inside Kubernetes as it doesn't support the Container Runtime Interface. For that reason, to make it possible to use Docker inside Kubernetes, an adapter called *Dockershim* had to be implemented to adapt the CRI to Docker internals and vice versa. This architecture adds an extra hop in the communication between the kubelet and the containers and therefore latency, and last but not least, the Dockershim needs maintenance. This resulted in Docker being deprecated as a container runtime after version 1.20 of Kubernetes, and at some point, it will be removed as a container runtime from new versions of Kubernetes. The most popular choice for a container runtime is containerd, which is actually a part of Docker.

Wait, but that is confusing! Let me clarify that we should look at containers from two different perspectives – local development of container-based applications and having those containers running inside Kubernetes. Until recently, almost everything around containers used to be Docker, and probably that is why Docker means different things to different people. However, after Kubernetes has deprecated and will eventually remove Docker as a container runtime, you have to just switch to containerd, in case you haven't. And the images you build with Docker will still work. The reason behind this is that Kubernetes works with Open Container Initiative (OCI) images, which all Docker images are. Both containerd and CRI-O are able to work with OCI-compliant images no matter how you build them. Standards are a good thing!

Nowadays you can run Kubernetes anywhere – on your laptop, on-premises, in the cloud, or even on several Raspberry Pis. Each of the public cloud platforms has a Kubernetes offering. In Microsoft Azure, it's called *Azure Kubernetes Service (AKS)*. Google Cloud Platform named it *Google Kubernetes Engine (GKE)*. You should have a better idea of how Kubernetes works by knowing what each cluster component does.

If you have Kubernetes clusters running production workloads on-premises, you have to manage all those machines. However, if you choose one of the cloud offerings, you will find out that most of the infrastructure is being abstracted by the platform. For example, you don't have to do anything to ensure the high availability of your control plane in AKS. Those have been abstracted away from you and managed by Microsoft. You just allocate a couple of worker nodes, and your cluster is ready to go. The master nodes are invisible and you don't pay for them. The same applies to GKE as well – master nodes are managed by the platform. Taking this further, Virtual Kubelet is an implementation of the Kubernetes kubelet agent that enables Pods to be running on other technologies. For example, you can use serverless container platforms like *Azure Container Instances* to run some of the workloads in your Kubernetes cluster. Virtual Kubernetes is the enabler for the so-called Nodeless Kubernetes. It alleviates the problems created by cluster management, capacity planning, auto-scaling, and so on. Therefore, you will care only about the application-related things, like building the container images properly and describing them as Kubernetes objects.

Container Images

In Chapter 2: Introduction to Dapr, you saw that when we initialized Dapr in Self-hosted mode by using the Dapr CLI, it started several containers – Redis, Zipkin, and Dapr Placement service. They were somehow running locally, but I didn't walk you through to understand what happened behind the scenes. In order to run a container, you will need a *container image,* which is a binary package of the program and its dependencies. Container images can be stored locally or pulled from a *container registry*. There are two types of container registries – public and private container registries. There are plenty of images publicly available on *Docker Hub*, the world's largest public container registry. If you want to run your application as a container, first, you have to build an image and push it to a container registry, so you can share it with your team or with the public. A fully managed private container registry offering exists in every major public cloud. In Microsoft Azure, for example, it is called *Azure Container Registry*. Alternatively, you can even host one on your own by using some of the open source container registries.

Running a Docker Container

Now let's get practical and see how to start a blog in seconds. *Ghost* is a free and open source blogging platform written in JavaScript. One of the easiest ways to install Ghost is by using Docker. Ghost is published on Docker Hub, and it is among the most popular images there.

Let me take a step back and tell you a story. I've been using Ghost for my blog `www.gatevnotes.com` since 2017. My blog is actually a Self-hosted Ghost on *Azure App Service*. At the time I decided to give Ghost a try, there wasn't an easy way to deploy Ghost in Azure App Service. I spent days making it work and maintaining it as new Ghost versions were released. It is publicly available in my GitHub, and many folks have used it; however, let's see now how containers can save you time by learning how to start Ghost in seconds as opposed to days.

Prerequisite   You will need Docker to be installed on your machine. More info here: `https://docs.docker.com/get-docker/`.

---

1. First, pull the latest version of the Ghost image locally by running `docker pull ghost`.

2. Then, you should be able to see that the Ghost image is present locally by running `docker images`.

3. Once you have downloaded the image, you can run a container by using the following command: `docker run -d --name my-ghost -e url=http://localhost:3001 -p 3001:2368 ghost`. The command sets the name of the container to be `my-ghost`, sets an environment variable for the URL of the blog, specifies that the TCP port `2368` in the container is mapped to port `3001` on the Docker host that is your machine, and at last provides the image to be used.

4. At this point, you should have a brand-new instance of Ghost accessible on `http://localhost:3001` and running on your machine in a container. You can check the container by invoking `docker ps` to list all running containers.

Building a Docker Image

Using already built images is easy enough. However, to put your applications inside an image, you have to know how to build one. Although Docker images are perceived as a single unit, internally they are constructed by a series of filesystem layers. Each layer builds on top of the state of the previous one and specifies what changes to be done as part of the current layer. This helps to optimize the storage and the transfer of images because multiple images can depend on the exact same layer and therefore this layer will be downloaded only once.

In order to build an image, all the steps must be specified as a sequence of commands inside a Dockerfile. Let's build one for the Hello service that we implemented in Chapter 2: Introduction to Dapr. In the hello-service folder that you should have already created by following the steps, create a new file named *Dockerfile* as shown in Listing 3-1. Please have in mind that a Dockerfile doesn't have an extension!

Listing 3-1. The contents of Dockerfile

```
FROM node:14
WORKDIR /usr/src/hello
COPY . .
RUN npm install
CMD ["node", "app.js"]
```

Create also a *.dockerignore* file (notice the dot) to specify what files to be ignored by the COPY command, as shown in Listing 3-2. In this case, it doesn't make sense to pollute the container image by copying the NPM packages into it. To save some space, the container itself will download them because after all, they are publicly accessible.

Listing 3-2. The contents of .dockerignore

```
node_modules
```

Let's explore the commands in the Dockerfile one by one:

1. FROM specifies the parent image to build from. In this case, it is the node image from Docker Hub that has version 14, the LTS (Long Term Support) version of Node.js along with a lot of tools needed for the development of Node.js applications.

2. WORKDIR creates if not existing and sets the working directory for all successive commands

3. The COPY command copies the source code of the application into the image except what you have specified to be ignored in the .dockerignore file. In this case, it is the node_modules directory.

4. RUN specifies that npm install should be executed to install all dependencies of the application.

5. The CMD command specifies what command to be executed when running the container. Since it is a Node.js application, the simplest way to start it is by running node app.js.

Open a terminal in the hello-service directory and run docker build -t hello-service . that builds the image for you by following the steps in the Dockerfile. Great, you have now built an image with your application! You can start a container by running docker run --rm --name hello -p 8088:8088 hello-service. You can verify it works by opening http://localhost:8088/sayHello in your browser. The --rm switch indicates that the container should be deleted once it exits.

There are some best practices to follow when writing your Dockerfile in order to optimize the work that is being done every time you build an image. They typically result in faster builds and better reuse of underlying layers. However, they are not in the scope of this chapter. You can find some of them described here: https://docs.docker.com/develop/develop-images/dockerfile_best-practices/.

Optimizing the Size of a Docker Image

Maybe you noticed that the size of the hello-service image is ~945 MB. That's a huge image for such a tiny application that consists of a few lines of code. The main reason for this is typically the parent image that is used. The node:14 image is about ~943 MB as it contains a lot of tools you need for Node.js development – git, node, npm, yarn, bash, and a number of other binaries that you don't need if you just want to run an application. Note that, since I am using the LTS version, the sizes may have changed at the time you read this. It also installs a lot of packages because the image node:14 derives from Debian 9 (codenamed Stretch). You can gain a better understanding of all image layers by running docker history --format "{{.CreatedBy}} -> {{.Size}}" --no-trunc hello-service. Reading this top to bottom, you will figure out that the layer that installs the NPM packages is just 2.32 MB and the layer that copies the application files is only 15 KB. This explains the delta of ~2 MB between the node:14 image and the hello-service image you just built.

Let's switch the parent image to be *node:14-alpine* and run the `docker build -t hello-service .` once again. This image is based on Alpine Linux, which is only 5 MB in size. The result is that our hello-service image is about 118 MB in size, of which 5 MB is for Alpine and about 103 MB for the node itself. Much better!

Finally, if you want to stop the hello container, execute `docker kill hello`. It will not only stop the container but also delete it because of the `--rm` flag we applied upon executing docker run.

There is also some room for further improvements in size. Multistage Docker builds allow you to use intermediary steps during the image building process. With multiple `FROM` statements in the same Dockerfile, you can use different parent images during the build stages, and you can selectively copy files into further stages. By doing this, the unneeded stuff is excluded from the final image. So you have one bigger image containing all the tools needed to build an application, and then you copy only the compiled version to another image that contains the minimum set of runtime dependencies. Of course, that works best for compiled programming languages.

Pushing to Remote Registry

Now you have an image that resides in your local Docker registry. But images are only useful when they can be consumed from any machine. Otherwise, you need to manually transfer them to target machines. Imagine how painful it will be to transfer this image to hundreds or thousands of Kubernetes nodes.

Depending on your application, you may choose to push it to a public container registry or a private one. The process will be pretty much the same with both types.

Let me show you how to push to Docker Hub:

1. First, log in to the container registry by running docker login. If you are about to push to another registry than Docker Hub, provide the location of the server, for example, docker login myregistry.azurecr.io.

2.   Create an alias of the image: `docker tag hello-service <your-docker-hub-username>/hello-service`. If you are pushing to another registry than Docker Hub, you also need to specify the fully qualified path to the registry, for example, *myregistry.azurecr. io/myservicesns/hello-service*.

3.   Run `docker push <your-docker-hub-username>/hello-service`.

As an exercise, build the images for the other two services we have implemented: world-service and greeting-service. Then push them to Docker Hub as you are going to need them in Chapter 4: Running Dapr in Kubernetes Mode where I will walk you through piecing the services together. Note that the Greeting service depends on Dapr in order to discover the two other services, so if you try running it, it will fail as we don't have Dapr yet.

Get Started with Kubernetes

Kubernetes runs anywhere. So you have a lot of options to choose from.

There are two options to get a working local Kubernetes cluster for testing:

- If you use Docker Desktop, enabling Kubernetes will create a single-node cluster for you. Kubernetes components will run as containers in Docker. In order to do that, first make sure you are using Linux containers, in case you are on Windows, then go to Settings ➤ Kubernetes, and check "Enable Kubernetes." Also applicable for Windows, enabling Windows Subsystem for Linux 2 is always a good idea because of its great performance. Docker Desktop will also install `kubectl` for you, the Kubernetes CLI tool that allows you to run commands against your Kubernetes cluster.

- *Minikube* runs a single-node Kubernetes cluster in a Virtual Machine on your computer. You will need to install kubectl separately. More info here: `https://kubernetes.io/docs/tasks/tools/install-minikube/`.

There is also a Kubernetes offering in each of the major public cloud platforms:

- Azure Kubernetes Service in Microsoft Azure

- Google Kubernetes Engine in Google Cloud

- Elastic Kubernetes Service in Amazon Web Services

Whatever you choose to use, whether locally or in the cloud, you will need to have the Kubernetes command-line tool (kubectl) installed on your machine. You will use it to run commands against your Kubernetes cluster to deploy applications and manage cluster objects.

If you use Docker Desktop, it will install kubectl for you and set its current context to the Kubernetes cluster in Docker Desktop. Of course, Enable Kubernetes must be switched on in the settings of Docker Desktop. For any other Kubernetes clusters, you will most likely have to install kubectl if you don't have it on your machine and authenticate against the cluster. More info here: `https://kubernetes.io/docs/tasks/tools/install-kubectl/`.

To validate that kubectl can access your Kubernetes cluster, run `kubectl cluster-info`; and if it is correctly configured, the output will be similar to the following:

```
Kubernetes master is running at https://kubernetes.docker.internal:6443
KubeDNS is running at https://kubernetes.docker.internal:6443/api/v1/
namespaces/kube-system/services/kube-dns:dns/proxy
```

Kubernetes Objects

By now you have some understanding of what the architecture of a Kubernetes cluster is along with all the different components running in it. Also, you learned how to build and publish container images. It's time to start using Kubernetes to run some containerized workloads on it. Let's go through some of the most common types of objects that you will likely use for every application:

- Pods

- Services

- Deployments

Pods

I already mentioned that containers run in *Pods*. Pods are the smallest deployable unit in a Kubernetes cluster scheduled on a single worker node. A Pod contains one or more application containers that share the same execution environment, volumes, IP address, and port space. Kubernetes objects are declared in manifest files using JSON or YAML format. YAML is the most commonly used one.

Let's create a new file and name it pod.yaml as it will contain the manifest in YAML, as shown in Listing 3-3 for a Pod that has a container running the hello-service image that you have already published to Docker Hub.

Listing 3-3. The contents of pod.yaml

```
apiVersion: v1
kind: Pod
metadata:
 name: hello-pod
 labels:
  app: hello
spec:
 containers:
 - image: <your-docker-hub-username>/hello-service:latest
   name: hello-container
   ports:
   - containerPort: 8088
```

Note that we can add several containers to a Pod manifest; however, it is not needed for the services we have implemented.

To deploy this manifest, you need to execute the following command, kubectl apply -f pod.yaml, assuming the file *pod.yaml* is present in the current directory. This will submit the Pod manifest to the API server, the Pod will be scheduled to a healthy node, and the container will be started.

Then you will be able to see it by running kubectl get pods:

```
NAME        READY   STATUS    RESTARTS   AGE
hello-pod   1/1     Running   0          1m05s
```

Initially, the status that you see may be *Pending,* but with time it will transition to *Running,* which means that the Pod is successfully created and the containers in it are running.

This Pod is not currently exposed to the outside world. So if you want to access it, you will have to set up port forwarding to it by using kubectl:

```
kubectl port-forward hello-pod 8088:8088
```

As long as the previous command is running, the Pod will be accessible on localhost:8088; however, to reach the single endpoint of the Hello service, you need to go to `http://localhost:8088/sayHello`.

You can also examine the logs of the Pod by running `kubectl logs hello-pod`.

There are many more things that you can do with Pods – setting up probes, managing container resources, mounting volumes, and so on. However, Pods are ephemeral and their state is usually not persisted. A Pod can be terminated at any time, or it can be deleted and recreated on another node.

Services

As I already explained, Pods are mortal – they come and go. You may want to replicate your workload by creating several identical Pods. In order to make them accessible from the outside, you will need to put a load balancer in front of this group of Pods. The *Service* object distributes the traffic across a group of Pods based on a label that you tagged your Pods with. Labels are key-value pairs that can be applied to Kubernetes objects. If you go back to the Pod manifest, you can see that it has the app label applied.

If we want to create a service for our hello-service application, it will have the definition shown in Listing 3-4.

Listing 3-4. The contents of service.yaml

```
apiVersion: v1
kind: Service
metadata:
 name: hello-service
spec:
 selector:
  app: hello
 ports:
```

```
- protocol: TCP
  port: 80
  targetPort: 8088
```

To create this service that represents all Pods labeled with `app: hello`, you have to run

```
kubectl apply -f .\service.yaml
```

And then you can verify it has been created by running

```
kubectl get services
```

Services are of several types depending on where you want to expose them. The default one is *ClusterIP*, which makes your service reachable only within the cluster. To access a service from outside of the cluster, you have to use either the *NodePort* or *LoadBalancer* service type. You will typically use the LoadBalancer type whenever you want to expose a publicly accessible Service from a Kubernetes cluster hosted in the cloud.

Deployments

Although it's entirely possible to define and create individual Pods, you most likely won't be doing that as managing them one by one is a tedious task.

A Deployment defines the application Pod and its containers. It also specifies how many replicas of the Pod are needed. By creating a Deployment, you specify the desired state of your application. Once you create it, Kubernetes makes sure that the actual state matches the desired one. Depending on the way you configure the Deployment, it also helps when transitioning your applications from one version to another by performing *rolling updates*. Rolling update is a strategy where Kubernetes gradually creates one or more Pods at a time with the new version and terminates one or more of the old Pods until all of them are running the latest version. This results in no downtime for your application.

Let's create a Deployment manifest for our Hello service, as shown in Listing 3-5.

Listing 3-5. The contents of deployment.yaml

```
apiVersion: apps/v1
kind: Deployment
metadata:
  name: hello-deployment
  labels:
```

```yaml
    app: hello
spec:
  replicas: 3
  selector:
    matchLabels:
      app: hello
  template:
    metadata:
      labels:
        app: hello
    spec:
      containers:
      - name: hello-container
        image: <your-docker-hub-username>/hello-service:latest
        ports:
        - containerPort: 8088
```

Like all Kubernetes objects, you apply it by running

```
kubectl apply -f .\deployment.yaml
```

When you run `kubectl get pods`, you will find those three Pods that were created by the Deployment. If we want to scale it out to five Pods, for example, we have to update the `spec.replicas` field to 5 and reapply it with the same command. As you can see, even the Deployment object works with *labels* and *label selectors* – the replicas' definition searches for Pods having the app label with a particular value. The service that we created previously will automatically discover all the new Pods created by this Deployment and will send traffic to them as well. The reason for this is the new Pods will also have the `app: hello` label that the service is looking for.

Packaging Complex Applications

I showed you how Kubernetes objects are defined in YAML manifests. Your entire application will likely consist of many YAML files. It will likely be configured in a slightly different way across environments such as dev, test, and production. Manually editing many YAML files is not always a good idea.

Helm is the package manager for Kubernetes that lets you define and then install even the most complex application that consists of many YAML files without dealing with any of them. The packages in Helm are called *Helm Charts,* and they contain all your YAML files in parameterized format. You can set values for those parameters during the time of deployment.

Artifact Hub is a public directory where you can find ready-to-use Helm Charts for popular software across many public Helm repositories. For example, installing a single-node MySQL database on a Kubernetes cluster is as simple as running the following commands:

```
helm repo add bitnami https://charts.bitnami.com/bitnami
helm install my-release bitnami/mysql
```

The first command adds the repository with all charts published by Bitnami where the `bitnami/mysql` chart is provided. The second one simply installs it.

Summary

In this chapter, you learned the basics of Kubernetes – what components a Kubernetes cluster consists of and what Kubernetes objects to use when deploying your applications to Kubernetes. Since Kubernetes orchestrates containers, we explored how to build Docker images, run them as containers, and push them to a container registry.

Now that you acquired some knowledge about Kubernetes, the next chapter will focus on getting Dapr to work in Kubernetes mode.

CHAPTER 4

Running Dapr in Kubernetes Mode

In Chapter 2: Introduction to Dapr, you learned how Dapr runs along with your application code and provides added functionality that is accessible via HTTP and gRPC. Then you got introduced to Kubernetes and its basic concepts.

The Self-hosted mode gives you the freedom and flexibility to run Dapr wherever you want. It is just a process running on a machine. Starting, operating, and scaling all pieces of your Microservices application are some of your responsibilities. In general, using Dapr in Self-hosted mode is recommended for development and testing. But in production, you will most likely utilize Kubernetes to ease out some of those responsibilities by using its declarative manner. This chapter will be about using Dapr as a first-level citizen of Kubernetes:

- Installing Dapr in Kubernetes mode

- Exploring the Dapr control plane

- Installing Dapr in production

- Dapr-izing applications in Kubernetes

- Configuring Dapr components

Let's start by understanding how to install Dapr in Kubernetes.

Installing Dapr in Kubernetes Mode

If you have followed the steps in Chapter 2: Introduction to Dapr, you will already have Dapr CLI already installed on your machine. In Chapter 3: Getting Up to Speed with Kubernetes, you learned how to use kubectl to interact with your Kubernetes cluster.

69

© Radoslav Gatev 2021
R. Gatev, *Introducing Distributed Application Runtime (Dapr)*, https://doi.org/10.1007/978-1-4842-6998-5_4

As a prerequisite, you need to have the dapr binary (Dapr CLI) at hand and have established a kubectl context to a running Kubernetes cluster. Let's get to work and install Dapr in a Kubernetes cluster. You have to simply execute the following CLI command:

```
dapr init --kubernetes
```

The following output will then be returned to you to indicate a successful installation:

```
Making the jump to hyperspace...
Note: To install Dapr using Helm, see here: https://docs.dapr.io/getting-
started/install-dapr-kubernetes/#install-with-helm-advanced

Deploying the Dapr control plane to your cluster...
Success! Dapr has been installed to namespace dapr-system. To verify, run
`dapr status -k' in your terminal. To get started, go here: https://aka.ms/
dapr-getting-started
```

Exploring the Dapr Control Plane

Installation was easy enough. Now let's explore what has been created for us in the Kubernetes cluster by using the Dapr CLI first. Note that all Dapr CLI commands that target Kubernetes provide the --kubernetes switch and its shorter alias -k. Some of the CLI commands do not support Self-hosted mode and thus do not provide a counterpart version without the --kubernetes switch. The command that lets you check the status of the Dapr control plane in Kubernetes is such an example:

```
dapr status --kubernetes
```

You already know that a Kubernetes cluster has master nodes that host the control plane components, that is, the brain of your cluster. Likewise, when Dapr is installed inside Kubernetes, it also has a control plane that holds the Dapr system services. The output of the dapr status command shows all components the Dapr control plane consists of:

```
NAME                    NAMESPACE     HEALTHY  STATUS    REPLICAS
dapr-sentry             dapr-system   True     Running   1
dapr-dashboard          dapr-system   True     Running   1
dapr-placement-server   dapr-system   True     Running   1
dapr-operator           dapr-system   True     Running   1
dapr-sidecar-injector   dapr-system   True     Running   1
```

The Dapr Placement and Dapr Sentry services should sound familiar as they are also applicable for Dapr when it is hosted in Self-hosted mode. As you may remember, the Dapr Placement service is automatically started as a Docker container for convenience when you use Dapr in Self-hosted mode. Actors can be distributed across nodes in your Kubernetes cluster, and the Dapr Placement service keeps track of the distribution of the actors. Whenever you use the Actors building block, this service will play a major role. You will learn more about actors in Chapter 10: The Actor Model, which is dedicated to the Actor model.

The Dapr Sentry service is the *certificate authority* for all Dapr applications. Dapr ensures that the communication inside the system of Dapr sidecars and also between Dapr sidecars and Dapr system services (Dapr Placement service is one such example) is secured by using *Mutual TLS* (mTLS) authentication. To establish secure two-way communication, at the time when a Dapr sidecar initializes, it generates an ECDSA private key and a Certificate Signing Request (CSR), which is then sent to Dapr Sentry. Dapr Sentry receives the CSR and turns it into a certificate by signing the CSR using the private key from the trust bundle that is available only to the Dapr Sentry service. The trust bundle contains two certificates – the root certificate and issuer certificate, the latter being used for signing workload certificates. The root certificate stays on the top of the certificate chain and serves as the trust anchor from which the *chain of trust* is derived. This also means that the issuer certificate is practically signed with the private key of the root certificate, which makes it an intermediate certificate. That is how trust is established between two parties without revealing their private keys.

Dapr Sentry automatically generates self-signed root/issuer certificates if they are not provided at the time of installation. Dapr also can handle the rotation of root certificates and workload certificates without any downtime. The default period of validity of workload certificates is 24 hours, while the two auto-generated certificates from the trust bundle are valid for 1 year.

Since Dapr Sentry is part of the Dapr control plane, mTLS is enabled by default when you host Dapr in Kubernetes. Conversely, in Self-hosted mode, mTLS is disabled by default as you don't have the Sentry service running on your machine. In case you want to enable mTLS for the Self-hosted Dapr, you have to either build Sentry from the source or download a pre-built binary and start it. Another important difference in the behavior of Sentry between Kubernetes and Self-hosted modes is the location where root and issuer certificates along with the private key of the issuer certificate are stored. In Kubernetes mode, the certificates are stored in a Kubernetes Secret; thus, they are only available to the control plane resources. In Self-hosted mode, they are stored under some path on the filesystem. Kubernetes Secrets are yet another type of Kubernetes object that allows you to store, manage, and control the access to sensitive information like passwords, tokens, keys, and so on.

Dapr Sidecar Injector and *Dapr Operator* are services unique for Dapr in Kubernetes mode. They are needed because of the way things are represented inside Kubernetes. An application is not simply a locally running process; instead, it is a process running inside a container, wrapped as a Pod, that may be replicated multiple times across Kubernetes worker nodes. The Dapr Sidecar Injector service makes sure that whenever it detects a Pod marked with a Dapr-specific annotation, it will inject a Dapr sidecar container in that same Pod. The Sidecar Injector is an implementation of the *Kubernetes Admission controller,* which intercepts requests to the Kubernetes API and executes some validation logic or modifies the objects before they are persisted. Out of curiosity, you may want to peek at the way it is configured to monitor for the creation of any Pods by running `kubectl describe MutatingWebhookConfiguration`. Later in this chapter, I will show you how to deploy to Kubernetes the distributed Hello World application that we have implemented in Chapter 2: Introduction to Dapr.

If you recall, components and configuration are files somewhere on the local filesystem that are being parsed and used by Dapr when it runs in Self-hosted mode. In Kubernetes mode, the exact same files are used as manifests that are applied to Kubernetes. Dapr extends the Kubernetes API by providing *Custom Resource Definitions* (CRDs) for both component and configuration resources. Having a *CRD*, your custom resource becomes a first-class citizen of Kubernetes that you can manage just like any other object, for example, Pod, Deployment, and so on. Components and configurations are always defined as CRDs no matter if you have Dapr running in Self-hosted or

Kubernetes mode. Or in other words, they can be applied to any Dapr installation, regardless of its hosting mode.

As you already know, components determine how the building blocks function – they specify what end service to be used and how to connect to it. By modifying the definition of a component, you effectively change the internal strategy of a building block. In the same way, the Configuration object allows you to control the way Dapr works. For example, by modifying the Configuration manifest, you can configure mTLS settings and how long a workload certificate should be valid or change the way distributed tracing works. When you use custom resources in Kubernetes, you will most likely have an operator that is going to be the controller of those custom resources. In the same way, you have human operators and site reliability engineers who are looking after some applications and services. They have the knowledge of how a complex application works, how to deploy it and manage it, and what specific actions to do in case of any problems. By implementing an operator, you can incorporate the domain-specific knowledge into an automation inside Kubernetes. For example, the operator (or controller) will run as yet another Deployment in your cluster and can make application-specific decisions and actions. It can allocate more replicas of some service if certain thresholds are reached or conditions are met. Another example would be knowing when and how to do backups or knowing what specific steps to take whenever the configuration of the application changes. In case any Dapr Component object has been changed, the Dapr Operator will notify all sidecars, and they will try to hot-reload the component.

Note   At the time of writing, the hot-reload feature is halfway implemented. Being a hot topic, it will most likely be implemented soon. Before that is implemented, you have to restart (or recreate) your Pods to make them pick up the updated versions of components and configurations by using `kubectl rollout restart deployments/<DEPLOYMENT-NAME>`, for example.

Let's have a look at the Kubernetes objects for the Dapr system services. By default, the control plane resides in the namespace dapr-system. Of course, if you don't want to use the dapr-system, you can specify the name of the namespace to be used at the time of running the `dapr init` command. Namespaces in Kubernetes are intended to provide logical separation for groups of objects inside a cluster. If you have a variety of resources belonging to different projects, teams, or environments, you will most likely benefit from using *namespaces*. The names of the resources within a namespace should be unique, but it is entirely possible to have a resource with the same name in a different namespace. If you don't specify a namespace when using kubectl, the `default` namespace will be implied for all commands. Execute the following command, and you will find out what resources were created for the Dapr control plane:

```
kubectl get all --namespace dapr-system
```

You will find out that a Deployment with one replica and a Service have been created for each Dapr system service – Operator, Placement, Sentry, and Sidecar Injector. Although the Dapr Dashboard is not really a control plane service, because of convenience, it is present as well. To open the dashboard, run `dapr dashboard -k`, and it will set up port forwarding for you and open the address in a browser. Don't forget the `-k/--kubernetes` flag; otherwise, it will open the Dapr Dashboard from your Dapr installation in Self-hosted mode. If you have installed Dapr in a nondefault namespace, you have to specify it via the `-n/--namespace` flag.

It's very slick to install Dapr using the CLI, but there are some other options as well.

Installing the Dapr Helm Chart

At this point, you might be thinking that the initialization via the CLI applies a couple of Deployment manifests, a few CustomResourceDefinition manifests, and so on. If that's the case, you are not that far away from the truth indeed, except that those manifests are packaged into the Dapr Helm Chart. You can still deploy Dapr using the Dapr CLI, but if you prefer to use Helm, you also can.

Let's see how to deploy a highly available Dapr control plane. This means that instead of running just one Pod for each system service, there will be multiple of them; by default, they are three replicas. This is needed because the Dapr control plane can prove to be a single point of failure for your services because they are relying upon it for communication, state management, and so on. Make sure your production cluster has at least three worker nodes; otherwise, you won't be able to achieve high availability although there will be multiple replicas of the system services running on it.

If you are going to use the same Kubernetes cluster, please uninstall the previously installed Dapr control plane by running `dapr uninstall --kubernetes`.

The steps to install Dapr with Helm are as follows:

1. First of all, you have to install Helm 3 on your machine. The official documentation guides you through the various installation options: `https://helm.sh/docs/intro/install/`. It's yet another binary that you must have downloaded or installed via a package manager.

2. Helm Charts are coming from different repositories. Dapr provides versioned Helm Charts from a GitHub repository. Let's add it and retrieve the information about all charts available in it:

```
helm repo add dapr https://dapr.github.io/helm-charts/
helm repo update
```

3. Now that you have all prerequisites, let's deploy a highly available Dapr control plane using the following command. Helm Charts allow you to specify values at the time of installation by using the `--set` flag and passing a custom value from the command line. That's how parameterization happens in Helm. It's a good idea to specify the version of Dapr you want to install (but make sure to install the latest stable version as at the time of writing the book it is 1.0.1) and also set the `--create-namespace` switch to create the dapr-system namespace, in case it doesn't exist:

```
helm upgrade --install dapr dapr/dapr --version=1.0.1 --namespace dapr-
system --create-namespace --set global.ha.enabled=true --wait
```

4. Lastly, let's validate how many Pods were created:

```
kubectl get pods -n dapr-system
```

The output of the last command will be something like this, the AGE column having been omitted for readability:

```
NAME                             READY STATUS  RESTARTS
dapr-dashboard-fccd6c8cc-cjm5f   1/1   Running 0
dapr-operator-886df997-79z4z     1/1   Running 0
dapr-operator-886df997-7f6nq     1/1   Running 0
dapr-operator-886df997-jflkg     1/1   Running 0
```

```
dapr-placement-server-0                 1/1    Running 0
dapr-placement-server-1                 1/1    Running 0
dapr-placement-server-2                 1/1    Running 0
dapr-sentry-7767c445f8-44gbt            1/1    Running 0
dapr-sentry-7767c445f8-9bbzn            1/1    Running 0
dapr-sentry-7767c445f8-sd8ql            1/1    Running 0
dapr-sidecar-injector-5ccd6b5466-dk2dp 1/1    Running 0
dapr-sidecar-injector-5ccd6b5466-gql46 1/1    Running 0
dapr-sidecar-injector-5ccd6b5466-szcpm 1/1    Running 0
```

Notice that every Dapr system service consists of three Pods. The three Pods of each service provide redundancy, and requests are load balanced between them. One exception is the Placement service that tracks where actors are instantiated across the cluster. It implements the *Raft consensus algorithm,* and therefore one of the Pods is elected as a leader, while the others are followers. If the leader goes down, another Pod will be appointed as a leader, and in the meantime, the failed Pod will come back as a follower.

There is just one replica of the Dapr Dashboard as it is not mission-critical. You can increase the number of replicas by specifying the `dapr_dashboard.replicaCount` chart value. Please have in mind that the `dapr init -k` command from the Dapr CLI also supports all chart options by specifying the `--set` flag, which expects a comma-separated string array of values, for example, `key1=val1,key2=val2`.

Some time will go by after you have installed Dapr, and there will be newer versions coming out. You need to know how to upgrade your Dapr control plane to a newer version.

Zero-Downtime Upgrades

Upgrading Dapr without any downtime is almost as easy as its installation is. However, a Helm release upgrade may ditch some objects depending on how the chart has been implemented and what values were provided. CustomResourceDefinitions are one of the Kubernetes objects that are tricky to be updated by Helm. This also applies to the certificate bundle of Dapr that is needed for mTLS communication. Whenever you are upgrading Dapr, you would want to reuse the old certificates so that it won't cause an interruption. But this is all handled by both Dapr CLI and the Helm Chart itself.

Now let's upgrade the Dapr Helm release to a newer version. In Helm's terms, a release is an installation of a chart. But first, don't forget to get the new version of the Dapr Chart by running

```
helm repo update
```

Then simply run `helm upgrade` and specify the new version you want to upgrade the Dapr release to:

```
helm upgrade dapr dapr/dapr --version <NEW-VERSION> --namespace dapr-system
--wait
```

At this point, the Dapr control plane will be running the newer version of Dapr. But if you have any sidecars running at the time you do the upgrade, they will still use the old version of the Dapr sidecar. You have to trigger a recreation of those Pods to pick up the new version of the Dapr sidecar container. You can do it by performing a rolling restart for the Deployment object: `kubectl rollout restart deployments/<DEPLOYMENT-NAME>`. This command will create a new set of Pods defined by this deployment. The existing Pods will be functional until the new Pods are up and running. After that, the old Pods will be deleted.

Uninstalling Dapr

Finally, let's also cover the uninstallation of Dapr. I don't recommend you to do this as you are going to need Dapr to be installed to be able to run the distributed Hello World application later in the chapter.

Dapr can be uninstalled by both the Dapr CLI and Helm. If you used Dapr CLI to install it, you can uninstall it by running `dapr uninstall -k`. In case you installed the Helm Chart, uninstall it by running `helm uninstall dapr --namespace dapr-system`.

Note   It's not recommended to try uninstalling Dapr manually. Always use the Dapr CLI or Helm. By trying to do it manually, you will most likely forget to delete some of the Dapr-related things, which will put your cluster in a very bad state, which may cause issues when you later try to install Dapr.

Now that you know how Dapr runs in Kubernetes mode, let me show you how applications are actually using it.

Dapr Applications in Kubernetes

Let me show you how the distributed Hello World app can be hosted in Kubernetes. No changes are required to run the application in Kubernetes. The only prerequisite is to have the Docker images for the three services published in Docker Hub under your account. You must have published them as part of the examples in Chapter 2: Introduction to Dapr.

As you would normally do, create a YAML manifest for each of the services. Let's explore Listing 4-1, the Deployment manifest of the Hello service, which you can store as a file named hello.yaml.

Listing 4-1. Deployment manifest of the Hello service

```
apiVersion: apps/v1
kind: Deployment
metadata:
  name: hello-deployment
  labels:
    app: hello
spec:
  replicas: 1
  selector:
    matchLabels:
      app: hello
  template:
    metadata:
      labels:
        app: hello
      annotations:
        dapr.io/enabled: "true"
        dapr.io/app-id: "hello-service"
        dapr.io/app-port: "8088"
    spec:
      containers:
      - name: hello-container
```

```
image: <YOUR-DOCKER-HUB-USERNAME>/hello-service:latest
ports:
- containerPort: 8088
```

Since we deploy everything in Kubernetes, it is perfectly fine for all services to listen on the same port as you won't have any conflicts as opposed to being in Self-hosted mode. But I decided to reuse the same code from Chapter 2: Introduction to Dapr and the containers built and published to Docker Hub in Chapter 3: Getting Up to Speed with Kubernetes, which means that all three services run on different ports although each one of them is hosted in a separate container.

Have you noticed those annotations starting with dapr.io? The *Admission controller* will catch every *creation* of a *Pod* and will pass the control to the Dapr Injector service, which will inspect the Pod for any dapr.io annotations. The most important annotations are dapr.io/enabled, dapr.io/app-id, dapr.io/app-port, dapr.io/protocol, and dapr.io/config. Those may look familiar to the flags available when executing dapr run. If dapr.io/enabled is *true*, the Sidecar Injector service will inject another container for the Dapr runtime as a sidecar container inside that Pod. The dapr.io/app-id, dapr.io/app-protocol, and dapr.io/port specify, respectively, the Dapr Application ID, the protocol used by the application, and the port to be used when invoking the service. Among those are annotations for configuring Dapr sidecar settings such as the log level, memory and CPU limits, and liveness and readiness probes. The dapr.io/app-port specifies the port that the application listens on. If you don't expect any other services calling into this application or if it doesn't listen on a port, you simply don't specify this annotation. The dapr.io/config specifies which Configuration CRD to use for the Dapr sidecar of this service. You can find the full list of all available annotations in Dapr docs at https://docs.dapr.io/operations/hosting/kubernetes/kubernetes-annotations/.

Please follow the same logic and specify the manifests for the World and Greeting services and save them as world.yaml and greeting.yaml, respectively.

In the case of the distributed Hello World example, the Greeting service will be the only service that is client-facing. This means that you don't have to define dapr.io/app-port because it will be directly accessed via a Kubernetes service from the outside. Add the following definition of the Service object at the bottom of greeting.yaml, but make sure to include the --- separator that allows you to have multiple resources in a single manifest file:

```
---
kind: Service
apiVersion: v1
metadata:
  name: greeting-service
  labels:
    app: greeting
spec:
  selector:
    app: greeting
  ports:
  - protocol: TCP
    port: 80
    targetPort: 8090
  type: NodePort
```

It targets the Pods that are tagged with the app selector with value greeting, exposes port 80, and targets port 8090 in the matching Pod(s). If your Kubernetes cluster runs locally, you would be better off using the NodePort service type as opposed to LoadBalancer, which requires a unique public IP per Service. The LoadBalancer type comes in handy whenever you have a Kubernetes cluster in the cloud such as Azure Kubernetes Service.

In order to apply the manifests of the services that the distributed Hello World application consists of, navigate to the directory where they are located and execute the kubectl apply -f . command. This will apply the manifests in the default Kubernetes namespace. Once that has been done, run kubectl get service greeting-service to get the NodePort on which the greeting-service listens on. In my case, it listens on port 31196, so opening http://localhost:31196/greet results in seeing the outputs from both Hello service and World service that were combined by the Greeting service.

This is the experience of having your Dapr application running inside Kubernetes. You don't have to think about what is available on your machine and whether any service dependencies will conflict with any others. Now let's inspect the logs of the Dapr sidecar running along with the Greeting service. We can find the name of the pod by executing kubectl get pods -l 'app=greeting'. Now that you know the name of the pod, have a look at its logs by running kubectl logs <greeting-pod-name> daprd. You will notice that many things were initialized like mTLS, various middleware, name resolution, actors, workload certificates generated, and others.

Have in mind that at this point, you cannot use the Actors building block. The reason is that there isn't any state component for persisting the state of actors defined. You saw how Dapr in Self-hosted mode created a Redis container and had the default state component configured to point to it just for convenience. That's not the case with Kubernetes as it is meant to be used as a production environment. You have to deploy Redis in Kubernetes yourself, or you can use an external service to persist the state of all actors.

Dapr and Service Meshes

If you are familiar with service meshes, some of the Dapr features may look very similar to what the service meshes provide. Some of the popular service meshes are Istio, Linkerd, and Open Service Mesh. Service meshes provide a set of features that address network-related concerns when communicating across services such as routing, traffic flow management, and Mutual TLS communication between services. Since a service mesh knows the ins and outs of your service-to-service communication, it also provides distributed tracing out of the box as Dapr does. Moreover, both Dapr and service meshes use the sidecar container pattern to implement their capabilities.

Although there is some overlap because of the distributed tracing and the mTLS, service meshes stay more on the networking infrastructure, whereas Dapr provides a language-agnostic programming model that helps you develop your Microservices application.

Dapr and service meshes can work side by side. You have to decide what features to use from each of them. For example, you may decide to let the service mesh provide mTLS authentication, which means that you have to tell Dapr to disable its mTLS. There are several options to do so:

- If you are installing/upgrading Dapr using its Helm Chart, you can disable mTLS by specifying --set global.mtls.enabled=false.

- If you are installing Dapr via the Dapr CLI, provide an additional flag for mTLS configuration dapr init --kubernetes --enable-mtls=false.

At the time of writing, Dapr is known to work side by side with service meshes like Istio and Linkerd. However, we won't be exploring how to use service meshes together with Dapr in this book.

Isolation of Components and Configuration

Components and configurations are namespaced objects. In Kubernetes, Dapr leverages the Kubernetes namespaces, but namespaces are also applicable for Self-hosted mode. This allows you to manage the security of and access to components. When you create a component inside a given namespace, only the Dapr applications running inside this namespace will be able to use it. Components also provide a way to set up fine-grained access control by explicitly specifying which apps can reach a component.

There is one global configuration that resides in the namespace of the Dapr control plane. But you can have a Configuration CRD per Dapr application, or several applications can share a single Configuration CRD. The configuration has to be created inside the same namespace where the Dapr application lives. Having an application-specific configuration allows you to control how the tracing works for this application, what middleware to be used, and what rules will apply when you use service-to-service invocation.

Summary

In this chapter, you learned how Dapr functions when hosted in Kubernetes mode.

The Dapr system services are building the so-called Dapr control plane, or the brain of Dapr. Two of the system services applicable for Dapr in Self-hosted mode are still present in Kubernetes – Dapr Sentry and Dapr Placement services. There are two additional services needed because of the way Kubernetes works – the Dapr Sidecar Injector and the Dapr Operator. The Sidecar Injector service makes sure there is a Dapr sidecar container for each Dapr application. Dapr Operator deals with the updates of any Component and Configuration CRDs, which control the way the Dapr sidecar and Dapr building blocks work.

You also learned about the ways to install Dapr in Kubernetes and later on perform zero-downtime upgrades. Once you had the Dapr control plane up and running in the Kubernetes cluster, it was about time to show you how to deploy the distributed Hello

World application that was implemented in Chapter 2: Introduction to Dapr without any code changes. In order to distinguish it as a Dapr application, the Dapr annotation had to be applied to the Pods of the three services. Once that was done, it became clear that once you have packaged your applications in container images, running them inside Kubernetes is a lot easier compared with Self-hosted mode because you don't have to think about port conflicts, installing local dependencies, and starting all application parts one at a time.

Later on, you learned how Dapr can work side by side with service meshes and how to deal with the isolation of components and configuration when you have a lot of applications and therefore have to meet various needs.

Now that you know how to develop and deploy Dapr applications, in the next chapter, you will gain some experience debugging them.

CHAPTER 5

Debugging Dapr Applications

Knowing how to configure your local development environment to be able to develop and debug applications seamlessly using Dapr is very important for your productivity. In this chapter, I am going to show you several different ways to run and debug Dapr applications locally, in a Docker development container, or in Kubernetes.

Dapr CLI

Dapr CLI is the tool that I keep showing you throughout the book. It's rather primitive when you want to start multiple applications as you need to keep several terminals open. Furthermore, you have to keep track of local ports and Dapr Application IDs.

However, this gives you the most control of the setup because you can easily change pretty much everything – you can change Dapr ports, you can choose to use the default components location, or you can specify another path that contains the components. The command with which you start your application along with a Dapr sidecar is dapr run. For example, the Hello service that is one of the services from the distributed Hello World application that we implemented in Chapter 2: Introduction to Dapr is started with the following command, given that you have navigated to the project directory:

```
dapr run --app-id hello-service --app-port 8088 -- node app.js
```

However, you can use the Dapr CLI just to start a Dapr sidecar for you because, for example, you want to start the application with Visual Studio 2019 and debug it there. In order to do this, you have to omit the command that you otherwise specify in the end to start your application:

```
dapr run --app-id hello-service --app-port 8088 --
```

© Radoslav Gatev 2021

R. Gatev, *Introducing Distributed Application Runtime (Dapr)*, https://doi.org/10.1007/978-1-4842-6998-5_5

After you run the command, you have to start the application, for example, from Visual Studio in Debug mode. Obviously, this method gives you the most control, but it's not the easiest one if you are going to do it repeatedly.

Dapr Extension for Visual Studio Code

There is a Dapr extension for Visual Studio Code that helps you start Dapr applications alongside a Dapr sidecar. The extension itself also supports some of the basic functionality that the Dapr CLI supports, like seeing the current active Dapr applications. Additionally, via the Visual Studio Code extension, you can invoke GET or POST methods by leveraging the Service Invocation building block or publish messages via the Publish and Subscribe building block.

You can also use the extension to scaffold Dapr tasks, needed for launching a Dapr sidecar with your application. In order to do so, open the command palette (Ctrl/Cmd+Shift+P) and select *Dapr: Scaffold Dapr Tasks* as shown in Figure 5-1. This results in opening a wizard that will guide you through some basic information about your application like Dapr ID and the port that it is listening on and will eventually result in creating a *Launch Program with Dapr* debugging configuration. This will directly call daprd and pass some flags that are configurable. The extension itself creates the configuration in .vscode\launch.json where it defines how to start a Dapr application in debugging mode. This means that when the configuration is selected, you can put a breakpoint somewhere in the app.js file and by simply pressing F5 it will start the application and put it into Debug mode, without any custom commands. It's the easiest way to start a Dapr application and debug it.

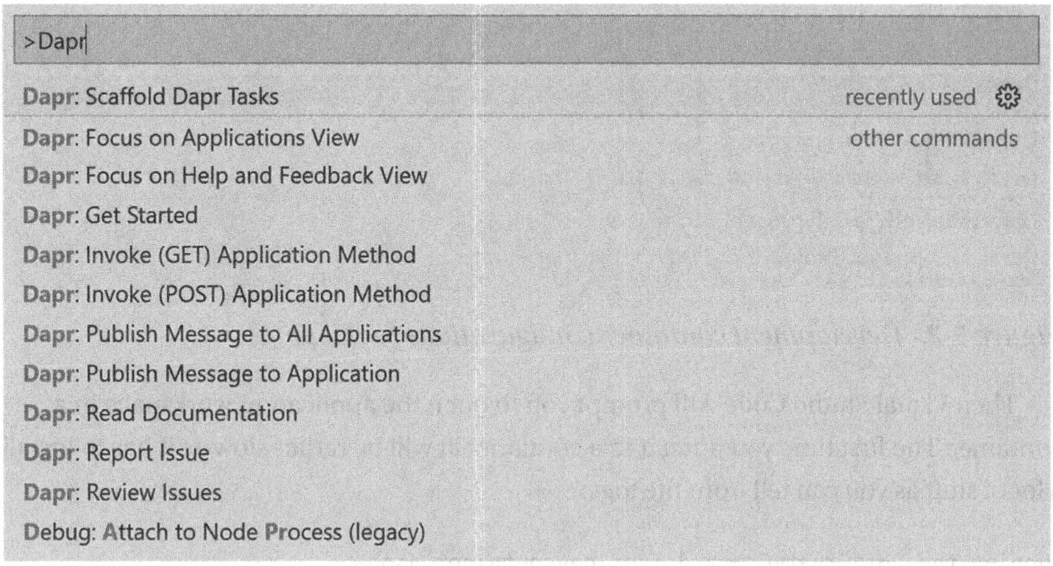

```
> Dapr|

Dapr: Scaffold Dapr Tasks                                    recently used  ⚙
Dapr: Focus on Applications View                             other commands
Dapr: Focus on Help and Feedback View
Dapr: Get Started
Dapr: Invoke (GET) Application Method
Dapr: Invoke (POST) Application Method
Dapr: Publish Message to All Applications
Dapr: Publish Message to Application
Dapr: Read Documentation
Dapr: Report Issue
Dapr: Review Issues
Debug: Attach to Node Process (legacy)
```

Figure 5-1. *Commands supported by the Dapr extension for VS Code*

Additionally, the scaffolding creates a folder that contains any Dapr components that are used by the application. When you start debugging, it will make sure to process all components from that folder.

You can find the already configured for debugging Hello service in the source code of the book under the following path: Chapter 5/Dapr-extension/hello-service.

Development Container

Another option is to develop entirely inside a Docker container. This means that you don't need to have any of the development tools and dependencies on your local machine. Instead, everything is going to happen in a development container that Visual Studio Code is going to interact with. There are a couple of pre-built containers for Dapr development. Dapr will be installed in the container and added to the path. It will also make sure to start other dependencies like a container running Redis, Zipkin, and the Dapr Placement service.

In order to do this yourself, you need to install the *Remote – Containers extension* in your Visual Studio Code. Then, open the command palette (Cmd/Ctrl+Shift+P) and select *Remote-Containers: Add Development Container Configuration Files*. Then select *From a predefined container configuration definition*, search for Dapr, and click *Show All Definitions*. The Dapr predefined configurations will show up as depicted in Figure 5-2. Choose the one that fits the language you used for implementing your application. At the time of writing, the two definitions are for C# and Node.js.

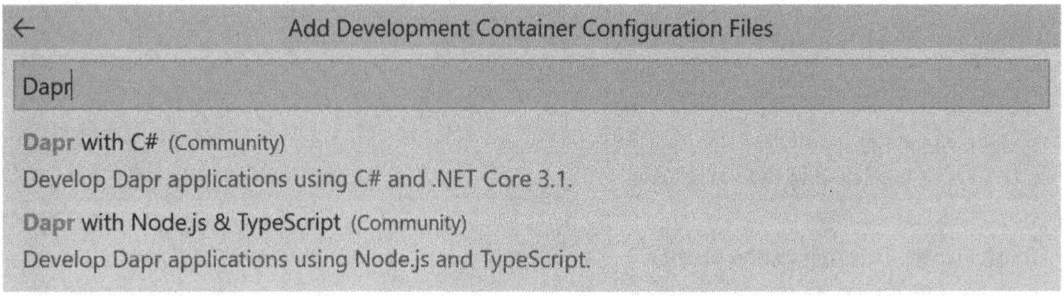

Figure 5-2. *Development container configurations for Dapr*

Then Visual Studio Code will prompt you to open the application workspace in a container. The first time you open it in a container, it will be rather slow as it has to install a lot of stuff as you can tell from the logs:

```
Running the PostCreateCommand from devcontainer.json...

[176564 ms] Start: Run: docker exec -i -t -u node -e SSH_AUTH_SOCK=/
tmp/vscode-ssh-auth-535f46918c49e0796e88a30ea3d75aab296fd5d0.sock -e
REMOTE_CONTAINERS_IPC=/tmp/vscode-remote-containers-ipc-535f46918c49e
0796e88a30ea3d75aab296fd5d0.sock -e REMOTE_CONTAINERS=true -e LOCAL_
WORKSPACE_FOLDER=c:\Chapter 5\Remote-containers\hello-service -w /workspace
d12bf642c03a7408dd40e93537598e02bab85adf37be6657b8159e14cf755064 /bin/sh -c
dapr init
⌛  Making the jump to hyperspace...
↘  Downloading binaries and setting up components...
Dapr runtime installed to /home/node/.dapr/bin, you may run the following to add
 it to your path if you want to run daprd directly:
    export PATH=$PATH:/home/node/.dapr/bin
✓  Downloaded binaries and completed components set up.
ℹ☐  daprd binary has been installed to /home/node/.dapr/bin.
ℹ☐  dapr_placement_dapr-dev-container container is running.
ℹ☐  dapr_redis_dapr-dev-container container is running.
ℹ☐  dapr_zipkin_dapr-dev-container container is running.
ℹ☐  Use `docker ps` to check running containers.
✓  Success! Dapr is up and running. To get started, go here:
    https://aka.ms/dapr
-getting-started

Done. Press any key to close the terminal.
```

Then pressing F5 will launch your application in Debug mode and set up port forwarding to the development container so that you can access your application on localhost.

You can find the already configured for running in a development container Hello service in the source code of the book under the following path: Chapter 5/Remote-containers/hello-service. When you open the project directory in Visual Studio Code, it will detect the configuration and prompt you by suggesting to reopen the folder in a container.

Bridge to Kubernetes

Most of the time, you will have a Microservices application that consists of a number of services. Some of them will have a dependency on a database or some other external service. You can use multitarget debugging in Visual Studio Code for starting multiple applications. However, having the application processes up and running is just a small part of what you will likely need in a complex architecture.

Bridge to Kubernetes is a tool that enables local development against a Kubernetes cluster. In simple terms, it sets up port forwarding to your local machine so that each Kubernetes service appears as if it was hosted locally. This makes it possible to substitute a certain service with a locally running application as a counterpart that you can debug. A single Kubernetes cluster that has the entire application stack deployed can be shared and utilized by multiple developers. To start using this, you will first need to install the *Bridge to Kubernetes extension* for Visual Studio Code or Visual Studio 2019.

However, a known limitation of Bridge to Kubernetes is that it doesn't work well with Pods that have multiple containers. Dapr utilizes the sidecar pattern for making the Dapr runtime accessible to each service, as it injects a daprd container in each Dapr-annotated Pod. This is somewhat problematic for Bridge to Kubernetes as you cannot fully utilize it for any services that are invoked via the system of Dapr sidecars since it cannot intercept the traffic between sidecars and applications. When you set up Bridge to Kubernetes for debugging a particular service, you have to trigger it yourself by sending an appropriate request to its ports on localhost.

Like the other Visual Studio Code extensions, this one also provides a command that sets the configuration up. It launches a wizard that will prompt you to select the Kubernetes service that you want to redirect to your machine, the local port where this service will be running, and the launch configuration.

As an example, I will show you how to debug the Greeting service of the distributed Hello World application. Note that I have deployed the entire application to Azure Kubernetes Service (AKS) because the idea is that several developers will share it. And I have pointed my kubectl context to it so that any kubectl command will point to AKS. There is one workaround before you will be able to debug a service locally. The Greeting service depends on its Dapr sidecar to call the Hello and the World services. That's why you need to expose the daprd container of some service that you won't be debugging. In my case, this will be the Dapr sidecar of the Hello service. Create a new file named dapr-sidecar-service.yaml that contains the manifest of the Kubernetes service that exposes a Dapr sidecar:

```
apiVersion: v1
kind: Service
metadata:
 name: dapr-sidecar
spec:
 type: LoadBalancer
 selector:
  app: hello
 ports:
  - name: dapr-http
    port: 80
    protocol: TCP
    targetPort: 3500
```

And don't forget to create in Kubernetes by running kubectl apply -f .\dapr-sidecar-service.yaml.

Bridge to Kubernetes can be configured by creating a KubernetesLocalProcessConfig.yaml file that is situated in the root of the application workspace. In this file, you can specify what environment variables to be made available to the application that you are going to debug. In my case, this will be the local address of the `dapr-sidecar` service that will be locally accessible on 127.1.1.1. This means that when you hit this IP address on port 80 via HTTP, it will actually go and call the remote dapr-sidecar service that is running inside AKS. This is configured in the following way:

```
version: 0.1
env:
  - name: DAPR_SIDECAR_HOST
    value: $(services:dapr-sidecar)
```

Of course, this will require some changes to be made in the application itself. It is not safe to assume that Dapr will be accessible on localhost at port 3500 as it is typically in Kubernetes. Bridge to Kubernetes will set up port forwarding to some random local address as I already mentioned. That's why you have to get the whole address from the environment variable that was made available by the configuration file:

```
const daprHost= process.env.DAPR_SIDECAR_HOST;
const invokeHello = `http://${daprHost}/v1.0/invoke/hello-service/method/
sayHello`;
const invokeWorld = `http://${daprHost}/v1.0/invoke/world-service/method/
sayWorld`;
```

Then when you press F5, Bridge to Kubernetes will set up your local debugging environment. It will require some permissions as it is going to manage the ports on your machine. If you have Docker Desktop running, make sure to quit it as it will prevent Bridge to Kubernetes to initialize successfully. Then opening `http://localhost:8090/greet` will let you debug the Greeting service while it is calling the other two services that are actually running inside a Kubernetes cluster.

You can find the Greeting service project configured for debugging with Bridge to Kubernetes in the source code of the book under the following path: Chapter 5/Bridge-To-K8s. Make sure to change values of `targetCluster` and `targetNamespace` in .vscode\tasks.json to reflect what is appropriate to your current context. As it comes to AKS, after you configure your kubectl context to point to it, you have to deploy Dapr and the manifests of the Hello World application just like in Chapter 4: Running Dapr in Kubernetes Mode.

Note   Please have in mind that the ability of Bridge to Kubernetes is pretty limited, at the time of writing the book. However, in my opinion, it is an important use case for debugging because you don't need to have the whole Microservices application running locally to be able to debug it. I find this pretty useful for complex applications.

Summary

In this chapter, I showed you several ways to debug your Dapr applications. You can debug everything locally by either using the Dapr CLI or the Dapr Visual Studio Code extension. Another option is to run and debug your applications inside a development container. And for the most sophisticated architectures, you can use Bridge to Kubernetes to debug a service locally while other parts of the application are running remotely inside a Kubernetes cluster.

You learned about the nature of the Microservices architecture. Later on, you were introduced to Kubernetes and how Dapr helps during the development of distributed applications. I also covered the concepts of Dapr and its two hosting modes – Self-hosted and Kubernetes – and what tricks to use for debugging during the development of Dapr applications.

The next part of the book will be a deep dive into the details of each building block that Dapr provides starting with the Service Invocation building block.

PART II

Building Blocks Overview

CHAPTER 6

Service Invocation

Developing an application based on the Microservices architecture implies having many smaller services that work as a whole. A significant part of their responsibilities goes to being able to communicate with each other. Some of them will use a loosely coupled means of communication by broadcasting some messages to all interested parties. Others, instead, would want to invoke a particular service by making a direct request to it. Service discovery and service invocation are the essentials that you will need whenever implementing such a Microservices application.

Fortunately, Dapr provides a building block for invoking other Dapr applications. In this chapter, you will learn what this building block does and how it works. Some services may be exposing an HTTP endpoint, while others understand gRPC. Dapr supports HTTP and gRPC both on the caller and the callee sides. Additionally, those two services might be running in different security boundaries. Because that makes things much more complex, I will show you how to make *cross-protocol* and *cross-namespace* calls. You might be willing to control access to some services very carefully as they may contain some very critical information or functionality that shouldn't be available from everywhere. We will explore how to leverage access policies in order to make certain services accessible only by a particular set of services that are eligible for calling in.

Overview

Imagine that there is Service A that performs several tasks and one of them is getting some result from Service B. There are a couple of challenges coming from this need:

- First of all, Service A must be able to locate the address of Service B. Both services may be colocated on the same machine or not.

- If both services are RESTful services, it's a matter of issuing an HTTP request. However, Service B may be a gRPC service, which means that Service A will need to have a gRPC client stub in order to call into

95

© Radoslav Gatev 2021

R. Gatev, *Introducing Distributed Application Runtime (Dapr)*, https://doi.org/10.1007/978-1-4842-6998-5_6

Service B. Maybe this won't feel very natural for the implementation of Service A if the majority of services are based on HTTP.

- The communication between the two services must be secure.

- In the nature of the cloud-native applications, transient faults are anticipated. Thus, client applications should expect and embrace such failures and handle them by using the *Retry pattern*. The Retry pattern relies on the premise that if you retry a failed operation after some reasonable delay, it will likely have been self-healed and therefore succeed. Of course, there are different strategies for defining the maximum number of retries and the duration of the delay. Some handy libraries provide you with such retry logic, for example, Polly for .NET applications.

- In a complex Microservices application, you would want to be able to understand where your cross-service communication starts and ends. And preferably this should be a visual experience.

Now let's see how those things will be if you use Dapr's Service Invocation building block. As you already know, each Dapr-ized service has a Dapr runtime companion running beside it as either a sidecar process or a sidecar container. All of the above-mentioned challenges are addressed when you call the /invoke endpoint of the Dapr sidecar as shown in Figure 6-1:

1. First, Service A makes an HTTP/gRPC call to its Dapr sidecar and specifies which application to be called, a particular method name, and some data. Assuming the protocol is HTTP and the Dapr sidecar listens on port 3500, the request URL will be the following: `http://localhost:3500/v1.0/invoke/<dapr-app-id>/method/<method-name>`.

2. Once the request reached the sidecar, it resolves the address of the sidecar target service by using the name resolution component that finds the particular location of the sidecar of Service B. There is more information on name resolution further in the chapter.

3. The request is forwarded to the sidecar of Service B. Note that sidecar-to-sidecar communication happens only via gRPC.

4. Dapr Sidecar B invokes the method of Service B. If you recall when starting the application with `dapr run`, you have to specify the port number that your application listens on. The same applies in Kubernetes mode where you use the `dapr.io/app-port` annotation. The actual URL for the request to Service B will be `http://localhost:<app-port>/<method-name>`.

5. The response of Service B is captured by its Dapr sidecar.

6. The sidecar of Service B forwards the captured output to Dapr Sidecar A.

7. Dapr Sidecar A returns the response to the calling service. For Service A, it seems like the response is coming right from its Dapr sidecar although a complex communication flow has happened behind the scenes.

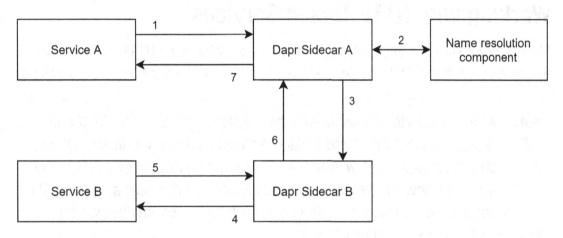

Figure 6-1. *Service invocation via Dapr sidecars*

Dapr acts like a *reverse proxy* between the caller service and the callee service. Furthermore, it will also try to resolve transient failures received from Service B by retrying the request up to three times with a backoff time period between calls.

Since all the communications flow through the Dapr sidecar, it is easy for it to provide a distributed tracing functionality. We are going to explore distributed tracing in depth in Chapter 12: Observability: Logs, Metrics, and Traces. For the same reason, Dapr can help you control the number of processed simultaneous calls on the application side whether it is coming from service invocation, pub/sub, or bindings.

The rate limiting takes effect when you specify the number of concurrent requests in the app-max-concurrency flag for Self-hosted mode or the dapr.io/app-max-concurrency annotation in Kubernetes mode. In this way, you can assume that only a configured number of requests at a time go through any method of the service without having to implement complex logic for managing concurrency.

The distributed Hello World example we explored earlier already uses the Service Invocation building block. However, let me show you how you can implement services based on HTTP and gRPC and how it looks from the consumer side.

As a matter of fact, the functionality provided by the Service Invocation building block is part of the foundation of Dapr as it needs to use direct service invocation as part of other building blocks, for example, the Publish and Subscribe and the Actors building blocks. You just don't call the service invocation API directly because it is internally utilized by the logic of the respective building blocks.

Working with HTTP-Based Services

Most of the services that are still being implemented are based on HTTP. Let's see how we can create a simple ASP.NET Core Web API, which we are going to invoke using Dapr.

Note   As a prerequisite, you will need to have installed Visual Studio 2019 with .NET 5; or if you prefer to use a code editor like Visual Studio Code, install just the .NET 5 SDK, which you can download from https://dotnet.microsoft.com/download. The following steps will be applicable for the latter case as running CLI commands is easier to follow than clicking through the project creation wizard of Visual Studio that might get updated.

---

1. First, start by creating a new folder for the project and navigate to it in a terminal.

2. Run the following command to scaffold an ASP.NET Core Web API project on .NET 5:

```
dotnet new webapi -f net5.0
```

3. Explore the ASP.NET Core project:

   a. A WeatherForecastController was created with a Get method, which
   returns a forecast for the next five days.

   b. Explore Properties/launchSettings.json that indicates what port your
   application will listen on.

4. Open Startup.cs and comment out the line app.
   UseHttpsRedirection(); because the Dapr sidecar and the
   service don't have to communicate over HTTPS. The reason for
   that is that they live inside the same security boundary.

5. Change the Get method of WeatherForecastController so that it
   accepts the number of days you want a forecast for:

```
[HttpGet]
public IEnumerable<WeatherForecast> Get(int daysCount)
{
        var rng = new Random();
        return Enumerable.Range(1, daysCount).Select(index => new
        WeatherForecast
        {
                Date = DateTime.Now.AddDays(index),
                TemperatureC = rng.Next(-20, 55),
                Summary = Summaries[rng.Next(Summaries.Length)]
        })
        .ToArray();
}
```

6. Now let's run it as a Dapr application, which also starts a sidecar
   process:

```
dapr run --app-id weather --app-port 5000 -- dotnet run
```

7. Leave that command running in this terminal as you are going to
   make requests to it.

Now let me show you how you can invoke the Weather Forecast service from another service:

1. First, open a new terminal and start a Dapr sidecar for your caller service: `dapr run --dapr-http-port 3500 --`. At this point, you will have two Dapr sidecars running in different terminals. Note that the single flag specified for `dapr run` specifies the port number that we want the second sidecar to be listening on.

2. Invoking the Weather Forecast service is a matter of calling the service invocation API exposed by the sidecar of the caller service. Note that as a caller, you don't have to know what address and what port the target application uses. Since the Weather Forecast service provides a GET method, you can simply open a browser at the following address: `http://localhost:3500/v1.0/invoke/weather/method/weatherforecast?daysCount=10`.

As you already know, the communication will flow from the caller sidecar to the callee sidecar, which will invoke the target method at `http://localhost:5000/weatherforecast?daysCount=10`. After that, the result will be propagated back to the caller app by the Dapr sidecars.

To recap, the service invocation API has the following endpoint `http://localhost:<daprPort>/v1.0/invoke/<appId>/method/<method-name>` that accepts POST/GET/PUT/DELETE requests:

- `daprPort` is the port number where the Dapr sidecars listen on.

- `appId` is the Application ID under which you have started the target application. Since cross-namespace calls are also supported, if you want to call a Dapr application that resides in another namespace, you have to specify it as <appId>.<namespace>.

- `method-name` is the method of the target service. In case your service exposes the method under a nested path like `/api/v1/methodname`, you have to pass the full path as a method name.

Whatever HTTP request method your service accepts, the same HTTP request method must be used when sending the request to the service invocation API. The body of the request along with the headers will be sent to the target application. Service invocation supports the following HTTP request methods – GET, POST, PUT, and DELETE.

Name Resolution

Making a request to another service is a matter of specifying the Dapr ID of that service and the method name. But behind the scenes, Dapr has to locate the specific sidecar, which is *a representative* of the target service. In Self-hosted mode, Dapr uses *Multicast DNS* (mDNS), whereas in Kubernetes it uses the built-in *Kubernetes DNS*. Anyway, the name resolution component is pluggable, and you can substitute it with a custom implementation that fits any other needs albeit being rather unusual.

Multicast DNS in Self-Hosted Mode

Multicast DNS is useful for resolving hostnames to IP addresses in small networks. It's often called *zero-config networking* as it allows you to register and discover services in the local network while leveraging standard IP protocols like UDP without the use of a DNS server. Each network participant announces its address to the others. Instead of trusting a single name resolution server, you trust what all network peers will tell you.

As we explored, Dapr in Self-hosted mode supports running multiple Dapr sidecars on the same host. In this case, the name resolution is mainly used to resolve the port number of the Dapr sidecar and not the address. But Dapr in Self-hosted mode also supports joining multiple machines in the same network and having Dapr sidecars across different instances. Not only that, but if you have multiple instances of the same Dapr App ID running on the same machine or dispersed across different machines, the mDNS component will round-robin between all instances of the same application.

Kubernetes Name Resolution

When Dapr runs in Kubernetes, a Pod that has been annotated with the `dapr.io` annotations will have an allocated companion Dapr sidecar container injected into it. For each application deployment, there will be a Kubernetes service that is representing all the Dapr sidecars that were injected in the Pods no matter whether you have replicated your Pods or not. Kubernetes services are the backbone of Dapr name resolution inside Kubernetes.

Let's see how the name resolution works in Kubernetes mode once we have the Weather Forecast service deployed as a Dapr application:

1. First, let's examine the Dockerfile we will use for building an image for the Weather Forecast service. It leverages the multistage build feature in Docker to produce a smaller image size. In the first stage, the parent image is dotnet/sdk, which contains all tools and dependencies needed for developing and building an application. The copy of the .csproj file and the copy of all other source code files are separated into different layers for a purpose – the source code files will likely change more frequently than the project file. This means that you won't have to restore NuGet packages if there are no changes in the project file since the last build. The first stage ends with a publish of the application, which results in having the application compiled for production and having all static files such as .js, .css, images, and so on copied into the out folder. The second stage takes the published application from the first stage and copies it over to the filesystem of the second one. The second stage is based on the dotnet/aspnet image, which contains just the runtime stuff so that you can run ASP.NET Core applications, and therefore it is way smaller compared to the SDK image.

```
FROM mcr.microsoft.com/dotnet/sdk:5.0 AS build-env
WORKDIR /usr/src/app

COPY *.csproj ./
RUN dotnet restore

COPY . ./
RUN dotnet publish -c Release -o out

FROM mcr.microsoft.com/dotnet/aspnet:5.0
WORKDIR /usr/src/app
COPY --from=build-env /usr/src/app/out .
ENTRYPOINT ["dotnet", "WeatherForecastHTTP.dll"]
```

2. To keep the image size small, you can define a `.dockerignore` file to ignore some files and folders when copying files to the filesystem of the image. For .NET projects, those folders are typically the `bin` and the `obj`. But you can include any other files that should be ignored. It won't make a huge difference since this is a very tiny project; however, you should know there is such an option.

3. Now it's time to build the Docker image. Open a terminal and navigate to the project folder where the files `Dockerfile` and `.dockerignore` are located and run

    ```
    docker build -t weatherforecast .
    ```

4. Since you are going to deploy this service to Kubernetes, it must be published to a container registry. In this case, it will be Docker Hub, so make sure you are logged into Docker Hub. The first command creates an alias of the local image in a format that is applicable to the container registry you are about to use. Docker Hub doesn't have to use a fully qualified domain name (FQDN), but just your Docker Hub username (Docker ID). The second command actually pushes the image to Docker Hub.

    ```
    docker tag weatherforecast <your-docker-hub-username>/
    weatherforecast
    docker push <your-docker-hub-username>/weatherforecast
    ```

5. Next, create a new file named deployment.yaml to contain the Kubernetes Deployment manifest that will deploy the `weatherforecast` image into a Pod, which will be marked with the `Dapr` annotations. Note that the port is 80 instead of 5000 because the file `launchSettings.json` that specifies the port for development is not published for production, so if the port has not been specified, it will use port 80 as provided by the `ASPNETCORE_URLS` environment variable in the `dotnet/aspnet` parent image.

    ```
    apiVersion: apps/v1
    kind: Deployment
    metadata:
    ```

```
        name: weather
    spec:
      replicas: 1
      selector:
        matchLabels:
          app: weather
      template:
        metadata:
          labels:
            app: weather
          annotations:
            dapr.io/enabled: "true"
            dapr.io/app-id: "weather"
            dapr.io/app-port: "80"
        spec:
          containers:
          - name: weatherforecast
            image: <your-docker-hub-username>/
            weatherforecast:latest
            ports:
            - containerPort: 80
```

6. The final step will be to apply this Deployment into your
    Kubernetes cluster by running

```
kubectl apply -f .\deployment.yaml
```

Now that you have the Weather Forecast service deployed as a Dapr application in
Kubernetes mode, let's find out how the name resolution works in Kubernetes.

In order for a request to /v1.0/invoke/<dapr-app-id>/method/<method-name> to
be resolved, the Dapr sidecar has to find the address of the other sidecar that represents
the dapr-app-id. As already specified in the Pod annotations, the Dapr ID is weather.
The Dapr sidecar is actually exposed to the other Dapr sidecars via a Kubernetes
service. When you run kubectl get services, you will be able to see the weather-dapr

service that was automatically created behind the scenes. You will be able to see how it is configured, for example, what is the selector and what ports it targets, by running `kubectl describe service weather-dapr`. Let's play with the name resolution:

1. Firstly, create a new file named dnsutils.yaml for a Pod manifest that will let you explore the DNS configuration:

```
apiVersion: v1
kind: Pod
metadata:
  name: dnsutils
  namespace: default
spec:
  containers:
  - name: dnsutils
    image: gcr.io/kubernetes-e2e-test-images/
    dnsutils:1.3
    command:
      - sleep
      - "3600"
    imagePullPolicy: IfNotPresent
  restartPolicy: Always
```

2. Open a terminal in the folder where you created the file and run `kubectl apply -f .\dnsutils.yaml`.

3. When the Pod is running, you can check how the name resolution is configured by examining the `resolv.conf` file:

```
kubectl exec -ti dnsutils -- cat /etc/resolv.conf
```

4. The former command will output something like the following depending on the type of Kubernetes cluster you use, but pay attention to the search domains, which will be used to complete a partial query in order to form a fully qualified domain name (FQDN):

```
nameserver 10.96.0.10
```

```
search default.svc.cluster.local svc.cluster.local
cluster.local
options ndots:5
```

5. Then let's try to resolve the name of the service that exposes the
    Dapr sidecar of the Weather application by using `nslookup` and
    passing just the name of the service created by Dapr:

```
kubectl exec -i -t dnsutils -- nslookup weather-dapr
```

6. And the output should be something like the following:

```
Server:         10.96.0.10
Address:        10.96.0.10#53

Name:   weather-dapr.default.svc.cluster.local
Address: 10.1.2.32
```

It seems like it was able to find the FQDN of the `weather-dapr` service that resides in
the default namespace and also its IP address.

Cross-Namespace Invocation

So far we have applied the manifests of the Dapr applications into the default
namespace. But in reality, you may end up using different namespaces for various
reasons – separation of environments, having different versions of the same application
running side by side, canary deployments, or just for keeping different software stacks
separate.

It's entirely possible to invoke a Dapr application running in a different namespace
than the one of the calling party. In order to do that, you have to include the namespace
name to the Dapr App ID in `/v1.0/invoke/<dapr-app-id>.<namespace-name>/
method/<method-name>`. In fact, if you don't specify a namespace, the way name
resolution works in Kubernetes is it assumes it is the default one.

Let me show you how it works. I will show you how to deploy the same Weather
Forecast service to a different namespace and call it from the sidecar of the Weather
Forecast service running in the default namespace. Sounds very interesting, isn't it? I
assume you have already deployed the service into the default namespace by following
the previous examples.

1. Create a new namespace named another-ns, for example:

   ```
   kubectl create namespace another-ns
   ```

2. Make sure your terminal is in the folder that contains the YAML file. Apply the same manifest but this time into the new namespace:

   ```
   kubectl apply -f .\deployment.yaml -n another-ns
   ```

3. The Dapr sidecar container by default listens on port 3500, so let's do a port forwarding to the deployment of the Weather Forecast service from the default template. As a reminder, when you don't specify a namespace, kubectl assumes it is the default one:

   ```
   kubectl port-forward deployment/weather 3500
   ```

4. Now open a browser and enter the following address that will invoke the Weather Forecast service in the another-ns: http://localhost:3500/v1.0/invoke/weather.another-ns/method/weatherforecast?daysCount=5

5. You should be able to see the JSON response with the forecast for the next 5 days. This means that the Dapr sidecar (from the default namespace) that you were calling directly was able to locate the weather-service in the another-ns namespace.

Cross-namespace access comes as a very handy feature in Kubernetes hosted mode. However, it isn't so useful for Self-hosted as there isn't such a concept of having isolated namespaces, although Dapr will try to mimic the support for namespaced components.

Working with gRPC-Based Services

gRPC is an open source *Remote Procedure Call* framework that was initially started by Google. It uses Protocol Buffers both as an *Interface Definition Language (IDL)* and a *message format*. Protocol Buffers is yet another project initiated by Google, which aims for serializing structured data in a binary format that is smaller and therefore faster when transferred compared to traditional formats like JSON and XML. The messages and procedures are defined in .proto files, which then can be passed through a compiler and to produce an auto-generated output that can be used for any language supported by the given compiler. You can generate code that will be used on the server side or generate code to be used by any client, which is often called gRPC stub.

gRPC uses HTTP/2 as its transport protocol, so it inherently leverages its performance optimizations such as binary framing that is a great fit for Protocol Buffers, the ability to send multiple requests and *responses* over a single TCP connection, and the ability to initiate pushes from the server. So HTTP/2 not only provides many performance optimizations when compared to HTTP/1.1 but also enables gRPC to support streaming scenarios like server streaming, client streaming, and bidirectional streaming.

gRPC is gaining more and more popularity among Microservices applications because of its high performance. I've seen several projects substituting some of their RESTful services with gRPC-based ones and realizing the performance gains. Dapr also supports communication over gRPC. In fact, the communication between sidecars happens only via gRPC. Applications can call the Dapr runtime via either HTTP or gRPC.

So far we have used only the HTTP API of the Dapr sidecar. Let's see how to make use of the gRPC support from both client and server perspectives.

Implementing a gRPC Server

Let me show you how to implement a gRPC-based application that is capable of working with Dapr. Since gRPC is only meaningful when you have the Protobuf interface, Dapr introduced a common interface called Appcallback, which can handle all requests coming from the Dapr sidecar. The gRPC server that you implement regardless of the language and technology must implement this interface so the Dapr sidecar knows how to call into your gRPC server. The reason is that deserializing a Protobuf message without the .proto file is mission impossible because the format doesn't carry the structure of the data like JSON and XML do.

For this example, I will use ASP.NET Core again and Dapr in Self-hosted mode.

1. First, create a new folder for the project. In my case, I named it GreetingGRPC.

2. Navigate to the project folder and run the following in a terminal to scaffold an *ASP.NET Core gRPC service*:

   ```
   dotnet new grpc -F net5.0
   ```

3. Open it in Visual Studio 2019, Visual Studio Code, or another editor of your choice. The template contains a simple service that we won't use. You can safely delete it.

4. Next, let's add the Appcallback proto file as a reference in our project straight from the Dapr master branch on *GitHub*. appcallback.proto also refers to some messages defined in common.proto, so it needs to be imported as well. In order to import those Protobuf references, we will use dotnet-grpc, which is a *.NET Core global tool* for managing Protobuf references. Before adding any references, you have to install the tool first:

```
dotnet tool install -g dotnet-grpc
dotnet-grpc add-url -s Server -o dapr/proto/runtime/v1/
appcallback.proto https://raw.githubusercontent.com/dapr/dapr/
master/dapr/proto/runtime/v1/appcallback.proto
dotnet-grpc add-url -s Server -o dapr/proto/common/v1/common.proto
https://raw.githubusercontent.com/dapr/dapr/master/dapr/proto/
common/v1/common.proto
```

5. Now that we have imported the proto for the Appcallback service, it will generate an abstract class whose methods we need to implement. Create a new file named AppCallbackService. cs under the Services folder with the following contents and implement the OnInvoke method, which is the entry point for method invocation:

```
public override Task<InvokeResponse> OnInvoke(InvokeRequest
request, ServerCallContext context)
{
        switch (request.Method)
        {
                case "SayHello":
                        {
                                var dataString = request.Data.
                                Value.ToStringUtf8();

                                var dataDefinition = new { Name =
                                "" };
                                var data = JsonConvert.Des
                                erializeAnonymousType(data
                                String, dataDefinition);
```

```
                        var result = new { result =
                        $"Hello, {data.Name}!" };
                        return Task.FromResult(new
                        InvokeResponse()
                        {
                                ContentType =
                                "application/json",
                                Data = new Any()
                                {
                                        Value =
ByteString.CopyFrom(JsonConvert.SerializeObject(result),
                                        Encoding.UTF8)
                                }
                        });
                }
            default: return base.OnInvoke(request, context);
        }
    }
}
```

6. The code is deserializing the input data and serializes the result
   into JSON. You have to install the Newtonsoft.Json package:

   ```
   dotnet add package Newtonsoft.Json
   ```

7. Make sure to provide a simple implementation of
   ListTopicSubscriptions to return an empty list. The Dapr sidecar
   calls this method at startup to check for any subscriptions:

   ```
   public override Task<ListTopicSubscriptionsResponse>
   ListTopicSubscriptions(Empty request, ServerCallContext
   context) =>
               Task.FromResult(new ListTopicSubscriptions
               Response());
   ```

8. Now that you have implemented the AppCallbackService, you
   should register in Startup.cs by adding the following line:

   ```
   endpoints.MapGrpcService<AppCallbackService>();
   ```

9. Lastly, let's run this gRPC service as a Dapr application. Open a
   terminal in the project directory and run the following command:

```
dapr run --app-id greetinggrpc --app-port 5000 --app-
protocol grpc -- dotnet run
```

Note   If you have previously installed an older version of dotnet-grpc, it won't be
updated when you run `dotnet tool install`. And when you try downloading
the proto files, it may fail with the following exception:

`Unhandled exception: System.IO.FileNotFoundException: Could`
`not load file or assembly 'System.Collections.Immutable,`
`Version=5.0.0.0, Culture=neutral, PublicKeyToken=b03f5f7f11d50`
`a3a'. The system cannot find the file specified.`

The solution for this problem is to uninstall the tool by running `dotnet tool`
`uninstall -g dotnet-grpc` and then reinstall it, which will install its latest version.

The gRPC application is running now. Note that we don't have a Protobuf definition
for our service; instead, the method name and the parameters come dynamically in the
InvokeRequest argument.

Most applications talk to their Dapr sidecars via an unencrypted channel because
they are a part of one security boundary and they should trust each other. But the gRPC
service template comes with TLS enabled on port 5001. If you want to make the sidecar
talk to port 5001 over TLS, you should also specify the switch `--app-ssl`:

```
dapr run --app-id greetinggrpc --app-port 5001 --app-protocol grpc --app-
ssl -- dotnet run
```

Invoking gRPC Service from HTTP

At the beginning of the chapter, I promised that you are going to learn how to make *cross-
protocol* invocations. gRPC and HTTP do not have feature parity. The HTTP verbs like
GET or POST don't mean a thing in gRPC. The query string that you pass for the HTTP
request cannot be translated directly to gRPC. For this reason, the OnInvoke method we
implemented accepts a parameter of type InvokeRequest that has a property named
HttpExtension, which contains the Verb and the QueryString.

The gRPC service is implemented in such a way that it doesn't depend on any specifics of HTTP. Therefore, you can call it from either HTTP or gRPC. The method name and the data it accepts are used by the gRPC service because they remain supported across both protocols. When the caller invokes its Dapr sidecar via HTTP, the method name is in the URL, and the data comes from the HTTP request body. Of course, you will have to follow the HTTP semantics and choose methods that support sending data in the HTTP body, like POST or PUT.

Let's see how it works. Start a Dapr sidecar that is going to be used only for calling the gRPC service. Open another terminal and run `dapr run --dapr-http-port 3500 --`

Now that the Dapr sidecar is up and running, you can use cURL, Postman, or any other tool to issue a POST request to the gRPC service. In this example, I will use cURL:

```
curl -X POST http://localhost:3500/v1.0/invoke/greetinggrpc/method/SayHello
-d "{'name': 'world'}"
```

The output will be in a JSON format: `{"result":"Hello, world!"}`.

See how simple it is to call a gRPC service from HTTP! As a caller, you are not messing with any proto files, Protobuf compilation, and so on. But still, your gRPC-based service has to be implemented in such a way that it doesn't expect any of the HTTP-specific properties.

Implementing a gRPC Client

To implement any client to a gRPC service means that you have to deal with client stub generation for the language you intend to use based on the Protobuf definition of the service you are about to call. The Dapr language-specific SDKs have already done this for you. Some of them are curated on top of the proto-generated code; others are just proto-generated. There are Dapr SDKs for a number of languages. If your favorite language is not supported, you just have to download the proto files and look for a Protobuf compiler.

In this example, I will show you how to use the .NET SDK to invoke the service.

1. First, create a new folder for the client application and create a new .NET console application by running

   ```
   dotnet new console -f net5.0
   ```

2. Install the latest version of the Dapr.Client NuGet package. At the time of writing, the latest version is 1.0.0:

```
dotnet add package Dapr.Client --version 1.0.0
```

3. Substitute the implementation of the Program class with the following code. In the Main method, it creates a DaprClient instance, prepares the input data, invokes the method of the gRPC service, and outputs the result in the console. The result is strongly typed for a reason – in case any type that is used for input data or output data does not implement the interface IMessage that is for proto-generated messages, Dapr will try to use JSON as a serialization medium:

```
class ResultMessage
{
        public string Result { get; set; }
}

static async Task Main(string[] args)
{
        var client = new DaprClientBuilder()
                .Build();

        var data = new { Name = "Reader" };
        var output = await client.InvokeMethodAsync<object,
        ResultMessage>("greetinggrpc", "SayHello", data);
        Console.WriteLine(output.Result);
}
```

4. Don't forget to add a using statement for Dapr.Client at the top of the file:

```
using System.Threading.Tasks;
using Dapr.Client;
```

5. Finally, let's run it with Dapr and see the result displayed in the console. Note that I don't specify --app-id nor --app-port as this will be just a client application: dapr run -- dotnet run.

6. In the logs, you should be able to find the output of the application right after the Dapr logs:

```
You're up and running! Both Dapr and your app logs will appear here.
```

`== APP == Hello, Reader!`

The result is that you used gRPC to call the service without really knowing what the underlying code of the .NET Dapr SDK does.

Securing Service-to-Service Communication

It may seem like every application that has access to a Dapr sidecar can call just about any other application that is represented by a Dapr sidecar. And you will be right, but that is the default behavior of Dapr.

Service invocation permissions can be controlled by specifying *Access Control Lists (ACLs)*. ACLs are defined in a `Configuration` object that can configure the called Dapr applications. Once you have defined a configuration for an application, you specify the path to the config file in the `--config` flag for `dapr run` when using Self-hosted mode, or in Kubernetes mode, you apply the Configuration manifest and then reference the Configuration CRD name in the `dapr.io/config` annotation. In my opinion, this feature is not particularly useful for Self-hosted mode when it runs on just one machine because after all the processes running on the same hosts can directly access each other. If you want to configure ACLs for your Dapr applications, you must have mTLS enabled.

The configuration is specified in such a way that for a given application, you can specify what the other applications that are eligible or not to call all methods or a specific method of the application. The policies defined in the ACLs are evaluated at the time you call an application. In order to find the matching policies, Dapr Sentry generates a *SPIFFE ID* to describe the identity of each Dapr application. SPIFFE stands for *Secure Production Identity Framework for Everyone* and is widely used with mutual authentication in dynamic environments like those of the distributed applications. Since Dapr already enforces Mutual TLS, it is very easy to leverage it and use SPIFFE IDs so that each Dapr application (via its sidecar) can introduce itself when calling other Dapr applications. In this way, the authorization can be enforced by matching the SPIFFE ID to the policies in the configuration of the called Dapr application.

The Sentry service generates and attaches a SPIFFE ID for each workload certificate it issues for a Dapr sidecar. This is the reason mTLS must be enabled. The SPIFFE ID has the following format: `spiffe://<trustdomain>/ns/<namespace>/<appid>`. Let's explore what a SPIFFE ID consists of. The trust domain is a way to create a higher-level grouping of several applications. This is the first evaluation level used to match an ACL policy. If there isn't any trust domain specified for an application, the default one is called **public**. The trust domain of a Dapr application can be specified in its configuration. You already know what namespaces and Dapr App IDs are – the mandatory attributes of every Dapr application. In the future, this mechanism may make it possible to securely consolidate Dapr applications running on various hosting environments as long as they share the same trust anchors used by their respective Sentry services.

Let's implement ACLs for the distributed Hello World application that I showed you how to implement in Chapter 2: Introduction to Dapr and later on we deployed to Kubernetes in Chapter 4: Running Dapr in Kubernetes Mode. To recap, once you deploy it to Kubernetes, all the three services are accessible by any other Dapr applications that might be deployed into the cluster in the future. Let me show you how to specify that the endpoints of the Hello service and the World service can be accessed only by the Greeting service and all other requests to those two services be denied. You have to create Configuration manifests for both Hello and World services. Let me show you how it looks just for the Hello service; however, you can also find the Configuration manifest for the World service in the source code of the book. The configuration assumes all three services are in the public trust domain and in the default namespace:

```
apiVersion: dapr.io/v1alpha1
kind: Configuration
metadata:
  name: helloconfig
  namespace: default
spec:
  accessControl:
    defaultAction: deny
    trustDomain: public
    policies:
    - appId: greeting-service
      defaultAction: deny
      trustDomain: public
```

```
    namespace: default
    operations:
    - name: /sayHello
      httpVerb: ['GET']
      action: allow
```

Then you have to add dapr.io/config: helloconfig to the annotations of the Deployment manifest for the Hello service that you have from Chapter 4: Running Dapr in Kubernetes Mode. This will tell the Dapr sidecar to use the Configuration CRD that you just defined. Finally, you have to apply those two manifests into your Kubernetes cluster – the configuration and the deployment. Then follow the same steps to configure the access to the World service. You don't have to create configuration for the Greeting service as if you don't specify a trust domain, public will be the default one.

Access Control Lists specify what action to be taken – communication can be either *allowed* or *denied*. As you can see from the ACLs for the Hello service, they are defined on three levels: there's a global policy that applies to all calling applications, followed by a list of application-specific policies, one per calling application you want to control, and below every application-specific policy, you can define a list of fine-grained policies to control access to specific operations of the application you currently configure. The policies are evaluated for a match from the most specific policy to the least specific one, in the following order until a match is found:

1. Action that is applied for an operation with a specific name and specific verbs (verbs are applicable only to HTTP, of course), accessed by a specific calling application.

2. In case a match at an operation level was not found for the current operation that is being invoked, default action for the calling application is applied.

3. In case a match at an application level has not been found for the current calling application, the global action is applied.

Let me explain the different options for the configuration of Access Control Lists:

- defaultAction – The global action that takes effect if no other policy matches. Can be allow or deny.

- trustDomain – The trust domain assigned to the application. If not assigned, public is the default one.

- policies – List of policies per calling application:
  - appId – The Dapr App ID of the calling application.
  - trustDomain – The trust domain of the calling application.
  - namespace – The namespace of the calling application.
  - defaultAction – The default action is applied if there is a match in the calling application but no specific operation was matched or there aren't any operations defined.
  - operations – List of operations, provided by the called application, for which the access is controlled for the current calling application:
    - name – The name of the method in the called application. It supports wildcards, for example, /op1/*.
    - httpVerb – The HTTP verbs that can be used by the calling application. A wildcard can be used to match all HTTP verbs, for example, ["*"]. This is not applicable for gRPC services.
    - action – Whether to allow or deny when a specific calling application is trying to invoke a specific operation on the current application.

Securing Dapr Sidecars and Dapr Applications

Now that you know how to specify ACLs for cross-service communication in Dapr, you might be wondering how you can authenticate the request reaching Dapr sidecars and the respective applications.

As you already know, Dapr sidecars are what provides the Dapr API. Typically you won't expose your Dapr sidecars publicly, but if you do, everyone who has network access to a Dapr sidecar will be able to consume the Dapr API. For this case, you have to configure sidecars to use token authentication and expect a token on every incoming request. The token is in JSON Web Token (JWT) format, and you will be responsible for the initial generation and rotation after that. The token that Dapr expects to receive upon every request must be present as an environment variable named DAPR_API_TOKEN for Dapr in Self-hosted mode or stored as a Kubernetes Secret. Once you do this, Dapr sidecars won't allow any request that doesn't have a valid token. Alternatively, you can utilize an OAuth 2.0 middleware, if you want to enable OAuth 2.0 authorization for your Dapr sidecars. You will learn how to do it in Chapter 13: Plugging Middleware.

Some building blocks like the Service Invocation, Publish and Subscribe, and Resource Bindings building blocks rely on being able to directly invoke your applications. If for some reason you need to expose your applications publicly, you may want to know whether a request came from a Dapr sidecar to allow it or something else tries to invoke it and therefore reject it. You can instruct Dapr to send a predefined JWT as a header in the HTTP requests to your application or as metadata in gRPC requests. You will be responsible to generate the token initially and then rotate it. To enable this, you have to set an environment variable named APP_API_TOKEN to hold the JWT for Dapr in Self-hosted mode or use a Kubernetes Secret.

Summary

Being able to discover and call other services is one of the most important needs in the world of distributed applications. In this chapter, you learned how the Service Invocation building block eases direct cross-service communication. You saw it in action for both HTTP- and gRPC-based services that are called via the Dapr system of sidecars via either gRPC or HTTP. We explored how name resolution works and how Dapr applications can be invoked across namespaces. By intertwining gRPC services with HTTP clients and vice versa, you know how cross-protocol communication was made possible by Dapr. You also learned how to control access to Dapr applications by defining Access Control Lists and also require authentication for any request coming to a Dapr sidecar or an application.

In the next chapter, we are going to explore how the Publish and Subscribe building block makes asynchronous communication possible.

CHAPTER 7

Publish and Subscribe

Communication and collaboration are vital for Microservices applications – whether it is synchronous or asynchronous. In this chapter, I am going to elaborate on what Publish and Subscribe is and when it is useful. I will walk you through the Dapr capabilities for implementing Publish and Subscribe and what are the supported messaging systems. Note that I will collectively refer to message brokers and streaming platforms that are supported by Dapr as messaging systems. Then I will show you how to build a system of three services where one of them is producing events and the others are consuming and processing them. At the end of the chapter, I will briefly touch on the future of the Publish and Subscribe building block in Dapr.

What Is Publish/Subscribe?

Publish/Subscribe or Pub/Sub is a messaging pattern where there are two types of parties involved – publishers and subscribers. The publishers send their messages to a messaging system where those messages can be categorized, filtered, and routed. Publishers don't know anything about the subscribers; they just publish a message that carries some type of payload. The messaging system allows keeping this data temporarily until it is processed. Then subscribers are declaring their interest in receiving all messages of some kind. Usually, messages are published against a topic that is defined by the publisher. Depending on the messaging system, there are various options for filtering messages based on their content.

There is a slight difference between messages and events. When the publisher expects that the information will be delivered and processed and then a certain outcome is achieved by some action, that is messaging. In a message-driven system, the message is virtually addressed to one or more receivers that are obliged to process it. An event is a signal emitted by some party in order to alert that a particular state was reached. In an event-driven system, an event published to an event stream can be received by zero or

119

© Radoslav Gatev 2021
R. Gatev, *Introducing Distributed Application Runtime (Dapr)*, https://doi.org/10.1007/978-1-4842-6998-5_7

more listeners that are interested in the events of this stream. There is a slight nuance between *event-driven* and *message-driven systems,* as one focuses on ingesting into event streams, while the other focuses on addressing recipients. However, for this chapter, I am going to use both interchangeably.

I already mentioned *topic* as a term. While we are talking about messaging, there is also another popular term – a *message queue.* At times, you might hear someone using both of those terms interchangeably. However, they serve different purposes. The queue provides an intermediary location for message producers to buffer messages until they are picked up by consumers. A single message is being picked by a single consumer to do some processing work. Until the consumer acknowledges that the message has been processed, the message is then hidden from other consumers by entering in a locked state. In case the consumer does not acknowledge the message to be processed, after some timeout, it is returned to the queue and is ready to be picked up by other consumers. If, at the time, there are no available consumers, the message will be kept for some time so that it can be picked up at a later stage. You can also define an expiration policy so that in case the message has not been picked up, it expires.

In contrast, topics are like a broadcasting station. Messages are emitted by various publishers, and they land into various topics. This routing process can happen dynamically according to some predefined rules, depending on the particular messaging system. Those messages will be delivered to zero or many subscribers that are listening for messages on a particular topic. This means that from each message, there might be different actions that are taking place at the same time. This is where the Publish and Subscribe pattern fits. Each of the subscribers may read the messages from a given topic at its own pace. You may hear someone referring to this as the *fan-out* messaging pattern because the message is being effectively spread across a number of subscribers in parallel.

What Are the Benefits of Publish and Subscribe?

By using Publish and Subscribe, you can achieve several things:

- Loose coupling

  A publisher sends a message that carries some payload into a topic. In contrast with the direct service invocation, it doesn't know who and how many the end consumers of this message will be. The number of different consumers may even change with time, but that doesn't affect the publisher in any way. If you are using direct service invocation, you have to update the code so that it knows how to call some additional services that may want to process the incoming updates of a particular service. Taking this even further, at the time of publishing some message, some of its subscribers may not be running.

- Scalability

Each subscriber will go through the messages of a given topic at its own pace. Some of the subscribers may perform a lot of compute-intensive work and thus require very powerful hardware to back them up. Once they are ready to pick up some new work, they will gather the next incoming message for a given topic. Other subscribers that don't require heavy computations may process it almost immediately. This means that the messaging system can be seen as an interim location that keeps a list of tasks. If you think about what it would have been with direct service invocation, the target service will most likely be overwhelmed with work as it has to start processing the requests as they arrive.

- Dynamic targeting

As implied by loose coupling, a change in the consumers does not require the code of the publishers to be updated. In fact, you may repurpose the subscriptions without even changing the implementation of any of both sides.

- Retries

Let's imagine a message was picked up by some subscriber but then at a later stage, it failed. It may have faced some type of intermittent failure that it cannot recover from, or something unexpected happened. In this case, the subscriber will return some type of error, and the message will be returned back to the topic. When the subscriber has recovered, it may pick it up again.

- No polling needed

  The Publish and Subscribe pattern eliminates the need for doing continuous polling. Have you ever seen an application initiating some kind of operation and then repeatedly querying the state of this operation every second until it returns a result? This is not needed anymore because once something is done, the interested parties will get notified about it.

When Not to Use Publish and Subscribe?

As with any other thing, Publish and Subscribe is not a silver bullet. You need to know when it makes sense to use it but also when it doesn't fit the needs.

- Expecting a real-time effect

  While a message can be processed straight away, it may be delayed for a while depending on the availability of the subscribers. I've seen applications that publish to a topic and then subscribe for another topic just to get the result of a particular operation that the initial message incited. That's an anti-pattern. If you need the result of an operation immediately, you should be better off with a direct service invocation.

- Large messages

  Most of the messaging systems work well with messages of small size, typically up to a few hundreds of KBs. If you need something bigger, store it in blob/file storage or some type of database and just reference it in the message.

How Does Dapr Simplify Publish and Subscribe?

The typical process that you will follow once you have selected a *messaging system* that fits your needs will be to find a library that can be integrated into the code of your application. It has to support the language or framework that your solution is based upon. Of course, you have to think about connectivity no matter if you host the messaging system yourself or you use a cloud service. If, at some point, you want to try out a different messaging system, you have to start using its specific library and rework the code to wire it up to your solution. The new messaging system will also try to impose some of its concepts over your code.

Dapr provides a handy building block that eases the integration of such a messaging system for loosely coupled communication across your services. The building block represents an implementation of the adapter pattern that is wrapping the operations supported by each particular messaging system and provides via the interface of the Publish and Subscribe building block. This makes it easy for you to transparently use a target system without knowing its particular details.

The key to this building block is once again the system of Dapr sidecars. As you can see, all the communication flows through them as shown in Figure 7-1.

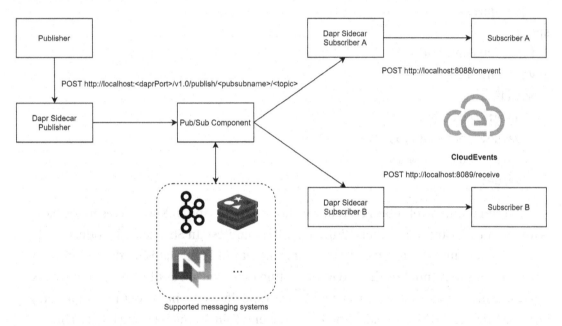

Figure 7-1. *Publish and Subscribe in Dapr*

The service that sends information to other services by sending a message is called a publisher. The publisher sends the message to its Dapr sidecar by stating which messaging system is targeted and the name of the topic inside it. This can happen either via HTTP by using the /publish endpoint of the Dapr API or via gRPC by invoking the respective function. The particular messaging system is one of the "supported messaging systems" as referred to in Figure 7-1. It is determined by the type of Pub/Sub component that was chosen.

Defining the Component

The component holds the information needed for connecting to the messaging system – URL, credentials, and so on. The specifics of the communication with a certain type of messaging system are implemented by the component.

For example, the default Pub/Sub component for Redis that you have in your Dapr components folder when you initialize Dapr in Self-hosted mode has the following definition:

```
apiVersion: dapr.io/v1alpha1
kind: Component
metadata:
  name: pubsub
spec:
  type: pubsub.redis
  version: v1
  metadata:
  - name: redisHost
    value: localhost:6379
  - name: redisPassword
    value: ""
```

You can use this definition both in Self-hosted mode and in Kubernetes mode as it is also a valid CustomResourceDefinition (CRD) manifest. In Self-hosted mode, the file is parsed each time when you call dapr run, whereas in Kubernetes mode, components have to be applied and thus the CRDs are getting materialized as objects in Kubernetes. The value of metadata.name is what you have to specify as the name of the component, and you provide it when invoking the /publish endpoint of the building block. The topic gets auto-created if it doesn't exist in the target messaging system. The value specified in spec.type is the name of the particular component implementation that handles the specifics of the messaging system. Then whatever you specify as a list of key-value pairs under spec.metadata is basically being sent to the underlying component implementation as input parameters. Those fields typically contain the information needed to establish a connection and to configure the behavior of the component. Later on, you can change the connection info, or you can even substitute the component type to talk to a different type of messaging system. Your services won't notice the difference as long as the name of the Pub/Sub component remains the same and you restart the

Dapr sidecar so that it picks up the new configuration. You don't need to change any of the existing code, and that is because you interact with the messaging system by using the *API* of the Publish and Subscribe building block.

You can find the source code of all components in the dapr/components-contrib repo at `https://github.com/dapr/components-contrib`. The components available to the Publish and Subscribe building block reside under the `pubsub` folder.

Note   In a future release, Dapr sidecars will be notified about changes in configuration and components so that they will be hot-reloaded automatically without having to restart sidecars manually.

You might have more than one pubsub component. You can create many pubsub components that are pointing to different messaging systems. After all, whenever you publish a message or subscribe to a topic, you always have to specify the name of the pubsub component. Keep in mind that components are namespaced. This means that the application will be able to discover any components that are deployed in the same namespace. For any cases of a big application, the services of which are spread across different namespaces need to communicate via the same message system, you have to create the same component in all the namespaces of the application involved.

Message Format

Once the message is received by the underlying messaging system, all subscribers are notified at their specific endpoints that are to be invoked whenever there is an incoming message on a new topic. The way this is achieved is by leveraging the system of Dapr sidecars. The Dapr sidecar initiates the request to its subscribed application, which then receives and consumes the message. The message received by the subscribers had been actually converted in a special format, right before it was ingested in the messaging system. This format conforms to the *CloudEvents* specification. CloudEvents is a CNCF (Cloud Native Computing Foundation, `www.cncf.io`) project that is a specification for describing event data in a common way so that it can be defined and processed across a variety of systems and services. Without having such a specification, loosely coupled communication won't be possible at all. The reason is that publishers tend to publish events in diverse formats and hence consumers must know how to process them on a case-by-case basis. The more a consumer knows about some custom proprietary format, the more tightly coupled the communication becomes. That's why CloudEvents greatly improves interoperability by setting the standards for describing event data.

Dapr only wraps the message data into CloudEvents in case if the data you are trying to publish is not a *CloudEvents* event. The CloudEvents spec defines a set of attributes that describe the data you are sending, or in other words metadata. This gives the context to the consumers so that they know what the type of the message is, where it originated from, what payload type it is, and how to serialize it. Let's take a look at an example message that contains the reading of a temperature sensor at a given moment. It was sent via the Publisher and subscribe building block of Dapr:

```
{
    "id":"e846390d-9bfe-4abd-a247-e2b42ad1d775",
    "source":"temperature-sensor",
    "type":"com.dapr.event.sent",
    "specversion":"1.0",
    "datacontenttype":"application/json",
    "data":{
        "eventTime":"2021-03-22T23:11:09.7134846Z",
        "temperatureInCelsius":30.421799
    },
    "topic":"temperature",
    "pubsubname":"sensors",
    "traceid": "00-5dce22d5dbe3354d871cbb1648115864-e5b9623f85147fd4-01"
}
```

A CloudEvents event can be represented in several formats – JSON, Avro, and Protobuf. In the case of JSON, a CloudEvents event is represented as a JSON object called an *envelope*, and the attributes as outlined in the specification are members of this JSON envelope. Dapr implements the following attributes:

- id – An identifier for the event being sent. It is unique among all events incoming from a given source.

- source – Identifies the organization, process, or application that produced the event.

- type – Specifies the type of the event in regard to the action it originated from, for example, `com.github.pull.create` or `com.dapr.event.sent`.

- specversion – The version of the CloudEvents specification for the current event. At the time of writing the book, it is 1.0.

- datacontenttype – The content type of the event payload in the data attribute. The payload may be in various formats like JSON, XML, or some binary format. Having specified the payload format makes it possible for consumers to deserialize the data properly.

- data – The event payload, serialized into the media format specified by the datacontenttype attribute.

- topic – An extension attribute injected by Dapr, specifies the topic in which the message was published.

- pubsubname – An extension attribute injected by Dapr, specifies the name of the pubsub component that talks to a messaging system.

- traceid – An extension attribute injected by Dapr and used by Dapr to identify the context for distributed tracing, which is going to be explored in Chapter 12: Observability.

Now that you know what the format of the messages is, let me walk you through the details of receiving a message.

Receiving a Message

Dapr follows the semantic of at-least-once delivery, which means that the message will be delivered to each subscriber at least once. If the delivery turns out to be successful, the subscriber has to acknowledge the message, which will be considered as delivered for this particular subscriber. But there are times when the message could not be processed by the subscriber or the subscriber is facing some intermittent issue at the time. In such cases, the messages are attempted to be redelivered. The retry should be expected by the subscriber, and so its logic must be implemented in an idempotent way. This means that multiple full or partial processing of the message won't cause any side effect except what is expected from single processing. If the operation cannot be implemented in an idempotent way, it should deal with any potential duplication that can be caused by any message delivered multiple times.

Note   If there are multiple running instances of a Dapr application that is subscribing to some topic when using Dapr in Kubernetes, Dapr will make sure to deliver the message to only **one** instance of that application. This behavior can be exploited in your favor, for example, whenever you want to drain a topic faster. You throw more instances of the subscriber application so that they process a higher number of incoming messages one at a time on each instance. This behavior is also known as the *competing consumers pattern*. Instead, if you want to prevent this behavior and make sure that every instance of a Dapr application receives the message, in your component's metadata section, specify a key named `consumerID` and assign the special value that contains the `{uuid}` tag that will be replaced with a randomly generated UUID (universally unique identifier) when a Dapr sidecar initializes. This will result in **all** application instances receiving **all** messages.

As I already explained, the message is delivered by calling the delivery endpoint of the subscriber. The response returned by this endpoint will determine whether the message is considered as successfully delivered or it should be retried once again. So if the Dapr sidecar receives anything other than HTTP status code 2XX, the message will be scheduled for redelivery. This means that something went wrong during the processing and you are relying upon the server to send a 4XX client error or 5XX server error. The only exception to the rule is status code 404 because there is no reason to reattempt calling a delivery endpoint that does not exist.

But if your application is smart enough to early detect that some message should be either retried or dropped, there is a way to do it. The message receiving endpoint should respond with status code 2XX, but it should also include a JSON payload as a response that controls the behavior with the following structure:

```
{
  "status": "<value>"
}
```

The value can be one of the following statuses:

- SUCCESS – The message was successfully processed. This is equivalent to sending HTTP status code 200 without any payload.

- RETRY – The message was not successfully processed and must be retried by Dapr.

- DROP – The message cannot be processed and should be dropped. Dapr logs this as a warning and drops the message.

Of course, similar semantics apply for gRPC as well. If the gRPC request succeeded, the message will be deemed successfully processed; otherwise, it will be retried.

Subscribing to a Topic

At this point, you might be wondering how to subscribe to a given topic. There are two ways to accomplish this – *programmatic* and *declarative*.

Programmatic Subscription

The programmatic subscription is done via the consumer application. It states what topics the consumer application is interested in and what endpoint it has for receiving the incoming messages. Upon startup, each Dapr sidecar issues a GET request to the /dapr/subscribe route of its application to collect all topics, if any, the application wants to subscribe to. If it subscribes to any, it returns a JSON array of all subscriptions with the following structure:

```
[
    {
            pubsubname: "pubsubComponent",
            topic: "topicName",
            route: "endpointName"
    }
]
```

Each object in the array represents a single subscription where pubsubname is the name of the pubsub component that targets a messaging system, the topic member is the name of the topic within the messaging system, and the value of route is the endpoint of the service that gets called whenever a new message is published.

Declarative Subscription

A potential downside of the programmatic approach is that you have to rebuild, publish, and deploy a new version of the Docker image of the service whenever you want to make a change in the subscriptions. To prevent this from happening, you may want to utilize the declarative way of specifying subscriptions, that is, the Subscription CRD. It has the following structure:

```
apiVersion: dapr.io/v1alpha1
kind: Subscription
metadata:
  name: my-declarative-subscription
spec:
  topic: topicName
  route: /endpointName
  pubsubname: pubsubComponent
scopes:
- app1
- app2
```

This component manifest defines a subscription to the same pubsub and topic and listens on the same route as from the programmatic subscription example. The difference is that the subscription is applied to two Dapr applications at once. This means that whenever a new message is published to this topic, a post request to the /endpointName endpoint of each application will be sent.

Controlling Time-to-Live (TTL)

As you already know, messages will be stored in the messaging system of choice until they are processed by a subscriber. If you need to enforce message expiration, you must set the TTL when you publish a message via the Dapr API.

The /publish endpoint supports a GET parameter named metadata.ttlInSeconds, which specifies the TTL in seconds for the message that is being published. There are messaging systems like Azure Service Bus that natively support it, and Dapr simply forwards the TTL to them. However, for any other messaging systems that do not support per-message TTL, Dapr handles it internally at the time of receiving the message. The result in both cases is that expired messages are not received by subscribers.

TTL can also be configured at the topic level in the component manifest. But have in mind that not all components support this feature.

Controlling Topic Access

You already know how to define a pubsub component that allows you to use some messaging system via the Publish and Subscribe building block. When you do so, all Dapr applications in the namespace can publish and subscribe to all topics of the Pub/Sub component.

But since the underlying messaging system may have a lot of topics you don't want to expose, you can control what applications can publish and subscribe to what topics. This can be done by setting three additional key-value pairs under the `spec.metadata` section of the component:

- allowedTopics – A comma-separated list of all allowed topics, for example, topic1,topic2.

- publishingScopes – Impose granular limitations by specifying which application can publish to what topics, for example, app1=topic1;app 2=topic1,topic2.

- subscriptionScopes – Impose granular limitations by specifying which application can subscribe to what topics, for example, app1=to pic1;app2=topic1,topic2.

What Messaging Systems Are Supported by Dapr?

At the time of writing the book, the following messaging systems are supported by Dapr:

- Apache Kafka – An open source distributed event streaming platform.

- Apache Pulsar – A cloud-native, distributed messaging, and streaming platform.

- Hazelcast – An in-memory computing platform that supports messaging.

- MQTT – Publish and subscribe to any broker that supports the MQTT protocol.

- NATS – An open source cloud-native messaging system. It is offered in two modules – the core NATS referred to as NATS and NATS Streaming referred to as STAN. NATS supports at-most-once delivery without persistence, whereas STAN is the opposite because it supports at-least-once delivery with historical data replay.

- RabbitMQ – An open source message broker.

- Redis Streams – Streams is a new data type introduced in Redis 5.0 that allows you to implement a history-preserving message broker. It is an append-only list of entries that supports consumer groups.

- AWS Simple Queue Service (SQS) – A fully managed message queuing service in Amazon Web Services.

- AWS Simple Notification Service (SNS) – A fully managed messaging service for both application-to-application and application-to-person communication in Amazon Web Services.

- Azure Service Bus – A fully managed enterprise integration message broker.

- Azure Event Hubs – A fully managed big data streaming platform and event ingestion service.

- GCP Pub/Sub – A fully managed real-time messaging service in Google Cloud Platform.

A Temperature Sensor Example

Let me show you how to build a sample application consisting of three services for measuring and reacting to changes in room temperature as shown in Figure 7-2. The Dapr components were not included there as they bring some complexity, and what you can see is just the logical communication flow. Of course, the communication happens by leveraging the Publish and Subscribe building block and the system of Dapr sidecars.

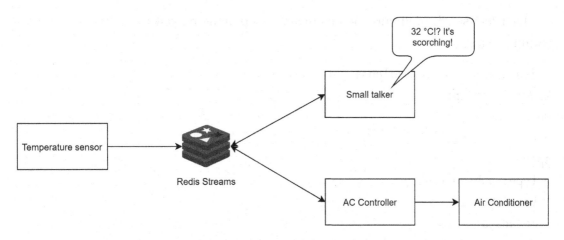

Figure 7-2. *A room temperature processing application*

The temperature sensor is a .NET Core console application that simulates temperature readings from a sensor and then publishes those readings as messages into Redis Streams by leveraging the Dapr .NET SDK. However, the temperature sensor doesn't really know how and into what system the message is being published. And that is because it makes a request to its Dapr sidecar in order to publish that message. The Pub/Sub component is configured to point to a Redis instance running in a container on the same machine.

After the message is persisted into Redis Streams, two subscribers are processing the incoming messages. The Small talker application is a Node.js application that simply receives the temperature readings and then depending on what the number is will say something obvious like "It's hot!" It subscribes to the topic by using the programmatic way of establishing a subscription. The other subscriber is the Air Conditioner Controller, which is an ASP.NET Core API that simulates the control of an air conditioner in the same room. However, this air conditioner is a dummy one as it doesn't support setting a target temperature to work toward achieving it. Instead, it has two states – started and stopped – and two modes – warm and cool. Depending on the temperature reported by the temperature sensor service, the AC Controller service will command the air conditioner. The AC Controller service utilizes the declarative subscriptions by being listed as a subscriber in a Subscription manifest. You can find the whole implementation of the application in the source code of the book.

First, let's see the definition of the pubsub component that talks to a Redis instance running in a container:

```yaml
apiVersion: dapr.io/v1alpha1
kind: Component
metadata:
  name: sensors
spec:
  type: pubsub.redis
  version: v1
  metadata:
  - name: redisHost
    value: localhost:6379
  - name: redisPassword
    value: ""
```

It's almost the same as the default Pub/Sub component that you get by initializing Dapr in Self-hosted mode. Note that you may have multiple Pub/Sub components of the same or different type, as long as their names are unique within a namespace. This component is named sensors; hence, you are going to use this name later on whenever publishing or consuming a message. The component file should be copied to the global components directory. As a reminder, when you execute dapr run, Dapr by default picks up all components in this folder; otherwise, you have to specify the path to the folder containing the components. The Dapr components folder is %USERPROFILE%\.dapr\ on Windows or $HOME/.dapr/bin on Linux and macOS.

Then let's examine the Main method of the temperature sensor console application that you can find in Program.cs:

```csharp
static async Task Main(string[] args)
{
        var jsonOptions = new JsonSerializerOptions()
        {
                PropertyNamingPolicy = JsonNamingPolicy.CamelCase,
                PropertyNameCaseInsensitive = true,
        };

        var daprClient = new DaprClientBuilder()
```

```
    .UseJsonSerializationOptions(jsonOptions)
      .Build();

var random = new Random();
var temperature = random.NextDouble() * MAX_TEMPERATURE;

while (true)
{
        temperature = GetTemperature(temperature, MIN_TEMPERATURE,
        MAX_TEMPERATURE);
        var @event = new
        {
                EventTime = DateTime.UtcNow,
                TemperatureInCelsius = temperature
        };

        await daprClient.PublishEventAsync("sensors",
        "temperature", @event);
        Console.WriteLine($"Published event {@event}, sleeping for
        5 seconds.");

        await Task.Delay(TimeSpan.FromSeconds(5));
    }
}
```

The GetTemperature method was omitted to keep the snippet short, but it simulates the reading of the current temperature from a hardware sensor. It will basically generate a random value that is close to the last temperature reading, so we don't see any dramatic temperature fluctuations. What the Main method does is that it sends a new message containing the current temperature along with a timestamp to the Publish and Subscribe API of Dapr by using the DaprClient class, which comes from the Dapr .NET SDK. The PublishEventAsync sends the event to the temperature topic of the sensors pubsub component. Note that via a single pubsub component, we can use many topics, for example, you may decide to start monitoring also the humidity by reading from another sensor and sending events to the humidity topic.

As you can notice, no logic wraps the event into a CloudEvents envelope. This is done once the event is received by the Dapr sidecar and it finds out that the payload is not already in CloudEvents format.

Next, let me run this application so that it starts ingesting events into Redis. A new terminal must be opened into the temperature sensor project folder, and the following is invoked:

```
dapr run --app-id temperature-sensor -- dotnet run
```

If everything is fine, you should see the application logs as the application will be producing an event every 5 seconds. Leave this terminal session working, and open another one. Let's explore how things look inside Redis. Run the following command to start an interactive shell session in the Redis container. The container is named dapr_redis and was created when you initialized Dapr in Self-hosted mode:

```
docker exec -it dapr_redis sh
```

Then, launch the Redis CLI by entering redis-cli. The Redis CLI allows you to run Redis commands. It is particularly useful for testing purposes when you want to explore the data in Redis. Once you are inside the Redis CLI, you can run commands like XLEN temperature, which will return the number of entries ingested into the particular stream. A Redis Stream is equal to a topic of a particular Pub/Sub component pointing to a Redis instance. You can further explore the information about a stream by using the XINFO command:

```
XINFO STREAM temperature
```

It will show how many entries there are, the number of consumer groups associated with the stream along with the first and the last entries, and some additional information. When using Dapr, by default the consumer groups will be named after the Dapr App IDs of the subscriber applications.

At this point, the temperature reading information is ingested into Redis, but there isn't anything consuming those events. Let's explore the Small talker application, which is a Node.js application. It serves on two endpoints – dapr/subscribe for announcing to Dapr that it wants to subscribe to the temperature topic and /temperature-measurement, which is the endpoint where new events are delivered:

```
app.use(bodyParser.json({ type: 'application/*+json' }));

app.get('/dapr/subscribe', (req, res) => {
    res.json([
        {
```

```
            pubsubname: "sensors",
            topic: "temperature",
            route: "temperature-measurement"
        }
    ]);
})
app.post('/temperature-measurement', (req, res) => {
    const temperature = req.body.data.temperatureInCelsius;
    let message = '';
    if (temperature > 31) {
        message = "It's scorching!";
        //... other if statements
    } else {
        message = "It's cold!";
    }

    let date = new Date(req.body.data.eventTime);
    console.log(`The temperature is ${temperature} degrees Celsius at
    ${date.toLocaleString()}. ${message}`);
    res.sendStatus(200);
});
```

In the preceding code snippet, an NPM package named `body-parser` is used for deserializing the events coming in CloudEvents format at the `/temperature-measurement` endpoint. Note that the media type is `application/*+json` because CloudEvents is delivered as application/cloudevents+json instead of application/json. After some logic that compares the current temperature to a predefined temperature range takes place, the message is logged, and the message is acknowledged by responding with HTTP status code 200. In this way, Dapr knows that the consumer has successfully processed the event.

Next, let's leave the application running in another terminal session: `dapr run --app-id small-talker --app-port 8000 -- node app.js`. It's important to specify the application port because the Dapr sidecar will invoke the delivery endpoint whenever there is a new event.

Last but not least, let's explore the AC Controller service that is implemented in ASP. NET Core. The code of the controller that is receiving the message is very simple and can be found in TemperatureMeasurementController.cs:

```
public IActionResult Post([FromBody] CloudEvent cloudEvent)
{
        dynamic data = cloudEvent.Data;
        var temperature = data.temperatureInCelsius;
        var airCon = AirConditioner.Instance;

        Console.WriteLine($"Temperature is {temperature} degree Celsius.");
        if (temperature < 21 || temperature > 23)
        {
                airCon.TurnOn();
                if (temperature < 21)
                {
                        airCon.SetMode(AirConditionerMode.Heat);
                }
                else
                {
                        airCon.SetMode(AirConditionerMode.Cool);
                }
        }
        else
        {
                airCon.TurnOff();
        }

        return Ok();
}
```

In the preceding code snippet, depending on some conditions about the temperature, the air conditioner is being turned on or off, and its mode is being changed in order to maintain a comfortable temperature in the room. The event is received as a CloudEvent, directly parsed from the body of the HTTP request. The CloudEvents support for ASP.NET Core comes from the CloudNative.CloudEvents.AspNetCore NuGet package. In order for it to work, you have to make sure to register the CloudEvents input formatter in `Startup.cs` so that it can deserialize the body of the request into a CloudEvents object and also suppress one validation that will otherwise cause your code to fail because the default validation in .NET 5 has changed:

```
services.AddControllers(options =>
{
        options.InputFormatters.Insert(0, new
        CloudEventJsonInputFormatter());
        options.
        SuppressImplicitRequiredAttributeForNonNullableReferenceTypes =
        true;
});
```

Before starting the AC Controller application, let's define its subscription by using the declarative approach:

```
apiVersion: dapr.io/v1alpha1
kind: Subscription
metadata:
  name: temperature-subscription
spec:
  pubsubname: sensors
  topic: temperature
  route: /TemperatureMeasurement
scopes:
- ac-controller
```

Under `spec` you basically provide the same info as in the programmatic approach – the name of the pubsub component, a topic inside it, and a delivery endpoint where new messages are sent. The difference here is that the subscription endpoint supports defining multiple subscribers at once. In this case, under `scopes` you can find just the `ac-controller`, which is the Dapr ID of the AC Controller service. Make sure to also copy this component manifest file into the Dapr components folder. Finally, let's run the AC Controller service as a Dapr application:

```
dapr run --app-id ac-controller --app-port 5000 -- dotnet run
```

Then by reading the application logs, you will track how the state of the air conditioner changes over time depending on the current temperature:

```
== APP == The AC is set to Cool mode.
== APP == Temperature is 10.511523 degree Celsius.
== APP == The AC is turned on.
== APP == The AC is set to Heat mode.
== APP == Temperature is 10.136372 degree Celsius.
== APP == Temperature is 9.497118 degree Celsius.
```

Switching Over to Another Messaging System

The sensors pubsub component is currently configured to use the Redis instance running in a container locally. But this might not feel very exciting. Let me show you how to switch to using Azure Service Bus without changing the code of any of the applications at all. I will use Azure CLI instead of the Azure Portal because CLI commands are way easier for showing examples as opposed to explaining what objects from the user interface to click. The appearance of the Azure Portal constantly changes.

1. You have to either install Azure CLI on your machine, or you can use the Azure Cloud Shell, which you can access at http://shell. azure.com. If you use the Azure CLI locally, you have to first log in by running az login. The Azure Cloud Shell will automatically do that for you.

2. Then, create a resource group in a region of your choice to logically contain your Service Bus resource. I am using West Europe:

   ```
   az group create -l westeurope -n my-service-bus-rg
   ```

3. Next, let's create the Azure Service Bus namespace in the resource group that we just created. It has to use the Standard tier so that Service Bus topics are supported. It's a good idea to not use the same name for the namespace as I do here because the name of the namespace must be globally unique:

   ```
   az servicebus namespace create --resource-group my-service-
   bus-rg --name dapr-pubsub-asb --location westeurope --sku
   Standard
   ```

4. Once the Service Bus namespace has been created,
    let's get a connection string to it. Copy the value of the
    `primaryConnectionString` property because you will need to
    specify it in the component metadata in the next step:

    ```
    az servicebus namespace authorization-rule keys
    list --resource-group my-service-bus-rg --namespace-name
    dapr-pubsub-asb --name RootManageSharedAccessKey
    ```

5. Now, let's update the sensors pubsub component to point to
    Azure Service Bus. Open the `pubsub-sensors.yaml` and change
    the type to `pubsub.azure.servicebus`. The name of the type
    follows the folder structure inside the dapr/components-contrib
    repository on GitHub.

6. Delete the objects `redisHost` and `redisPassword` as they are
    not relevant anymore for the Service Bus component. Instead,
    you should simply specify the connection string as an item
    with key `connectionString` and for value paste the contents of
    `primaryConnectionString`.

7. Finally, stop all three Dapr applications by pressing Ctrl+C, and
    rerun the same commands `dapr run` to make them pick up the
    new configuration of the `sensors` Pub/Sub component.

After you have done this final step, the temperature sensor application will start
sending the messages into a Service Bus topic named `temperature`. Dapr will create
it automatically for you. Then when the two consumer applications want to read the
messages in the topic, Dapr will create a new subscription for each of them. You can
explore all this visually by opening the Azure Portal and navigating to your Service Bus
namespace. There are also some useful charts that help you understand at what rate
messages are ingested and processed, as you can see from Figure 7-3.

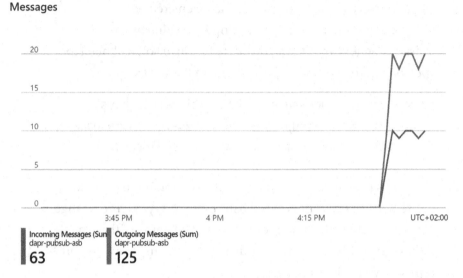

Figure 7-3. *Number of messages chart in Azure Portal*

Additionally, you can pass some additional configuration that is specific to the messaging system of your choice as additional key-value pairs in the metadata of the component. The supported keys vary depending on the type of pubsub component that is used. You can find all supported by consulting the source code of a given component in the `dapr/components-contrib` repository on GitHub or in Dapr docs (docs.dapr.io).

For example, by default, the maximum number of delivery attempts for an Azure Service Bus subscription is 10. After that, the message is moved to the dead-letter subarea of the subscription. You can control this number among others supported by specifying an item with the name `maxDeliveryCount` and the number as a value in the component manifest.

Be aware that the specifics are up to the messaging system of choice. For example, Apache Kafka offers persistent storage of data, whereas the message retention in Azure Event Hubs can be no more than 7 days. It's advisable to try not to rely on a specific behavior offered by a given component as this will make your application less portable across different messaging systems.

Limitations of the Publish and Subscribe Building Block

The Publish and Subscribe building block will be a good fit for most services that need to use the Publish and Subscribe pattern. However, there are a few missing functions that can be identified:

- No support for a dead-letter topic – Some messages will always cause errors no matter how many times you attempt to retry processing them. For such cases, in some of the messaging systems like Azure Service Bus, a dead-letter queue exists natively. It is a sub-queue of each topic that holds all the problematic messages that are sometimes called *poison messages*. The messages can be identified as problematic as soon as they fit some filtering condition, for example, maximum number of deliveries was exceeded or the TTL of the message expired. Currently, if you instruct Dapr to DROP a message, it always logs that the message is being dropped and that's it. Depending on the messaging system, the message may be also moved to a dead-letter queue. In cases when dead-lettering is not supported, Dapr has to acknowledge the delivery because there is nothing else that can be done. This is tricky mostly because not all messaging systems support dead-letter queues, for example, Redis Streams doesn't have a Dead-letter Stream. Dapr will always try to support the maximum common supported functionality by all end technologies. In certain cases when the underlying messaging system does not support dead-lettering, it will be reasonable to acknowledge the poison message from the source topic and move it to another topic to keep track of poison messages. But you have to implement this behavior as it is not yet supported by Dapr.

- The message queue pattern is not supported – The semantics of the message queue pattern where a single message can be picked up by a single consumer cannot be enforced. The current functionality provided by the Publish and Subscribe building block fits only the fan-out pattern that is typical for Pub/Sub. However, such behavior can be achieved using input binding from the Resource Bindings building block that we are going to explore in Chapter 9: Resource Bindings.

- No way to batch-receive a number of events – At the time of writing, a single call to the delivery endpoint carries a single event.

- No way to dynamically set up subscriptions – Currently, the subscriptions are set up at the time of starting up a Dapr application, and they cannot be changed during the lifetime of the application. But there may be some cases where certain conditions should dynamically create a subscription for a given application.

Summary

In this chapter, you learned how Dapr helps you to easily use the Publish and Subscribe pattern. After a brief overview of what Pub/Sub communication is and when it makes sense to be used and when it isn't a good idea, you explored how the Publish and Subscribe building block of Dapr works. You learned what messaging systems are supported by Dapr. Then, you put all this knowledge into practice by implementing a temperature processing system consisting of three services. One of the services used a programmatic subscription, while the other used a declarative one. Initially, the system of three services was using Redis Streams as a messaging system, but later on, I guided you to switch over to Azure Service Bus. The chapter wrapped up by touching upon some of the possible limitations that you may hit if you have any special requirements around Publish and Subscribe.

In the next chapter, you will learn how to use the State Management building block to persist the state of your services.

CHAPTER 8

State Management

At some point, services need to work with state. The way for persisting the state marks out how scalable they are going to be. In this chapter, I will walk you through a brief introduction to what is the difference between stateful and stateless services and what are the challenges for scaling them. As it typically happens, when you don't want to incorporate some functionality in your code, you use an external service that provides the functionality you need out of the box. You will learn how Dapr helps you persist the state of your services by leveraging external state stores. When you make it to the point to persist data of a distributed application, you must think over two important traits – concurrency and consistency. Once I cover how the State Management building block works, I will go through the state stores that are supported by Dapr. I will also touch on how the Actors building block that I am going to cover in Chapter 10: The Actor Model relies upon state management.

Stateful vs. Stateless Services

In the world of microservices, services live in containers, and the composition of all those containers logically forms the Microservices application. Some of those services may be producing a result by relying solely on the input that was sent into them without depending on any state. That is a stateless service as it doesn't care about the context of the current request and the outcome of any previous requests. For example, searching for some products in an online store can be served by a stateless service – you just type some keywords, and it makes a query to the database. This service may be replicated to several containers behind a load balancer, and it doesn't matter which of those replicas will process the incoming request.

After some time, a requirement to make this product service more intelligent may come. It may have to track where the user came from and what are their interests and even take into consideration if the user is logged in so that it knows even more details.

© Radoslav Gatev 2021
R. Gatev, *Introducing Distributed Application Runtime (Dapr)*, https://doi.org/10.1007/978-1-4842-6998-5_8

Based on the information it has collected, the service will make sure to grade and order the returned products accordingly. As a developer, you will be tempted to save all this information about the user locally and in memory. It's very easy to create a *static concurrent dictionary* that can keep the state locally among different requests. This makes the service a stateful one, which means that its instances won't be autonomous and interchangeable anymore. Each instance holds its portion of the whole state so that the load balancer has to examine every request and based on some condition to direct it to the respective instance that keeps the state information about a user. In such a scenario, the instances can effectively be called *shards*. Sharding is a technique used to split a large volume of data into multiple chunks called shards that are persisted on different servers. But the primary goal of sharding is to accommodate a volume of data that is so big that doesn't fit a single server. Sharding is very typical for databases, but it also brings a lot of challenges. For example, each shard becomes a *single point of failure*. You may want to replicate each shard to another server to make sure a failure or corruption in one shard does not deteriorate the whole sharded service. Furthermore, the load balancer needs a strategy to distribute requests to the available shards. This mapping between a request and a shard is done by a sharding function whose job is to resolve a request to a particular shard in a deterministic and uniform way. The sharding function is pretty much like the hashing function that is used by hash tables. You have to identify what part of the request to use as a sharding key – IP address, path, country, and so on. The sharding function will use this key to consistently determine which shard this request should be routed to. Let's assume that the initial number of shards was set up to be 5. With time those shards become full, and you need to add another shard to make them 6. Depending on the sharding function that you use, this might result in a change in the way all requests are being distributed across shards. Or you may need to implement a resharding process. This becomes very complicated for implementation unless you are building a new database technology, of course.

But there is a way to have a stateless service that still uses a state. I know it sounds confusing at first! This can be achieved by offloading the state persistence to an external service as shown in Figure 8-1. When you scale out such a stateless service, each replica will always manage to find the ID for a particular session in the state store. And you don't care what replica will service your request in the end. However, calling an external service will add some performance overhead; but in most cases, it will be negligible if the service and the state store are in close proximity. The service can be scaled out indefinitely; however, eventually, the bottleneck will become the common state store, which will have to be scaled as well to keep up with the load.

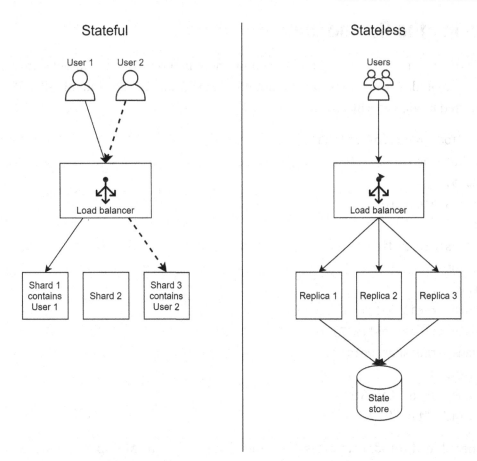

Figure 8-1. *Stateful and stateless services*

State Management in Dapr

Dapr simplifies the interaction with a state store by providing a State Management building block. You use the API of the building block to interface with all supported services. Some of them are Redis, Azure Cosmos DB, Couchbase, SQL Server, and many others. The state items are represented as key/value pairs. This means that after you save a state item, you can query its value by searching by its key.

Some of the benefits of using the State Management building block are the following:

- Utilizing external state stores without learning/installing/integrating their SDKs or APIs. You only interact with the Dapr APIs. Dapr handles the specifics of the target service.

- As a result, swapping one state store for another doesn't require any code changes.

Defining the Component

Before you can use the building block, a component that points to the target state store must be created. The default state component that is created when you initialize Dapr in Self-hosted mode looks like this:

```
apiVersion: dapr.io/v1alpha1
kind: Component
metadata:
  name: statestore
spec:
  type: state.redis
  version: v1
  metadata:
  - name: redisHost
    value: localhost:6379
  - name: redisPassword
    value: ""
  - name: actorStateStore
    value: "true"
```

The value of `metadata.name` is the name of the state store. Multiple state store components can be created and used by Dapr applications. Later on, when you want to execute some operation via the API, you have to reference the particular state store by specifying its name.

As with other components, the `spec.metadata` section contains the connection details and any options that are supported by the particular state store implementation. In the preceding example, `actorStateStore` is set to true, which means that this component will be used for persisting the actors' state. Only a single state store can be used by the Actors building block.

Note   Components are namespaced. This means that Dapr applications see all the components that exist only in the namespace where they reside. If you want to persist state to the same state store but from other namespaces, you have to create the same component. You can use the same name because names should be unique within a namespace.

Note   Additionally, components can be made available only to a select list of Dapr App IDs by listing them under the `.scopes` section of the component.

Controlling Behavior

Let me show you how you can control the behavior of the target state store. Some of the state stores support specifying the options for *concurrency* and *consistency*. Dapr tries to support them via the State Management building block on a best effort basis. You can also specify some options that are supported by a particular implementation of a state component. However, if you want to make your applications as universal as possible, you should restrain from specifying any particular options or metadata and embrace eventual consistency and last-write-wins as a strategy for concurrent changes. Let's see what this means.

Concurrency

To understand what the concurrency concerns are, let's imagine that multiple instances of a service have acquired the last state of an item from the state store. At some point, they may try to update it almost at the same time. For example, imagine that each instance counts the requests it receives getting the last count, increments it by one, and saves it in the same place. You may expect in the end the sum of all requests to be equal to the total requests received. But so many requests are coming that some of them are even processed in parallel by different instances of the same service. For those parallel requests, the last counter gathered from the state store will be equal to 10, for example. All the instances that have picked up 10 will try to update it to 11, that is, incrementing it by one. Because those instances don't know if the particular item was updated right before persisting the value, some calls may be missed by such a naïve counter.

But there is a way to prevent such conflicts from happening. Dapr implements *Optimistic Concurrency Control (OCC)* by using ETag or (Entity Tag) for items stored in a state store. ETag actually originates from HTTP where it also helps leverage the already cached data without making new requests. ETag is an identifier assigned to a specific version of a resource, in this case an item persisted in a state store. Performing OCC by using ETag happens in two steps:

- An ETag is returned whenever you get some item.

- When performing an update, you have to provide the ETag in order to attest to the version the update is based on. If the ETag provided in the update request matches the current ETag for the item in the state store (meaning that data has not changed in the meantime), the update will succeed.

ETag can be optionally provided only in mutating operations, which in Dapr are saving and deleting state.

Dapr supports two modes of concurrency, which you choose depending on whether you pass an ETag when performing a mutating operation:

- First-write-wins – If you specify an ETag to a mutating operation, the operation will only succeed if there is a match between the specified ETag and the latest one for the item in the state store. Otherwise, the operation is rejected.

- Last-write-wins – If you don't specify an ETag, this is the default behavior. The operation will always be performed. This can be useful when you know that collisions won't happen or performing an update based on a stale version doesn't cause any side effects for the integrity of the data you are saving.

For stores that don't natively support OCC with ETags, Dapr will try simulating the behavior as it stays in the middle between Dapr applications mutating state and the target state store. The implementation is up to the state store component. It is best to check whether the state store component you are about to use supports ETags or not.

Consistency

Dapr supports two consistency levels: *strong* and *eventual*. The consistency level can be specified as a hint to get, save, and delete operations.

When using strong consistency, you ensure that reads will return the most recent version of the data, and mutating operations will synchronously confirm the change with a quorum before completing the request. Strong consistency is considered slow but safe as operations will most likely have to span multiple replicas depending on the target state store. Note that not all state stores support strong consistent reads.

When using eventual consistency, the read operation can get data from any of the replicas of the state store (again, depending on the state store). This means that some read requests may return some obsolete value because replicas will converge to the latest value as time passes. For mutating operations, the change will be asynchronously reconciled with a quorum of replicas.

You have to decide which mode works best for your application depending on the state data it uses. Taking such a decision imposes a trade-off between consistency on one side and scalability on the other. The cost of strong consistency is a higher latency, as you are going to wait for multiple replicas to acknowledge; however, your data is always up-to-date. In contrast, eventual consistency performs faster but may return stale data from time to time.

Metadata

Different state stores support different features. For example, when using Azure Cosmos DB, you can specify the partition key as a metadata property as a part of any request to the Dapr State API. When you do so, you will be able to achieve better performance for your queries because, otherwise, Cosmos DB will have to scan all the physical partitions for a particular item. The `partitionKey` is a property of the metadata object that is supported on all operations of the State Management building block.

That was just one example of a supported metadata property. Other state stores support different properties. Don't get confused with the store-specific metadata that is configured in the component. The metadata of a component defines how it works (e.g., establishing a connection, controlling its behavior), whereas the metadata of a state request is used just for the current operation that is executed in the target state store.

Saving State

As is common, the State API is provided by the Dapr sidecar container or process (for Self-hosted mode) that stays next to each service. As shown in Figure 8-2, to persist some state you have to issue a POST request to the `/state/<your-state-store-name>` endpoint where you specify the name of the component. In Figure 8-2, the state component is named `myStateStore`.

The body of the request is an array of one or more key/value pairs. Those items will be processed individually while persisted in the state store. Note that both inserts and updates can be performed via this endpoint. In distributed scenarios, it is more useful to have an upsert endpoint as opposed to standalone insert and update endpoints.

Now let's see how to persist some state items. You can optionally specify options and metadata to be sent to the state store for each of the state items:

```
{
    "key": "callerIp",
    "value": "88.88.99.16",
    "etag": "27",
    "options": {
            "concurrency": "first-write",
            "consistency": "strong"
    },
    "metadata":{
            "metadataKey": "metadataValue"
    }
}
```

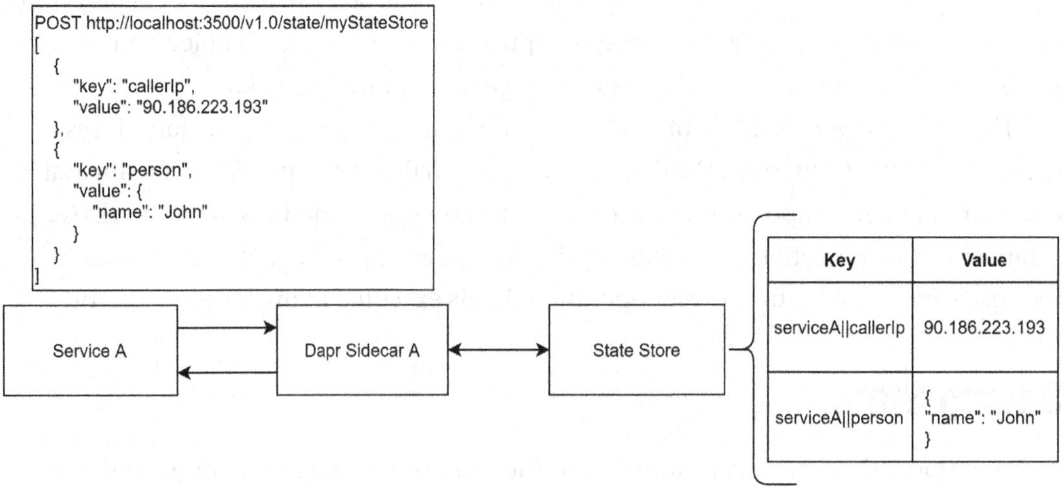

Figure 8-2. *Persisting state*

In the target state store, the items were persisted using keys derived by the Dapr App ID and the original key of the state item following the convention `<App ID>||<state-key>`. This makes it possible to use the same state store for persisting the state of multiple applications without having any key collisions. In case the state store is being used for persisting state of actors, the keys will follow a slightly different format: `<App ID>||<Actor type>||<Actor id>||<state key>`.

Having the Dapr App ID automatically inserted at the beginning of the state key originally specified means that by default your Dapr applications won't be able to share state data. In other words, Service A cannot access Item1 that is persisted by Service B, as the requests originating from Service A will have the following key `Service-A||Item1` while the state item will be persisted under the `Service-B|Item1` key.

For most applications, this will be useful. But Dapr allows you to configure the state sharing behavior by specifying a state prefix strategy. A prefix is what is inserted in front of the key you specify when calling any endpoint of the State API. By default, it is the Dapr App ID.

But you can use the name of the state store component as a prefix. This makes it possible for all applications regardless of their Dapr App IDs to work with the state data persisted via the same state component.

The next and the most relaxed prefix strategy is to not use a prefix. In this way, applications will be able to access any state data, regardless of whether it is persisted via Dapr or by an external application.

To control the state prefix strategy, you have to specify a metadata item named `keyPrefix` in the state component configuration, and the three possible values we just explored are, respectively, `appid`, `name`, and `none`.

Note   As a best practice when you use Dapr in Self-hosted mode and want to use the State Management building block, make sure to always specify a Dapr App ID. Otherwise, upon each execution of `dapr run`, a new App ID will be generated. If you rely on the default prefix strategy that leverages the App ID, having auto-generated IDs is not a good idea as you won't be able to access the persisted state later on.

Getting State

There are two endpoints for retrieving state – one for gathering individual items and another that supports bulk requests.

Getting Individual Items

Now, revisit Figure 8-2 to understand the current state of the data in the state store. Issuing a request with cURL to get the state item with the key person looks like this:

```
curl -X GET 'http://localhost:3500/v1.0/state/myStateStore/
person?consistency=strong'
```

The response is the following JSON object:

```
{"name":"John"}
```

Note that I have specified the consistency mode as a parameter, which is optional. The ETag of the item is returned as a response header. The single prerequisite if you want to use the Optimistic Concurrency Control is you have to pass this ETag to any consecutive requests that are mutating this item.

Getting Items in Bulk

Sometimes, you need to retrieve a couple of items. Instead of sending an individual request, Dapr offers a bulk endpoint, where you can specify the keys for which you want to gather values.

A request with cURL looks like the following:

```
curl -X POST 'http://localhost:3500/v1.0/state/myStateStore/bulk' -H
'content-type: application/json' -d '{\"keys\": [\"callerIp\", \"person\"],
\"parallelism\": 10}'
```

What Dapr will do behind the scenes is it will issue N number of requests to the state store, where N is the number of keys that you specified. That's why there is an optional property that you can specify to control the number of requests that are executed in parallel. The reason for providing a way to limit the parallel requests is that you can overwhelm the target state store if you specify too many keys. For state stores like Cosmos DB, you should make sure that it has enough capacity of request units so that it performs all requests without any throttling.

The response in my case contains the following payload:

```
[
    {
        "key":"person",
        "data":{
            "name":"John"
        },
        "etag":"26"
    },
    {

        "key":"callerIp",
        "data":"90.186.223.193",
        "etag":"24"
    }
]
```

It's entirely possible for some of the individual requests to fail for various reasons. In such cases, the object will be present in the resulting payload, but it will have an error property that holds the error message Dapr received at the time of sending the request to the target state store. Also, if such a key doesn't exist, it will still be returned but without a data property.

You can pass some metadata property to the target state store by providing it as a query parameter, as it is with the following example that targets Cosmos DB: http://localhost:3500/v1.0/state/myStateStore/bulk?metadata.partitionKey =mypartitionKey.

Deleting State

In order to delete state items, you have to issue individual DELETE requests for each key you want to delete. You can optionally pass the ETag in the If-Match header of the request.

Here you can see a request to delete a state item with the key that equals person. The optional parameter consistency is also included:

```
curl -X DELETE 'http://localhost:3500/v1.0/state/myStateStore/
person?consistency=strong'
```

Using State Transactions

You already know the basic operations that are supported by the State Management building block. As we explored the bulk operations, I must point out once again that bulk saving doesn't support transactions for all items that are specified. Some of them can be successfully persisted, while others may fail.

Dapr has another endpoint that supports transactions over a list of operations that are mutating any state items. Either all operations succeed at once or the whole operation fails and nothing is changed. Namely, the mutating operations in regard to transactions are upsert and delete.

Transactions are executed as POST or PUT requests on the /state/<store-name>/ transaction endpoint. As with any other endpoints, options are specified per state item. It supports specifying metadata as another property next to operations, and it applies to the whole request. Here is the body of a transaction that changes the name of a state item with the key person and deletes the state item with the key callerIp:

```
{
    "operations": [
        {
            "operation": "upsert",
            "request": {
                "key": "person",
                "value": {
                    "name": "James"
                }
            }
        },
        {
            "operation": "delete",
            "request": {
                "key": "callerIp"
            }
        }
    ]
}
```

As I already mentioned, the Actors building block uses a single state component to persist the state of the actors. An important detail is that this state store must support both transactions and ETags. In the next section, you will learn what stores are supported and what their capabilities are.

Supported Stores

Now that you know what the State Management building block offers, let me list all the supported state stores in Table 8-1 at the time of writing the book. All of the stores support the CRUD operations like upsert, get single, get bulk, and delete. And just a handful of them provide transactional support. Those state stores that support both transactions and ETags can be used to persist the state of actors, which will be covered in detail in Chapter 10: The Actor Model.

Table 8-1. *Supported state stores*

Name	CRUD	Transactional	ETag
Aerospike	✔	✘	✔
AWS DynamoDB	✔	✘	✘
Azure Blob Storage	✔	✘	✔
Azure Cosmos DB	✔	✔	✔
Azure SQL Database/SQL Server	✔	✔	✔
Azure Table Storage	✔	✘	✔
Cassandra	✔	✘	✘
Cloudstate	✔	✘	✔
Couchbase	✔	✘	✔
Google Cloud Firestore	✔	✘	✘
HashiCorp Consul	✔	✘	✘
Hazelcast	✔	✘	✘
Memcached	✔	✘	✘
MongoDB	✔	✔	✔

(continued)

Table 8-1. (*continued*)

Name	CRUD	Transactional	ETag
PostgreSQL	✔	✔	✔
Redis	✔	✔	✔
RethinkDB	✔	✔	✔
ZooKeeper	✔	✘	✔

Some of the state stores listed in the preceding require special attention. For example, when you use the state component for the SQL Server store, you will most likely provide the credentials of a user that is not part of the sysadmin or db_owner role. That is usually considered as the best practice – you grant only the minimum set of permissions that are needed. But in order for Dapr to work, it needs to set up a table where the state is saved. Therefore, the credentials for the user that you specify in the connection string must have the permissions for CREATE TABLE, CREATE TYPE, and CREATE PROCEDURE granted.

Another example is when you use Azure Cosmos DB for transactions. A peculiarity of Cosmos DB is that transactions can span items stored in a single partition. Hence, if you want to execute a transaction, you have to pass the partition key as metadata.

Summary

Having the ability to store some state is crucial. We outlined what are the differences between a stateless and a stateful service and the various considerations when it comes to scaling both. Next, you learned how the State Management building block makes it easier to use a target state store with the functionality it provides – persisting, getting, and deleting state. After we explored how to use the basic operations, I introduced you to the transactional support that some state stores have. During the course of the chapter, you learned how to work with concurrency and consistency and how to pass metadata items to the state store whenever executing a state operation.

In the next chapter, you are going to see how the Resource Bindings building block can help you integrate your Dapr-based applications with various external systems.

CHAPTER 9

Resource Bindings

So far, I have shown you how to interface with other services within your microservices-based application. This chapter will be about integrating with various external services. The communication typically happens in two ways – either an external service creates an event that a local Dapr service listens for or a local Dapr application makes a request to an external system. Dapr has a building block for talking to external systems, which logically can be split into two groups from a logical perspective – input and output bindings. I will enumerate the various systems that the Resource Bindings building block integrates with and whether it is for input or output or it is bidirectional. Then I will explain what the API of the Resource Bindings building block looks like. To demonstrate how things work, I will walk you through implementing a solution that monitors an Azure Blob Storage container for newly uploaded photos using Azure Event Grid; it performs object detection, then sends the recognized and tagged images to the same storage account, and also persists the objects identified to a state store.

The Need to Communicate with External Services

Let's face it. You cannot implement everything as a locally running service. Quite often, for example, it is not reasonable to host a bulky database that requires a lot of storage and processing power within your cluster. Or maybe you want to offload some of the functionality that is needed to a ready-made *Software as a Service (SaaS)* product instead of spending the effort to implement it from scratch on your own. Such decisions are taken as early as the time you are designing the boundaries of the services in the Microservices architecture and what capabilities will be provided by external systems or services.

External services come in all shapes and sizes. Some of them are accessible via RESTful APIs, while others may support GraphQL, for example. Most of them can be accessible via HTTP, while others may use AMQP, MQTT, or even some proprietary

© Radoslav Gatev 2021

R. Gatev, *Introducing Distributed Application Runtime (Dapr)*, https://doi.org/10.1007/978-1-4842-6998-5_9

protocols. You get the idea: there is a huge variety of services, each of them providing various communication options – APIs, SDKs, libraries, and so on. But more holistically, there are basically two reasons you want to do this – to receive some input from an external system and process it or to send a request to an external system and receive the result, if any. That's why the Bindings building block aims to provide a universal way to interact with external systems by generalizing the communication with them behind the Dapr API.

The building block can be divided into two subparts – *input bindings* and *output bindings*. Input binding is when an external system triggers an endpoint of a Dapr application. It typically happens when some events happen in this external system and your application must be notified in order to process the new events. The building block relies on a component of a specific type. I will describe the component structure in more detail later in this chapter. The trigger of the input binding is described inside the component manifest. For example, it can connect and listen to some message queue and get triggered whenever a new message is created. There are a lot of message queues that are supported by the Bindings building block. Another example can be when you want to receive and process tweets that match a particular query that was defined in the component. Depending on the component type you choose, you can achieve different things.

Output binding is when your Dapr application needs to gather some data from an external system or execute some action in the external system. Therefore, it calls its Dapr sidecar, which relies on the specific component that you have defined to talk with the external system. By using an output binding, you can execute a SQL SELECT statement, for example, and receive the result, or you can send a message to a queue, or you can send an SMS. Some of the output bindings return results, while others do not.

Supported Bindings

I will intentionally start by enumerating all supported external systems at the time of writing the book so that you get a better idea of what is possible by using this building block. For each supported external system, there is an implementation of a component. The components of the Bindings building block should implement at least one of the interfaces – either for input or output. Some of the components support both directions. Once you understand what Bindings components exist, I will walk you through the API of the building block.

I will categorize the supported components into several groups to make it easier to absorb the information because there are a lot of supported systems.

Generic Components

Table 9-1 contains all the supported external systems that are not a part of any of the public cloud platforms. Some of them can be hosted anywhere – on-premises or in the cloud. Others like Apple Push Notification Service and Twilio SMS are proprietary and therefore comply with the Software as a Service (SaaS) model. By looking at the table, you can tell whether the component supports input, output, or bidirectional bindings. Under the column Input triggers, I have listed the events that cause the input binding to be triggered. Under the column Output operations, you can see what operations you can execute via the output binding on a specific external system.

Table 9-1. *Supported generic bindings*

Name	Input	Input triggers	Output	Output operations
Apple Push Notification Service	✗		✔	Create – sends a push notification
Cron (Scheduler)	✔	Scheduled trigger	✔	Delete – stops the previously started Cron
HTTP	✗		✔	Performs an HTTP request. Supports the following HTTP verbs as operations: GET, HEAD, POST, PUT, PATCH, DELETE, OPTIONS, TRACE
InfluxDB	✗		✔	Create – writes a single point
Kafka	✔	A new message for a consumer group	✔	Create – publishes a message to a topic
Kubernetes Events	✔	New Kubernetes Events for a namespace	✗	

(continued)

Table 9-1. (*continued*)

Name	Input	Input triggers	Output	Output operations
MQTT	✔	New messages in a topic	✔	Create – publishes a message to a topic
MySQL	✘		✔	Exec – performs Data Definition Language (DDL) and returns the number of affected rows Query – executes SELECT statements and returns a SQL result set Close – closes the DB connection
PostgreSQL	✘		✔	Exec – performs Data Definition Language (DDL) operations and executes INSERT, UPDATE, and DELETE statements and returns the number of affected rowsQuery – executes SELECT statements and returns a SQL result setClose – closes the DB connection
Postmark	✘		✔	Create – sends an email
RabbitMQ	✔	New message in a queue	✔	Create – publishes a message to a queue
Redis	✘		✔	Create – performs SET to persist some data under a specified key
RethinkDB	✔	A state change in a table	✘	
SMTP	✘		✔	Create – sends an email
Twilio SMS	✘		✔	Create – sends an SMS to a telephone number
Twilio SendGrid	✘		✔	Create – sends an email
Twitter	✔	Tweet matching a predefined query	✔	Get – searches for tweets that match some parameters

As you can see from Table 9-1, there is a broad range of components that Dapr provides for the Bindings building block. Among them are message queues, common protocols, databases, notification services, mailing services, and even social networks. With time, the number of supported external systems will grow because you can implement a Bindings component for every system that exposes some kind of API that other applications could use.

You may have noticed that some of the external systems are supported by other types of components as well. For example, there is a Redis component for State Management, Publish and Subscribe, and Bindings. If you use all those building blocks, you can point the component to the same Redis instance, and you won't experience any conflicts. That is because each component type uses a different Redis data structure and applies different semantics. The Publish and Subscribe component uses Redis Streams, the State Management component uses Redis Hashes, and the Bindings component uses Redis Strings.

When it comes to Apache Kafka, there is also an implementation of a Publish and Subscribe component. The difference is very slight – the Bindings component expects a consumer group to be defined and reads only from it, whereas Publish and Subscribe enables you to leverage the fan-out messaging pattern where the consumer group is by default assigned to the App ID of each subscriber that consumes messages on its own pace. The Bindings component applies the message queue semantics of all messaging systems that are supported. This means that if you happen to have multiple services that can be triggered by the same input binding, they will compete for messages. The first service that takes a message and processes it successfully will acknowledge the message, so it won't be received by other services.

There is one outlier in Table 9-1. That is the Cron component. The Cron component does not interface with any external system. Instead, it provides a way to schedule the triggering of an endpoint. Let's say that every 30 minutes your application should check for new subscribers in your mailing list to send them a welcome email. In order to achieve this, you have to create a Cron component, and you can either use one of the shortcuts like "@every 30m" or the full CRON expression "0 30 * * * *". This means that it works the same way as the other input bindings; the difference is that it is not triggered by an external system but on a schedule instead. Then you have to create the respective endpoint that is going to be triggered. It should be named after the name of the component. Note that the scheduling depends on the start time of the Dapr sidecar – no matter if it is in Self-hosted or Kubernetes mode. Whenever a sidecar process/container is created, the clock of the Cron scheduler starts ticking away. As you know, Pods are ephemeral, so don't expect the Cron to happen consistently on the defined schedule. If a Pod is being recreated, the schedule can be twofolds late at most, and this can happen if the Pod was destroyed right before it was about to trigger the input binding. Then the new Pod will start counting from zero.

Public Cloud Platform Components

Let me start with the services from Microsoft Azure that are listed in Table 9-2. The example I am going to show you later in this chapter will be based off on Azure Blob Storage and Azure Storage Queues. Azure Event Grid will be also used to subscribe for any changes happening on Azure Blob Storage.

Table 9-2. *Supported bindings in Microsoft Azure*

Name	Input	Input triggers	Output	Output operations
Azure Blob Storage	✘		✔	Create – uploads a blob to a containerGet – reads the contents of a particular blob
Azure Cosmos DB	✘		✔	Create – creates a document
Azure Event Grid	✔	A new event for a subscription	✔	Create – publishes an event to a custom topic
Azure Event Hubs	✔	A new event for a consumer group	✔	Create – sends an event
Azure Service Bus Queues	✔	A new message in a queue	✔	Create – sends a message to a queue
Azure SignalR	✘		✔	Create – sends a message to specific users or groups of users
Azure Storage Queues	✔	A new message in a queue	✔	Create – inserts a message in a queue

Next, you can find all the supported services within Amazon Web Services listed in Table 9-3.

Table 9-3. *Supported bindings in Amazon Web Services*

Name	Input	Input triggers	Output	Output operations
AWS DynamoDB	✗		✔	Create – adds an item to a table
AWS Kinesis	✔	A new record in a stream	✔	Create – puts a single record into a stream
AWS S3	✗		✔	Create – uploads a file to a bucket
AWS SNS	✗		✔	Create – publishes a message to a topic
AWS SQS	✔	A new message in a queue	✔	Create – sends a message to a queue

The supported services from Google Cloud Platform are enumerated in Table 9-4.

Table 9-4. *Supported bindings in Google Cloud Platform*

Name	Input	Input triggers	Output	Output operations
GCP Pub/Sub	✔	New message for a subscription	✔	Create – publishes a message to a topic
GCP Cloud Storage	✗		✔	Create – uploads a file to a bucket

And there is one service supported in Alibaba Cloud that is listed in Table 9-5.

Table 9-5. *Supported bindings in Alibaba Cloud*

Name	Input	Input triggers	Output	Output operations
Object Storage Service	✗		✔	Create – uploads a blob to a bucket

Overview of the Building Block

At this point, you most likely have a good understanding of what external systems are supported and what are the capabilities of each one of them.

Let me mention some of the benefits of the Resource Bindings building block:

- No SDKs or libraries are required – you specify the component for the external service you want to use by putting in the metadata specific to the particular system. From there on, you leave it to the API of the building block.

- You can focus on the business logic instead of thinking about how to implement an integration with some external system.

- No inherited concepts and classes – standardized payload defined by the building block.

Binding Components

As usual, the component is what defines the specific behavior of the building block. Once you have chosen the specific component type you want to use, then you have to make sure to supply values for connection information properties and some other metadata specific to the particular external system that this component interfaces with. A single component can support both input and output bindings from/to an external system.

For example, the following snippet is a definition of a binding component for Kafka:

```
apiVersion: dapr.io/v1alpha1
kind: Component
metadata:
  name: mykafkabinding
  namespace: default
spec:
  type: bindings.kafka
  version: v1
  metadata:
  - name: brokers
    value: "http://localhost:9092"
```

```
- name: topics
  value: "someTopic1"
- name: publishTopic
  value: "someTopic2"
- name: consumerGroup
  value: "consumerGroup1"
- name: authRequired
  value: "false"
```

Let's first focus on the metadata section, which in this case is specific to the Kafka component. In order to connect to an external system, you have to specify its address and some authentication information. In the preceding case, Kafka runs locally, and it doesn't require any credentials. Some properties can be used for both input and output bindings, while others are specific to one of them. In the case of Kafka, the `topics` and `consumerGroup` elements apply only for the input binding, which consumes events from one or more topics by using a consumer group. The topic specified in `publishTopic` is used whenever the output binding is invoked, and that is the topic that ends up receiving the event.

The name of the component is being further referenced by any input and output binding requests.

Input Bindings

Input bindings are useful when a Dapr application needs to be triggered by an event that happened in an external system. Once you have defined a binding component that supports input bindings, Dapr will try to identify what applications can be triggered by this input binding. Remember there are namespaces and scopes applicable for components, so not all components can see all applications and vice versa. The Dapr runtime will try to execute an `OPTIONS` request to a route with the name of the binding component, and if it receives anything other than 404 Not Found, this will mean that the Dapr application subscribes to the input binding.

When the application registration is done, the input binding works as shown in Figure 9-1.

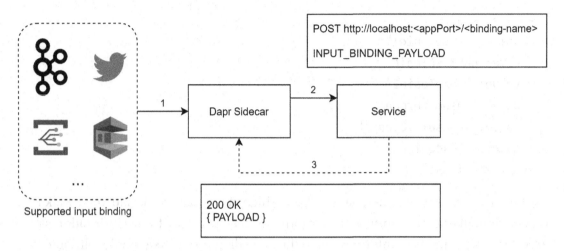

Figure 9-1. *Input binding*

On the left side, you can see that the flow is initiated by one of the supported external systems. When the input binding detects a new event that occurred, Dapr calls into an application endpoint with the same name as the binding component. The body of the request will contain the payload coming from the external system. That's where things start to get specific. You cannot really swap one component for another because the application processing the payload expects a payload with a specific structure.

When the service is done processing the payload, it should return a successful response with status code 200. It means that the input binding was successful, and the event should be marked as processed and removed. Otherwise, Dapr will assume that the event wasn't processed successfully and will try to redeliver it. As I just mentioned redelivery, maybe you are wondering what the event delivery guarantees are. This depends solely on the component implementation – it can be either exactly once or at least once.

Returning just status code 200 is enough for Dapr to know the event was processed successfully. There is more you can do just by providing a response body, although I don't recommend doing so for various reasons. However, this is currently supported, and we should explore it. For example, you can directly invoke one or more output bindings or *persist* some state in a state store. In the case of output binding, the limitation is that you cannot receive the response, since the output binding was invoked by the Dapr app response to the input binding trigger. It's a fire-and-forget kind of action.

The following JSON is an example of a response body that persists some data in a state store and invokes output bindings:

```
{

        "storeName": "stateStore",
        "state": stateData,

        "to": ['storagebinding', 'queuebinding'],
        "concurrency": "parallel",
        "data": outputBindingData
}
```

This will instruct Dapr to do two things – persist some data into a state store named stateStore and invoke output bindings named storagebinding and queuebinding by passing them some payload. Here stateData is a placeholder for an array of JSON state objects as state items will be applied in bulk. The outputBindingData is a placeholder for the JSON object that the output bindings that you are targeting expect. Note that you can specify more than one binding, but the data you pass to them is a single object. You should have this in mind as some bindings might expect a different input format. Currently, there is no way to pass metadata to those bindings. You will learn about what metadata can be supplied when I explain how the output bindings work. If you have specified multiple bindings, they can either be invoked in parallel or serial (one after another), which is specified by the concurrency property.

Note   The option to return a response with payload from a Dapr application upon processing an input binding trigger will be deprecated in Dapr v1.1.0 and removed after that. If you still need to persist some state or invoke an output binding, then simply use the respective endpoints from the Dapr API.

Output Bindings

Output bindings allow you to call an external service and optionally receive some data from it. After you have defined a component (or created the CRD in Kubernetes mode) that supports output binding, you simply reference it by name in any requests to it as shown in Figure 9-2.

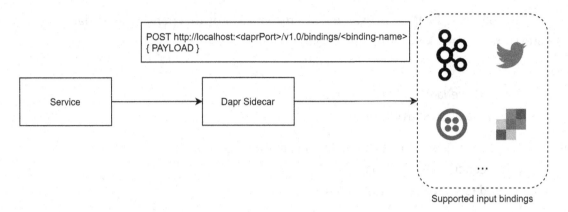

POST http://localhost:<daprPort>/v1.0/bindings/<binding-name>
{ PAYLOAD }

Service

Dapr Sidecar

...

Supported input bindings

Figure 9-2. *Output binding*

As you might have noticed, this time the components stay on the right side as the initiator is the Dapr application itself. It issues a POST or PUT request to the /bindings endpoint specifying the name of the binding that is targeted. This example shows how to use the HTTP-based API of the building block, but keep in mind that you can also achieve the same by calling the respective gRPC method.

The structure of the payload you are passing when invoking an output binding looks like this:

```
{
        "data": someJsonObject,
        "metadata": {
                "key1": "value1"
        },
        "operation": "create"
}
```

Although the payload has a generic structure, the values of the data and metadata properties are determined by the specifics of the external system you target and the binding component for it. The data property contains the data that the external system expects. It can be the contents of a file, a message, and so on.

The operation property states what operation you want to execute. There are several standard operations defined in Dapr – get, create, delete, and list. You can revisit the tables with the supported bindings to check what operations each component supports for output. Some components stick to the standard operations, while others define a set of custom operations.

The metadata property is a set of key-value pairs that specify certain properties that are used when performing the operation in the target external system. This typically contains information that is very specific to the component implementation and the target external system. If certain metadata items are not specified with the request payload, the component will usually try to get them from its metadata. Maybe you would want to try invoking an output binding without any metadata for the sake of keeping your code loosely coupled. But the reality is that you cannot fully invoke an output binding without passing some metadata. For example, imagine you want to persist some object in Redis by invoking the operation create. You pass the object value into the data property of the payload, and you do not pass any metadata. The request will fail because the Redis binding component doesn't know what key to use to persist the value. The list of examples goes on and on.

When implementing the endpoint to be triggered by an input binding or the code invoking an output binding, you always have to keep in mind what is the target external system you are invoking. You need to have a good grasp on what is supported, what is the schema of the input payload, and what data and metadata you can pass to the output binding.

Implementing an Image Processing Application

Now let me show you how to build an image processing service built with ASP.NET Core. The service will be triggered whenever a new image is uploaded to a specific path in an Azure Storage Blob container. Then the service downloads the image, and it invokes a pre-trained model for object detection – *YOLO version 4*. YOLO stands for *You Only Look Once* and is one of the models that are fast enough to be capable of detecting objects in real-time scenarios. If the model recognizes any objects in the uploaded photo, it will tag them by outlining a boundary box and will label them on top of the image. A lot of services and technologies will work hand in hand for that example. But from the perspective of the service we are going to build, it all goes through Dapr as opposed to directly talking to those services.

Overview

Since the interaction between various parties is quite wild, you can see what actions take place in the process by looking at the sequence diagram in Figure 9-3.

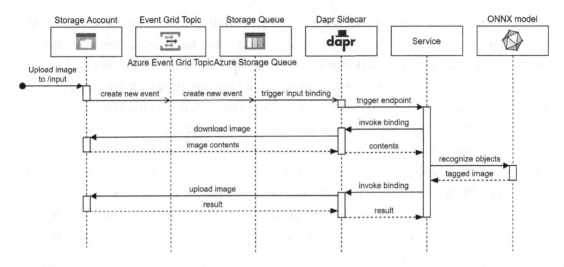

Figure 9-3. *A sequence diagram of an object detection service*

Let me describe the end-to-end flow of the application:

1. An image is uploaded to the /input path in an Azure Storage Container.

2. Azure Event Grid detects the uploaded image and creates a new message in an Azure Storage Queue.

3. The Dapr sidecar notices the new message in the Azure Storage Queue and triggers the service endpoint that is going to contain the main logic. We are going to explore its implementation.

4. The service receives the message that contains the information about the uploaded blob.

5. The service invokes an output binding to retrieve the image contents from Azure Blob Storage.

6. The service performs an ONNX model inference using ML.NET by providing the downloaded image.

7. The service receives a list of all recognized objects along with a local path to a tagged image in which all detected objects are outlined.

8. The service invokes an output binding to upload the tagged image into the /output directory of the Azure Storage Account.

The ONNX model that I use for object detection is YOLO version 4. This is a pre-trained model that can recognize objects from 80 classes. It is fast enough that it can be used for real-time object detection, for example, think about recognizing objects from a web cam stream.

ONNX is an abbreviation of *Open Neural Network Exchange.* ONNX is an open source format used to represent machine learning and deep learning models. The model format was initially introduced by Facebook and Microsoft in 2017, but later on, other companies joined the project as well. ONNX is a description of a model made in Protobuf format, which aims to ease the interoperability between machine learning frameworks and to allow hardware vendors to maximize the performance of model inference. In other words, ONNX enables you to build and train your model in a framework of choice and then convert it into ONNX and run it anywhere you want. For example, the YOLO v4 model was originally a pre-trained TensorFlow model, which was later converted into ONNX. The inference is the step that comes after training. During training, the model relearns a new capability, whereas during inference it applies this capability to some new data it has never seen. There are various runtimes that support ONNX models; among them are ONNX Runtime, NVIDIA TensorRT, and Windows ML. For this example, I will be using the support for ONNX Runtime in ML.NET. ML.NET is a machine learning library for .NET. Since the service will be implemented in ASP.NET Core, ML.NET is the perfect match for doing the inference of the ONNX model.

You might be wondering what the end result of a model inference will look like. As shown in Figure 9-4, those will be the objects detected when you upload this photo of two adults crossing a street and pushing a stroller with a very special dog riding it. As you can see, several object types were detected: person, fire hydrant, and traffic lights.

Figure 9-4. *Object detection: source image and tagged image*

Creating Resources in Microsoft Azure

As you can see from the sequence diagram (Figure 9-3), both Azure Event Grid and Azure Storage Queue are involved in triggering the input binding when a new file is uploaded. But in Table 9-2, they are both listed as services that are supported for input bindings. So why did I decide to use a storage queue as an interim location? I could have solely used Azure Event Grid without creating any messages into the Azure Storage Queue. While this is true, there is an important detail coming from the networking setup that your machine is using. Your machine is connected to a network in which you have a private IP address. This means that if a service like Azure Event Grid wants to directly trigger an endpoint of a service running on your machine, this won't be possible because you don't have a public IP that it can reach. You will end up using a tool like ngrok to open a tunnel to your machine.

Before I show you any code from the service, let me first guide you through the process of creating the Azure resources that will be needed. For the next script, you will either need Azure PowerShell installed on your machine, or you can directly open shell.azure.com and choose PowerShell. In the latter case, you have to comment out the Connect-AzAccount cmdlet as you will be automatically authenticated. Please make sure that before running the script, you have selected the correct subscription where you want to provision the resources in. You can check what the current subscription is by executing (Get-AzContext).Subscription. If you want to select another one, you can use the Select-AzureSubscription cmdlet:

```
$location = 'westeurope'
$resourceGroupName = 'images-detect-rg'
$storageAccountName = 'imgdetectstor'
$storageContainerName = 'images'
$storageQueueName = 'images'

Connect-AzAccount

$resourceGroup = New-AzResourceGroup -Name $resourceGroupName -Location
$location

$storageAccount = New-AzStorageAccount -ResourceGroupName
$resourceGroupName -Name $storageAccountName -Location $location -SkuName
Standard_LRS

$storageContainer = New-AzStorageContainer -Name $storageContainerName
-Context $storageAccount.Context

$storageQueue = New-AzStorageQueue -Name $storageQueueName -Context
$storageAccount.Context

$newEventGridSubParams = @{
        EventSubscriptionName = 'new-image'
        ResourceId            = $storageAccount.Id
```

```
        EndpointType            = 'storagequeue'
        Endpoint                = "$($storageAccount.Id)/queueServices/
                                   default/queues/$storageQueueName"
        IncludedEventType       = @('Microsoft.Storage.BlobCreated')
        SubjectBeginsWith       = '/blobServices/default/containers/images/
                                   blobs/input'
        SubjectEndsWith         = '.jpg'
}
New-AzEventGridSubscription @newEventGridSubParams

$storageAccountKey = (Get-AzStorageAccountKey -ResourceGroupName
$resourceGroupName -Name $storageAccountName)[0].Value
Write-Output "Copy the following key and use it in the Dapr components:
$storageAccountKey"
```

Feel free to change the values of the variables at the beginning of the script as the names of the storage accounts must be globally unique. Hence, make sure to change the value of $storageAccountName. Also, depending on where you are, you may want to choose another Azure region and set it to the $location variable. Note that I removed some conditional statements that prevent the partial execution for the sake of placing simpler code in the book. You can find the full version of the script that first checks whether a resource exists and then attempts to create it in the source code of the book. When this script finishes successfully, it will output the value of the first key of the storage account, which will be needed when creating the component manifests.

By now, in the resource group that you have created with the script, you should have a storage account with a single container named images and a single queue named images. An Event Grid System Topic has also been created to serve the subscription. The subscription is triggered for any file having the .jpg extension that is uploaded into the input folder in the storage container. If you open the Azure Portal, the resource group will look like as displayed in Figure 9-5. It's a good idea to explore the storage account resource to check whether a container and a queue were properly created.

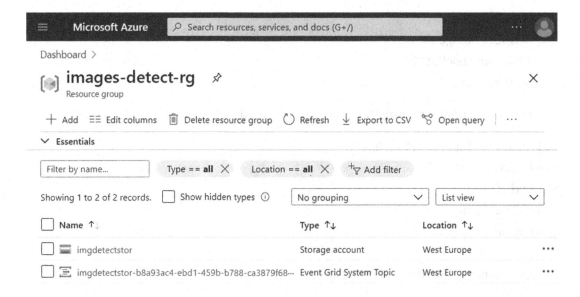

Figure 9-5. *The resources and the resources created by the script*

Creating the Dapr Components

It's time to create the component manifests for Azure Storage Queue and Azure Blob Storage because the Azure resources were just created. Let's start with the Azure Storage Queue. Make sure to provide values for the `<storage-account-name>` and `<storage-account-key>` placeholders:

```
apiVersion: dapr.io/v1alpha1
kind: Component
metadata:
  name: azqueue
  namespace: default
spec:
  type: bindings.azure.storagequeues
  version: v1
  metadata:
  - name: storageAccount
    value: "<storage-account-name>"
  - name: storageAccessKey
    value: "<storage-account-key>"
```

```
  - name: queue
    value: "images"
  - name: decodeBase64
    value: "true"
```

The component for Azure Blob Storage is defined as follows:

```
apiVersion: dapr.io/v1alpha1
kind: Component
metadata:
  name: azblob
  namespace: default
spec:
  type: bindings.azure.blobstorage
  version: v1
  metadata:
  - name: storageAccount
    value: "<storage-account-name>"
  - name: storageAccessKey
    value: "<storage-account-key>"
  - name: "container"
    value: "images"
  - name: decodeBase64
    value: "true"
```

Make sure to replace the storage account name and the storage account key with values that are applicable to your resources. As you can see, the azqueue component points to a queue named images, and the azblob component points to a container named images. Both components work with base64-encoded values as a payload. I have to point out that even if we are about to use the azblob component for performing output bindings and the azqueue component for responding to input bindings, this is not specified anywhere. If the component supports bidirectional bindings, it is up to your service code to decide how to utilize the binding via the Dapr API.

Implementing the Service

The image processing service will be implemented using ASP.NET Core. This time I won't guide you through the process of creating a new project as it is straightforward. The ONNX model inference is isolated in a class library project named ObjectRecognition that is referenced by the ASP.NET Core project. This chapter doesn't cover topics like how to use ONNX, but feel free to explore the code on your own because I know that using ready-made models feels very exciting. Just make sure that the ONNX model is located in the following path: ObjectRecognition/Model/yolov4.onnx. If it is not, you can download it from the ONNX Model Zoo: https://github.com/onnx/models.

The service consists of a single controller named ImagesController, which has a single Post action method that handles the input binding that is triggered by the Azure Storage Queue. Note the default route for the controller will be /images, which doesn't have anything to do with azqueue. To make that possible, note that the RouteAttribute was applied to the whole controller, which means it will resolve the requests coming from the Azure Queue component at /azqueue. After the PostAsync method receives the URL of the uploaded blob, the DownloadFileAsync method invokes the Blob Storage output binding in order to download the photo. Note that the operation property is get and the blobName is passed as metadata:

```
private async Task DownloadFileAsync(string pathInContainer, string
targetDownloadPath)
{
    var outpuBindingData = new
    {
        operation = "get",
        metadata = new
        {
            blobName = pathInContainer
        }
    };
    var json = JsonConvert.SerializeObject(outpuBindingData);
    var stringContent = new StringContent(json, Encoding.UTF8,
    "application/json");
    var httpClient = new HttpClient();
```

```
var response = await
httpClient.PostAsync($"http://localhost:{_daprPort}/v1.0/
bindings/{_storageBindingName}", stringContent);

using (var fs = new FileStream(targetDownloadPath, FileMode.
OpenOrCreate))
{
        await response.Content.CopyToAsync(fs);
}
}
```

Once the image is downloaded, it is saved to a temporary file that is later used for inference. The next step is to perform the ONNX model inference. As I already mentioned, the code that performs the inference is isolated in its own project. When the inference is done, the model saves a tagged image that has all recognized objects outlined, and a list with the counts of all recognized object classes is returned as well.

The next step is to upload the file to Azure Blob Storage by using the create operation of the output binding. The image is being serialized into base64 format, and the relative path to the blob inside the container is passed as metadata so that it knows where to upload the new file:

```
private async Task UploadFileAsync(string targetImageTempPath, string
targetUploadPath)
{
        string base64Image = await FileToBase64Async(targetImageTempPath);
        var outputBindingData = new
        {
                operation = "create",
                data = base64Image,
                metadata = new
                {
                        blobName = targetUploadPath
                }
        };
        var json = JsonConvert.SerializeObject(outputBindingData);
        var stringContent = new StringContent(json, Encoding.UTF8,
        "application/json");
```

```
using var httpClient = new HttpClient();
var response = await
httpClient.PostAsync($"http://localhost:{_daprPort}/v1.0/bindings/
{_storageBindingName}", stringContent);
}
```

After all those steps are performed, the request that initially triggered the Dapr application via an input binding calls `ControllerBase.Ok()` to produce an empty HTTP status code 200 response. In this way, Dapr is getting acknowledged that the triggered endpoint successfully processed the incoming request.

Running the Dapr Application

Now that we explored the most important snippets of code in the image processing application, let's see this in action. First, make sure that the components you created are in the default components directory of Dapr; otherwise, you should specify the path to the custom components directory by using the `--components-path` flag when calling dapr run.

Open a new terminal, navigate to the directory where the ASP.NET Core project named `ImageProcessor` is, and run the following command:

```
dapr run --app-id imageProcessor --app-port 5000 -- dotnet run
```

Alternatively, if you want to debug the whole application, you can start just the Dapr sidecar and launch the debugger manually (from either Visual Studio 2019 or Visual Studio Code). An important detail is to fixate the Dapr sidecar HTTP port by passing the optional flag:

```
dapr run --app-id imageProcessor --app-port 5000 --dapr-http-port 3500
```

Also, make sure the logs returned by both the application and the Dapr sidecar look good, that is, there are no errors logged.

Next, it is time to upload a new image to a folder named `input` in the storage container. There are two options – Azure Storage Explorer, which is a cross-platform desktop application, or its web counterpart in the Azure Portal – you can find Storage Explorer in the blade of the storage account we created earlier.

For this, I will open Azure Storage Explorer, locate the subscription where I created the storage account, and open the images container inside the storage account. Next, I will create a new folder named `input`, and I will upload a new image as shown in Figure 9-6.

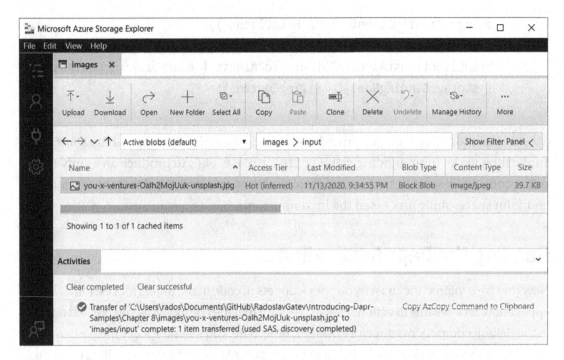

Figure 9-6. *Uploaded a new photo into the input folder under the images container*

After you have uploaded the photo, it's time to go back to the terminal session where the Dapr sidecar is running. If everything was successful, you should be able to see logs for each step that we discussed earlier. Now to see the tagged image, go back to Azure Storage Explorer and go one directory up the hierarchy. You should be able to see the output folder, which was created automatically where tagged images will be uploaded to. Your result image should already be here with all the recognized objects outlined. Lastly, if you open the terminal where you started the application, you should be able to see the operations performed by the application and also the recognized objects:

```
== APP == info: ImageProcessor.Controllers.ImagesController[0]
== APP ==       Input binding endpoint was triggered.
== APP == info: ImageProcessor.Controllers.ImagesController[0]
== APP ==       An image with the following url was uploaded:
https://imgdetectstor.blob.core.windows.net/images/input/you-x-ventures-
Oalh2MojUuk-unsplash.jpg.
== APP == info: ImageProcessor.Controllers.ImagesController[0]
```

```
== APP ==        Downloading the image to C:\Users\myuser\AppData\Local\
Temp\tmp7ADC.tmp.
== APP == info: ImageProcessor.Controllers.ImagesController[0]
== APP ==        Model inference started.
== APP == info: ImageProcessor.Controllers.ImagesController[0]
== APP ==        Model inference finished. The tagged image is:
C:\Users\myuser\AppData\Local\Temp\tmp833A.tmp.
== APP == info: ImageProcessor.Controllers.ImagesController[0]
== APP ==        Uploading the image back to Azure Storage at the following
location inside the container: output/you-x-ventures-Oalh2MojUuk-unsplash.jpg.
== APP == info: ImageProcessor.Controllers.ImagesController[0]
== APP ==        The following objects were recognized:
== APP ==        laptop: 6 times
== APP ==        person: 6 times
== APP ==        book: 1 times
```

Summary

In this chapter, you learned what the capabilities of the Resource Bindings building block are. There are two types of bindings that can be identified – input and output. There are ready-made components for external systems and services in several public clouds that support input, output, or bidirectional mode. Next, you learned how components are defined, and we explored the API that the Resource Bindings building block provides. Finally, I showed you how to build an image processing application based on ASP.NET Core that combines the integration capabilities of both input and output bindings. It integrates with both Azure Blob Storage and Azure Queue Storage and utilizes an ONNX object recognition model in the middle.

In the next chapter, you will learn about what the Actor model is and how Dapr simplifies it by providing an Actors building block.

CHAPTER 10

The Actor Model

In this chapter, you will learn what the Actor model is, when it is a fit, and when not. You will also understand what implications the virtual Actor model introduces. After all that, you will learn the specifics of the Actors building block of Dapr. Then you will put all the knowledge into practice, as I show you how to implement a sample application that automates your home and treats each object in it as an actor. It will be implemented entirely in .NET.

Overview of the Actor Model

As with every programming model or paradigm, there is a central concept that lays the foundations so that a certain outcome can be achieved. For example, functional programming places functions in the center of its computational model and avoids having a mutable state. Object-oriented programming (OOP) is another example, where everything is an object that has some state and behavior. In contrast with functional programming, the state of the objects is mutable.

As you might be able to tell, the Actor model is all about having actors at the heart of the programming model. Each actor knows how to do a certain type of processing, mutate, and retain its internal state and communicate with other actors by exchanging messages. If you want to draw a parallel between object-oriented programming (OOP) and the Actor model, you will find a lot of similarities. Like the objects in OOP, actors do have an internal state that is not shared with the other actors, which means that it cannot be directly changed from the outside. Does that remind you of one of the core principles of OOP, namely, encapsulation? Actors communicate by passing messages to other actors. At a very abstract level, the traditional OOP languages like C# and Java implement message passing as method calls.

© Radoslav Gatev 2021
R. Gatev, *Introducing Distributed Application Runtime (Dapr)*, https://doi.org/10.1007/978-1-4842-6998-5_10

However, there is one important difference between the two models. This is how they deal with concurrency. If we compare the Actor model to OOP in a single-threaded world, they will be almost identical on an abstract level, ignoring all technical details. However, it is not reasonable to write single-threaded applications as this means that at a given time, there will be only one task that is performed. Imagine your application starts a blocking operation to read something from the disk; this will render your single-threaded application unusable until it finishes processing the blocking operation. So apparently, concurrency is a must for modern applications. Actors were devised to be used in concurrent systems, whereas the OOP paradigm itself does not impose a specific way to achieve concurrency. If you want to achieve concurrency in traditional OOP languages, you have to spawn multiple threads that can do some work in parallel. But multithreaded programming requires mastery as it is fairly easy to introduce *race conditions,* for example, if your threads depend on some shared state. As a way to solve this problem, one has to introduce *locks* or *mutexes*. But it really depends on the developer's skills to early identify the problem that may likely occur. On the contrary, actors address the concurrency in a very simple manner. You can think about creating an actor as spawning a new thread, although that's not always the way it happens technically. There are some restrictions that actors impose – they have some dedicated memory to represent their state, but it's not shared with any other actor. Unlike threads, the only way to gain access to the actor's state is by sending a message to it. Since actors don't depend on anything from the current machine, it makes them easy to distribute, which means that they can run on different machines. Traditionally, concurrency is achieved by using multiple cores of the CPU, whereas the Actor model blurs the boundary of cores, CPUs, and even machines. As a result, this makes the implementation of distributed and concurrent applications simpler, and you don't have to care about complex stuff.

To summarize, actors are independent units of computation that communicate by sending or receiving messages and can make a decision based on their local persistent state. Although multiple actors can perform some logic at the same time, it is very important to highlight that each actor processes messages sequentially. This means that if a single actor receives multiple messages at the same time, it will process them one at a time. That's why the definition of the Actor model states that each actor has a mailbox that stores all messages. That's pretty much like a message queue. The operations inside every actor happen on turn-based concurrency, which creates the illusion of single-threaded processing. Having the guarantee that only one operation will be performed at a time protects against having the standard problems with concurrency. If you want to perform actions in parallel, you have to create more actors. Whether this makes any sense really depends on the problem you want to model, and I don't really encourage you to use actors if you solely need to achieve higher parallelism. Depending on the domain, actors can be modeled after various objects – actors can perform mathematical operations or models, for example, a finite-state machine, serve as digital twins of an IoT system, represent game objects, or even model technical concepts, for example, the Saga pattern that I described in Chapter 1: Introduction to Microservices.

If you were to model a parking system using the Actor model, you would most likely try to identify what are the various classes that build the digital model of a parking system. Let's assume these are parking sensors, a parking space containing one or more parking sensors, a parking lot that groups a number of parking spaces, parking levels, parking ramps, and so on. As the example implies, there is a hierarchy of objects because, for example, parking sensors are assigned to a single parking space, which is part of the parking lot. This means there is a tiered control, where the top-level actors assign subtasks to their child actors. The child actors are in fact supervised by the top-level actors. The number of actor instances can reach millions, while the number of actor types depends on the actual design. It follows pretty much the same logic as OOP; objects are instances of classes. The turn-based concurrency applies to actor instances and not actor types, as shown in Figure 10-1. The rule is that concurrent operations to the same actor instance are not allowed. Instead, they are processed sequentially.

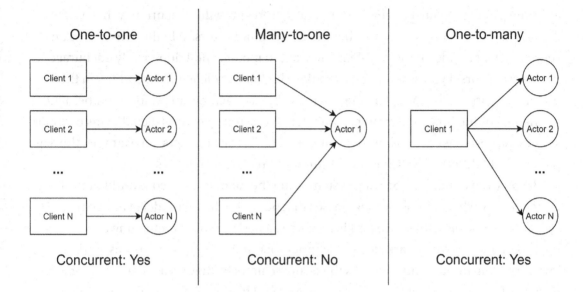

Figure 10-1. *Concurrency of actors*

When an actor receives a message, it can do three things:

- Create one or more actors.

- Send one or more messages to another actor it knows.

- Designate how to handle the next message.

Each actor has a unique address that is assigned at the time of creation. When you want to send a message to an actor, you send it to the actor's address. Actors can communicate only with actors whose addresses they know. An actor that creates other actors inherently knows their addresses, so it can directly send some messages to them. As actors are newly created, they have an initial state and behavior. With time, an actor will process messages that will cause state and behavior to change for any upcoming messages.

Advantages and Disadvantages

Now that you've learned what the Actor model is, let me identify some of its benefits:

- Easy to scale – Actors don't have any dependency on the local state or anything on the machine. This means that you just create new instances without trying to keep track of any boundaries. Actors can be placed on the same machine or any other machine. The actor runtime will decide what is optimal.

- Fault tolerance – If something unexpected happens like an exception is thrown while handling a message or the whole node that hosts the actor goes down, the actor can be either restarted or even recreated on a new node with its last known good state.

- Easy distribution – The actor you are trying to address can be running locally or in a node in a remote data center. It doesn't matter where it is located as long as it receives the messages.

- Easy synchronization – Actors do not depend on any shared state, which makes programming easier and prevents any race conditions.

As with everything in software development, a single decision brings advantages that usually solve some problem in the first place, but it also carries some trade-offs. Here are some of the disadvantages of the Actor model and some common pitfalls that one may fall into:

- Actors are susceptible to deadlocks – A deadlock may occur if an external process sends a message to an actor that then sends a message to another actor that makes a circular request to the first actor. Some of the Actor model implementations have a mechanism to deal with this. Dapr is one such example because it has a mechanism to impose a time limit on all actor operations. After that, it times them out.

- Overflowing mailbox – Because each actor instance can handle one message at a time, when the number of messages in the mailbox increases, the actor instance can become congested. If the actor instance cannot process them fast enough and the messages are ingested at a greater rate, the queue of waiting clients will grow bigger and bigger with time. However, this rather depends on the actual implementation.

- Too many actor types and/or instances – The Actor model implies that everything should be an actor, but the granularity depends on your design. Creating too many actor types generates a lot of overhead because they have to create and pass messages over the network. Creating too many actor instances doesn't necessarily mean that your system will be faster, but for sure you will waste some of the machine resources. Actors should not be used to achieve solely better concurrency. If this is the case, you should better find some construct for asynchronous programming, for example, Futures in Scala or Task in .NET.

- Testing and debugging become complex – Actor systems can grow very complex, and the flow of messages can become so wild. But this is generally applicable to any distributed system that involves cross-service communication.

When to Use It?

The Actor model is a powerful tool when you use it properly. However, if you apply it incorrectly, it can lead to having a more complex system. You need to be able to decide in what case to use the Actor model and when to use something else. For example, the most generic description of a use case will be when you have a great deal of concurrency and, at the same time, you want to manage the state. That is what actors are for.

When you decide to introduce the Actor model for your distributed application, you should be able to apply it to the entire application or a great part of it. There is no point in having just one actor type. The power of this programming model is unleashed when you have several actor types that work together as a system adhering to some hierarchy. Of course, this doesn't mean that everything in your system should be by all means converted to an actor of some type.

There are a lot of ways to misuse the Actor model. For example, when you want to gather the state of all actors in a given system, you will be tempted to query all of them separately. If this involves just a handful of actor instances, this isn't a problem. However, when the number of instances is in the hundreds, thousands, and even millions, this is an utterly suboptimal way to query state as you have to make as many calls as the number of actor instances. In such cases, it is better to directly query the database where the state of all actors is stored. This pretty much depends on how the actor implementation that you choose to use persists the state of its actors. By choosing Dapr, this is entirely possible as I am going to show you the structure of the keys under which the state is stored for each actor instance.

Actors are highly scalable, but they don't necessarily offer the best performance because of the nonconcurrent access to actor instances. Another common example of misuse is not storing any state or storing too much state. If your actors don't rely on some state, then you probably should revisit why you use the Actor model in the first place. On the contrary, if you store too much state, upon each operation that the actor performs, it will take more time to gather and persist the state. Therefore, this will prove to be a bottleneck. This also applies to any blocking I/O operations.

Actor Implementations

There are a lot of frameworks that provide you with the Actor model. There are even languages that provide out-of-the-box support for actors – the processes in Erlang are equivalent to actors. One of the most notable frameworks that implement the Actor model is Akka that runs on *Java Virtual Machine (JVM)* and therefore supports Java and Scala. There is a port of Akka for JavaScript called Akka.js and one for .NET called Akka. NET that supports C# and F#.

Other examples are Orleans that runs on .NET, Service Fabric Reliable Actors that supports .NET and Java, and, of course, Dapr that is language-agnostic. Each of the above-mentioned frameworks and languages imposes its own opinions about the Actor model albeit using the same foundation. I grouped the last three examples intentionally, as they have a common virtue. And it's not only that Microsoft created them.

Virtual Actors

The virtual Actor model was introduced by Project Orleans that was created by Microsoft Research. Virtual actors use the same analogy as *virtual memory* does – it allows clients to invoke a virtual actor by calling its address no matter where the actor is physically placed (if at all). This vastly simplifies the Actor model as callers don't have to think about where the actor is placed and how to balance the load and recover from failures. The actor runtime itself takes care of those concerns. When a request to a given actor arrives, the runtime checks whether such an instance exists somewhere in the cluster. If it cannot find the actor, it is activated in some node of the cluster, which means that an in-memory instance of the actor is being created. Over time, unused actors will be garbage collected. Albeit being unallocated from memory, once a virtual actor is created, it has a *perpetual existence,* and therefore its address remains the same. The reason for this is that the state of an actor always outlives the lifetime of the actor in-memory object. Whenever the next request to this address comes, the actor will be materialized in memory with the same state as before it was garbage collected.

Now that you know the idea of the Actor model and the concept of virtual actors, let me introduce you to the support the Actors building block in Dapr provides.

The Actor Model in Dapr

Dapr provides a language-agnostic implementation of the virtual Actor model. The actors can be implemented by using some of the SDKs that Dapr provides – .NET, Java, and Python. On the opposite side, actors can be invoked from any language via the HTTP or gRPC endpoint of Dapr API. The Actors building block works both in Self-hosted and Kubernetes modes. Behind the scenes, it combines the features of two other building blocks – Service Invocation and State Management – because actors have methods and state. The abstract idea of sending, receiving, and processing messages is instead realized by implementing methods that execute some logic and mutate the state.

To persist the state of the actors, the building block depends on a state store that must support transactions and ETags. If you want to check which state stores are those, you can revisit Chapter 8: State Management. The specific component that you want to be used for persisting the state of actors must be marked with `actorStateStore` set in the following way:

```
apiVersion: dapr.io/v1alpha1
kind: Component
metadata:
  name: statestore
spec:
  type: state.redis
  version: v1
  metadata:
  - name: redisHost
    value: localhost:6379
  - name: redisPassword
    value: ""
  - name: actorStateStore
    value: "true"
```

It is very useful to know how the state is persisted inside the chosen state store if you intend to issue any queries to get the state of all actors. The naming convention of the key for the state of each object follows the scheme `<APP-ID>||<ACTOR-TYPE>||<ACTOR-ID>||<KEY>` where

- App ID – The Dapr App ID of the application that hosts the actor.

- Actor type – Represents the type of the actor.

- Actor ID – The unique ID of the actor that allows you to address individual actor instances.

- Key – The name of the state key. The reason this exists is that actors can persist their state using multiple keys.

As I already explained about virtual actors, actors are being activated upon their first use, which means that an object representing the actor gets created in memory. After some time passes, Dapr scans for any actors that are idle and deallocates them. The exact address of an actor instance in Dapr is determined by its Actor ID and the actor type. Dapr does the heavy lifting for managing actors across all available nodes – it has to ensure that there is a single activation of a given Actor ID across the entire cluster, ensure that a single client can access an actor at a time, and keep track of where actors are placed. There is a system service inside Dapr called the Placement service that ensures actors work properly. It is only used by the Actors building block for keeping track of actors. If you don't plan to use the Actors building block, you can choose not to deploy it.

Dapr Placement Service

From a logical perspective, the Dapr Placement service is probably the most sophisticated service inside Dapr. Keeping a distributed state of a dynamically changing environment is not an easy task. Kubernetes nodes and pods come and go, but the actors distributed among them should remain working no matter what is happening with the underlying infrastructure. Let's keep it clear. Every application that utilizes Dapr is represented by a sidecar, but when we look at it from the Actor model standpoint, there are two types of sidecars: sidecars of actor hosts and sidecars of ordinary applications, or as we usually call them services. Actor hosts are those services that host the functionality of any actor type. They are basically another type of web service. On the other side, there are the ordinary Dapr sidecars that you are well used to. As part of their operations, they can choose either to invoke any particular actor instance or on the contrary not use actors at all. Let's peek into what is running behind the scenes in Dapr to make the Actors building block possible.

The early versions of Dapr used to support only a single instance of the Placement service. But since this used to be a single point of failure for the Actor model, something had to be done. The Placement service keeps the placement tables that contain the actor hosts and the actor instances that are spread across all actor hosts in the cluster. It also establishes a communication channel with all the Dapr sidecars, each of which keeps a local cache of the latest version of the placement tables. You can think of the placement table as a hash table. Using a *hash function*, it maps the actor type and Actor ID to a given actor host (represented by its sidecar), except that hashing is not so simple in this scenario. For the next couple of paragraphs, I will use servers, nodes, and Pods interchangeably while the meaning is actor host.

Kubernetes environments are of a very dynamic nature – Pods come and go, and even nodes can go down, and that is why you have several of them. This means that the internal address and number of Pods can vary at any given moment. Having a simple hash table that is based on the existence of individual Pods won't take you much further. The reason is that with any change in the number of Pods (which may occur frequently), the whole hash table will have changed. The naive modulo hashing function works well as long as the list of buckets remains stable. When a bucket is either added to or removed from the list (or an actor host Pod), the majority of requests will be resolved to another bucket, and only a small part of the requests will still be resolved to the same host. For a live environment, this means that actor instances must be reshuffled to keep up with the structure of the hash table, or the hash table itself must be remapped to fit the new list of buckets.

Instead, Dapr uses a modern hashing approach named *consistent hashing with bounded loads*. Consistent hashing is very often used whenever you have to shard a cache across a set of nodes, which is also called a distributed cache. By using consistent hashing, you will ensure that whenever a Pod is either added or removed, the majority of keys will still map to the same bucket (or Pod). It operates independently of the number of buckets by assigning the keys at a given position on an abstract circle called *a hash ring*. The request is not directly mapped to a given bucket; instead by using approximations, the hash is mapped to the closest bucket to it on the hash ring. But there is still one problem – the classic consistent hashing does not deal with load balancing across buckets. It's pretty much a random assignment to some bucket, which sometimes causes unlucky buckets to become overloaded. That is why the hashing algorithm is called consistent hashing with bounded loads. It deals with both of the problems – have a minimal number of moves whenever something in the environment changes and address the problem with load balancing across servers by setting a tight guarantee on the maximum load of each bucket. Eventually, the placement tables that use the hashing approach described in the preceding will be distributed to all Dapr sidecars to serve as a local cache.

Now that you know the concepts, let's take a look at the place where the placement tables are kept as a single source of truth – the Placement service. Having a state and a distributed system to manage it is usually a tricky problem as well. You cannot solve it by simply replicating the state manager because the state that the Placement service persists is applicable for the whole cluster. Instead, all instances of the Placement service have to agree on what the latest state is. There is a whole other category of algorithms that lets multiple participants reach a complete consensus on a thing, called *consensus algorithms*. The most famous one is *Paxos* while being also the foundation of distributed consensus algorithms. However, Dapr uses *Raft* that was designed to be easy to understand and also easy to apply because there are a lot of implementations of it that can be easily reused.

Nodes in Raft are in one of three states – *leader, follower*, or *candidate*. While the candidate is an intermediary state, there is one node appointed by quorum voting to be a leader, and the other nodes become followers. The leader is the conductor of the whole consensus-building process. Each server in the cluster has a log and a state machine. The state machine is the component that has to be made fault-tolerant and is further used by clients. In this case, the state machine, which is the application-specific part of the algorithm, represents the Actor placement tables in Dapr. However, internally, the changes are first made to a write-ahead log, and the consensus is actually reached on it. The reason for this is that by following the log entries, you can recreate the most recent state. All new state changes that come from clients are brokered by the leader at first, which translates them into a log entry and replicates them to all followers. Once a quorum of nodes (N/2+1) acknowledges that the log entry is persisted, it is considered as committed and applied to the finite state machine.

The interaction between actor host sidecars, the Placement service, and the ordinary Dapr sidecars is depicted in Figure 10-2. Let me walk you through what happens behind the scenes. On the left-hand side, you can see there are a bunch of actor hosts that are represented by their Dapr sidecars. Whenever a change in any of the actor hosts occurs, the Placement service has to be informed, which internally executes the Raft algorithm, and when consensus is reached eventually, all Dapr sidecars will receive the latest state. Such a change may be when a new Pod that is hosting actors of some type joins the cluster or maybe some Pod went down (in other words, leaves the cluster).

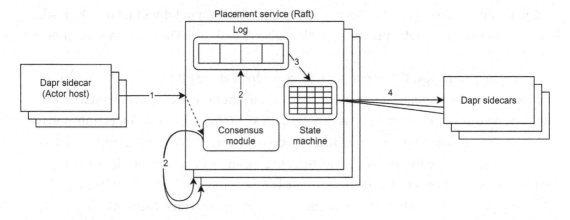

Figure 10-2. *The Placement service*

The whole process of such a change looks like the following:

1. Once a Dapr sidecar that hosts some actors is up and running, it establishes a gRPC streaming connection with the Placement service. It declares what types of actors it can host before the Raft leader of the Placement service.

2. The leader converts the request into a log entry and appends it to the local log. While doing so, it also sends the log entry to all followers and waits for their responses.

3. Once a quorum of all nodes successfully persists the log entry, the leader applies the log entry to the state machine or in this case the Actor placement tables.

4. Eventually, the leader disseminates the new state of the Actor placement tables to all Dapr sidecars by performing a three-phase commit:

    a. In the first phase, all Dapr sidecars are locked, which means that incoming requests will be held for a while.

    b. Then in the second phase, after all sidecars are locked, the update of the placement tables commences in all sidecars, so that they update their local copies of the placement tables.

    c. In the third phase, when the sidecar update is done, all sidecars are unlocked.

In this way, it is ensured that all Dapr sidecars use the same version of the Actor placement tables. That was enough to get an idea of the Placement service. Let's explore how the building block works.

The Lifetime of Actor Instances

Now that you learned about how the information about actor hosts and instances is spread across the whole cluster, let's see what the lifetime of an actor instance is. As Dapr implements the virtual Actor model, actors must be activated before you can use them. Then, at some point, the actor can become idle and will be subject to garbage collection.

The duration of the idle period and how often to scan for any idle actors are configurable per the actor host. Each Dapr host has an endpoint that is used for discovering all actors that it can host along with all configurations that Dapr expects to gather by issuing a GET request to `http://localhost:<app-port>/dapr/config`. This configuration is done out of the box for you when you use an SDK of your choice to implement an actor. Later on in the chapter, you will learn how to use the Dapr .NET SDK to implement some actors. The `/dapr/config` endpoint returns an output with the following structure:

```
{
  "entities": ["actorType1", "actorType2"],
  "actorIdleTimeout": "1h",
  "actorScanInterval": "30s",
  "drainOngoingCallTimeout": "30s",
  "drainRebalancedActors": true
}
```

The properties serve the following purpose:

- `entities` – The actor types that the host supports.

- `actorIdleTimeout` – Specifies how long an actor instance should be inactive before it is considered as "idle." Once marked "idle," it is up for a deactivation.

- `actorScanInterval` – Specifies how often Dapr scans for any idle actors.

- `drainOngoingCallTimeout` – Specifies how long to wait for an active actor to finish its operation before rebalancing occurs, for example, when the actor host is being scaled out to more instances.

- `drainRebalancedActors` – Specifies whether to wait for the duration specified by `drainOngoingCallTimeout` or not before deactivating an actor. If it is set to false, actor instances are deactivated imminently.

When is an actor considered to be active? One example is whenever a method of an actor is invoked. But actors in Dapr also support timers and reminders, which are means of scheduling periodic work. An actor can self-register a timer or reminder, or this can be done from the outside by a client. Then, timers and reminders are invoked either on the specified schedule at the time of creation, or they can be triggered by clients.

What is the difference between a timer and a reminder? A timer is stopped whenever an actor instance is deactivated. Dapr doesn't persist any information about any timers that were scheduled before the instance was deallocated. On the contrary, reminders are persistent – they are executed no matter what until they are explicitly unregistered or the actor is explicitly deleted via the API. The information about the reminders is persisted in the state of the actor. After any deactivations and failovers, the reminders are being recreated. Another important difference is that the execution of a reminder resets the idle countdown, whereas a timer doesn't do it.

Actors and reminders have two properties for scheduling:

- `dueTime` – Specifies when the reminder/timer should be executed for the first time after its registration.

- `period` – Specifies how often the reminder/timer should be fired after that. If it is empty, the reminder/timer is fired only once as configured by `dueTime`, and it won't repeat after that.

For example, if you want to register a timer or reminder that is fired 3 seconds after registration and then every 6 seconds, it will look like this:

```
{
  "dueTime":"0h0m3s0ms",
  "period":"0h0m6s0ms"
}
```

Concurrency

As you already know, only one operation can happen at a given time inside an actor instance. Although, from a technical point of view, every method or timer/reminder callback is asynchronous, those are not executed simultaneously. Instead, an operation can place a lock on a given actor instance only in case if there isn't any other active operation at the moment, as shown in Figure 10-3.

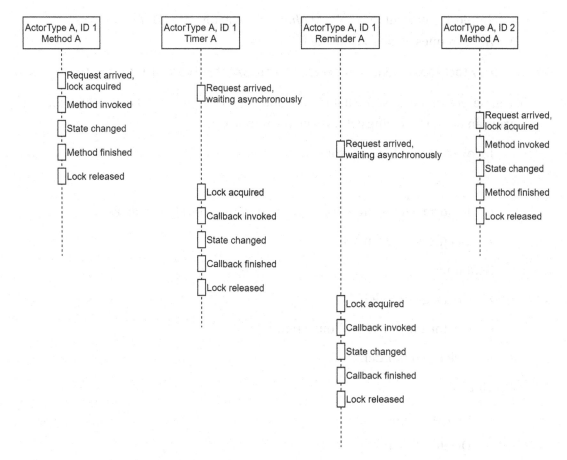

Figure 10-3. *Turn-based access*

As you can see, all operations on the actor with ID 1 happen sequentially, no matter if they are methods, timers, or reminders. If currently there is an ongoing operation in a given actor, at a time the new request comes, it waits asynchronously to take its turn. And in parallel, before all pending operations on the actor with ID 1 finish, the same MethodA executes on the actor with ID 2, but those are different instances of the same type.

Invoking Actors via the API

To perform any actor operations, you have to use the Actors API. It supports both HTTP and gRPC. The requests are channeled through the Dapr sidecar, which supports the following endpoints:

```
http://localhost:<daprPort>/v1.0/actors/<actorType>/<actorId>/<method|state
|reminders|timers>/<name>
```

For example, if you want to invoke *MethodA* of an actor with ID *ID1* and type *ActorTypeA*, the request will look like the following:

```
POST http://localhost:<daprPort>/v1.0/actors/ActorTypeA/ID1/method/MethodA
```

Of course, you can pass some data in the body of the request. And to summarize, as a client, you can do the following actions via the Actors API:

- Invoke a method of an actor.

- State

  - Perform a multi-item transaction to change the state of an actor.

  - Get the state of an actor.

- Reminders

  - Create a reminder.

  - Get the information about a reminder.

  - Delete a reminder.

- Timers

  - Create a timer.

  - Delete a timer.

As you notice, the API gives you access to pretty much any property of an actor. However, think twice before using any other endpoint than the one for method invocation on an actor. The reason is that the Actor model was designed to have a self-sustaining system of actors as the main unit of computation. Only an actor knows best how to manage its own state and when it makes sense to register or delete a reminder.

That was all about the Actors API from a client perspective. Let's take a look at how actors can be implemented.

Implementing Actors

An actor is an ordinary web service. Actors must implement a certain set of API endpoints via HTTP so that Dapr can interact with the actual actors on the host. It doesn't make a lot of sense to explain what these endpoints are because you will most likely use a certain Dapr SDK for implementing actors. The SDK will automatically implement those methods. It doesn't make sense to try to implement the hosting from the ground up.

I am going to show you how to use the .NET SDK to implement a set of actors representing a room (a smart one) and some devices in it as shown in Figure 10-4. I will also show you how to build a client application that will act like a person who just got back from work and enters the living room, turns on the lights, and turns on the air conditioner. The air conditioner is yet another actor type that is instantiated by the room actor. It has a temperature sensor as a discrete actor that it pings every 10 seconds (using a reminder) in order to know what the current room temperature is. When the room temperature converges with the target temperature, the air conditioner will become idle, to save on your electricity bill. What a smart room, huh?

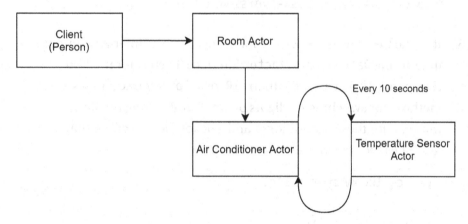

Figure 10-4. *Actor example*

Let's get started! We will create three projects in total – one class library for the actor interfaces, one for the ASP.NET Core API that is going to implement and host the actors, and another one that will be a console application acting as a client of the actor system. Since I am going to build a kind of home automation solution, every project name will be prefixed with Home. Before everything, make sure you have defined a state component that supports transactions to persist the state of your actors.

Defining the Actor Interfaces

Having a standalone project that holds just the actor interfaces is very useful as those interfaces will be referenced by the actual implementation in the Web API project and also by any clients that are using actors.

The following steps will guide you on how to create the class library that holds the actor interfaces:

1. Firstly, create a new project of type class library. If you prefer Visual Studio, you can go with its wizards; however, for any other case, use the following command:

```
dotnet new classlib -o Home.Actors -f net5.0
```

2. Add the latest version of the Dapr.Actors NuGet package, which at the time of writing is 1.0.0. Make sure to navigate to the project folder at first:

```
cd Home.Actors
dotnet add package Dapr.Actors --version 1.0.0
```

3. It's time to define the interface for each actor. The interface simply inherits the Dapr.Actors.IActor interface. Each actor method returns a Task. Let's start with the IRoomActor interface. It has methods for switching the lights on or off and getting the ID of the actor for the air conditioner and a Describe() method that describes the current state of the room:

```
public interface IRoomActor : IActor
{
        Task TurnOnLights();
        Task TurnOffLights();
        Task<ActorId> GetAirConActorId();
        Task<string> Describe();
}
```

4. Next, create the `IAirConActor` interface that will serve as the contract for the air conditioner. You can create additional classes for the definition of any state that is either obtained or persisted by the actor. For this example, I chose to encapsulate the internal state and created some methods for reading specific things. Note that the methods of the interface reference two enums that are defined below the interface:

```
public interface IAirConActor : IActor
{
        Task TurnOn();
        Task TurnOff();
        Task<bool> IsTurnedOn();
        Task SetTargetTemperature(double temperature);
        Task<double> GetTargetTemperature();
        Task<double> GetCurrentTemperature();
        Task SetMode(AirConMode mode);
        Task<AirConMode> GetMode();
        Task<AirConState> GetState();
}

public enum AirConMode
{
        Heat, Cool
}

public enum AirConState
{
        Idle, Working
}
```

5. Finally, create the ITemperatureSensorActor interface, which
    is very simple because it contains only a method Measure() for
    measuring the current temperature in the room:

```
public interface ITemperatureSensorActor : IActor
{
        Task<double> Measure();
}
```

Implementing the Interfaces

Now that you have defined the interfaces, it is time to implement them in an ASP.NET
Core Web API project:

1. Navigate to the root folder of the solution and create a new ASP.
    NET Core Web API project:

```
dotnet new webapi -o Home.ActorsHost -f net5.0
```

2. Navigate to the project folder and add the latest version of the
    Dapr.Actors.AspNetCore NuGet package, which at the time of
    writing is 1.0.0:

```
cd Home.ActorsHost
dotnet add package Dapr.Actors.AspNetCore --version 1.0.0
```

3. Add a reference to the project that contains the actor instances:

```
dotnet add reference ../Home.Actors/Home.Actors.csproj
```

4. Create a folder called Actors that will hold all your
    actor implementations. And then create a class named
    TemperatureSensorActor that extends the Dapr.Actors.Runtime.
    Actor base class. Make sure to define a constructor that accepts
    an ActorHost object, which is then passed to the constructor of
    the base class. A lot of functionality is inherited from the base
    class. For example, via the StateManager property, you can work
    with state, and there are methods for registering and unregistering
    timers and reminders and also a couple of virtual methods for
    reacting to lifetime events happening for an instance of the actor.
    The implementation of the TemperatureSensorActor is as follows:

```
public class TemperatureSensorActor : Actor,
ITemperatureSensorActor
{
        private const string STATE_NAME = "sensor_data";
        private const int MIN_TEMPERATURE = 1;
        private const int MAX_TEMPERATURE = 40;

        public TemperatureSensorActor(ActorHost host) : base(host)
        {
        }

        public async Task<double> Measure()
        {
                var currentState = await StateManager.
                TryGetStateAsync<double>(STATE_NAME);
                var currentTemperature = 0d;
                if (currentState.HasValue)
                {
                        currentTemperature = GetNextTemperature
                        (currentState.Value, MIN_TEMPERATURE,
                        MAX_TEMPERATURE);
                }
                else
                {
                        var random = new Random();
                        currentTemperature = random.NextDouble() *
                        MAX_TEMPERATURE;
                }

                await StateManager.SetStateAsync<double>(STATE_NAME,
                currentTemperature);

                return currentTemperature;
        }
```

```
private static double GetNextTemperature(double temperature,
int min, int max)
{
        // This method just generates the next temperature
        measurement. Check the source code of the book for
        the full implementation
}
```
}

5. Create a class AirConActor. Note that it also implements
    the IRemindable interface, which contains a single method
    ReceiveReminderAsync that is triggered whenever the reminder
    is fired. This enables reminders to be registered for this actor
    type. The OnActivateAsync method is fired right after an actor
    instance is activated and before any method is invoked. It is a
    great place to set the initial state of an actor or to register any timer
    or reminder. The reminder that we need continually monitors
    the temperature by calling the temperature sensor registered
    when the air conditioner is turned on and unregistered upon
    turning it off. Please note that the following code contains only
    the most important methods of the actor. You can find the full
    implementation in the source code of the book:

```
public class AirConActor : Actor, IAirConActor, IRemindable
{
        private const string STATE_NAME = "aircon_data";

        public AirConActor(ActorHost host) : base(host)
        {
        }

        protected override async Task OnActivateAsync()
        {
                await base.OnActivateAsync();

                var stateExists = await StateManager.
                ContainsStateAsync(STATE_NAME);
```

```
        if (!stateExists)
        {
                var data = new AirConData()
                {
                        TemperatureSensorActorId = ActorId.
                        CreateRandom(),
                        IsTurnedOn = false,
                        Mode = AirConMode.Cool,
                        TargetTemperature = 20d
                };
                await StateManager.SetStateAsync(STATE_NAME, data);
        }
}

// The implementation of the other non-essential methods is
omitted! Check out the source code of the book.

public async Task TurnOff()
{
        var state = await StateManager.
        GetStateAsync<AirConData>(STATE_NAME);
        state.IsTurnedOn = false;
        await StateManager.SetStateAsync(STATE_NAME, state);

        await UnregisterReminderAsync("control-loop");
}

public async Task TurnOn()
{
        var state = await StateManager.
        GetStateAsync<AirConData>(STATE_NAME);
        state.IsTurnedOn = true;
        await StateManager.SetStateAsync(STATE_NAME, state);
```

```
        await RegisterReminderAsync("control-loop",
        null, TimeSpan.FromSeconds(5), TimeSpan.
        FromSeconds(10));
    }

    public async Task ReceiveReminderAsync(string
    reminderName, byte[] state, TimeSpan dueTime, TimeSpan
    period)
    {
        var airConState = await StateManager.
        GetStateAsync<AirConData>(STATE_NAME);
        var sensorProxy = ActorProxy.Create<ITemperatureS
        ensorActor>(airConState.TemperatureSensorActorId,
        "TemperatureSensorActor");
        var currentTemperature = await sensorProxy.Measure();

        if (currentTemperature < airConState.TargetTemperature)
        {
            airConState.State = (airConState.Mode ==
            AirConMode.Cool) ? AirConState.Idle : AirConState.
            Working;
        }
        else
        {
            airConState.State = (airConState.Mode ==
            AirConMode.Cool) ? AirConState.Working :
            AirConState.Idle;
        }
        await StateManager.SetStateAsync(STATE_NAME, airConState);
    }
}
```

6. Create a new class RoomActor for the room actor. It manages the
    state of the lights and keeps an instance of the air conditioner
    actor. Please note that the following code snippet contains the
    essential methods only:

```
public class RoomActor : Actor, IRoomActor
{
        private const string STATE_NAME = "room_data";

        public RoomActor(ActorHost host) : base(host)
        {
        }

        protected override async Task OnActivateAsync()
        {
                await base.OnActivateAsync();

                var stateExists = await StateManager.
                ContainsStateAsync(STATE_NAME);
                if (!stateExists)
                {
                        var data = new RoomData()
                        {
                                AreLightsOn = false,
                                AirConActorId = ActorId.CreateRandom()
                        };
                         await StateManager.SetStateAsync(STATE_NAME,
                        data);
                }
        }

    // The implementation of the other methods is omitted!
}
```

7. Then register the actor runtime and all actor types in the ConfigureServices method in Startup.cs. You can optionally apply the actor configuration settings that I described earlier:

```
services.AddActors(actorRuntime =>
{
        actorRuntime.ActorIdleTimeout = TimeSpan.FromHours(1);
        actorRuntime.ActorScanInterval = TimeSpan.FromSeconds(30);
        actorRuntime.DrainOngoingCallTimeout = TimeSpan.FromSeconds(40);
        actorRuntime.DrainRebalancedActors = true;

        actorRuntime.Actors.RegisterActor<RoomActor>();
        actorRuntime.Actors.RegisterActor<AirConActor>();
        actorRuntime.Actors.RegisterActor<TemperatureSensorActor>();
});
```

8. Last but not least, you have to map the endpoints that must be implemented by actor hosts. Just add the following lines in the Configure method:

```
app.UseEndpoints(endpoints =>
{
        endpoints.MapActorsHandlers();
});
```

Implementing the Client

The actors are fully implemented. It's time to use them. The next steps will guide you on how to create a console application that invokes actor methods:

1. Navigate to the root folder of the solution and create a new console application:

```
dotnet new console -o Home.Person -f net5.0
```

2. Navigate to the project folder and install the latest version of the Dapr.Actors NuGet package, which at the time of writing is 1.0.0:

```
cd Home.Person
dotnet add package Dapr.Actors --version 1.0.0
```

3. Add a reference to the Home.Actors project that contains all actor interfaces:

```
dotnet add reference ../Home.Actors/Home.Actors.csproj
```

4. Update the Main method in Program.cs with the following code:

```
public static async Task Main(string[] args)
{
        var actorId = new ActorId("LivingRoom");
        var roomProxy = ActorProxy.Create<IRoomActor>(actorId,
        "RoomActor");
        await roomProxy.TurnOnLights();

        var airConId = await roomProxy.GetAirConActorId();
        var airConProxy = ActorProxy.Create<IAirConActor>(airConId,
        "AirConActor");
        await airConProxy.TurnOn();
        await airConProxy.SetMode(AirConMode.Cool);
        await airConProxy.SetTargetTemperature(24d);

        for (int i = 0; i < 20; i++)
        {
                Console.WriteLine(await roomProxy.Describe());
                await Task.Delay(15000);
        }

        await airConProxy.TurnOff();
        Console.WriteLine(await roomProxy.Describe());
}
```

The preceding code creates a proxy to an actor of type RoomActor that has an ID *LivingRoom*. The proxy gives you strongly typed support when calling the methods of an actor's interface. After the lights in the room are turned on, a proxy for the air conditioner actor is created. By calling the methods of the proxy, the air conditioner is being turned on and set to cooling mode with a target temperature of 24 degrees Celsius. Then the state of the room is repeatedly queried every 15 seconds so that you can observe the temperature changes.

Using the strongly typed interface of the actor proxy that provides a way to do RPC is called *Actor Service Remoting*. However, that is not the only way to use actors. Another way is to create an ActorProxy that is not strongly typed. You will have access only to the InvokeAsync method for invoking a method of an actor. You will have to specify the exact types of input and output data upon calling the method. Or you can directly query the HTTP API of an actor that I explained earlier in the chapter. Of course, the preferred approach is to leverage the actor interface with Actor Service Remoting as it is the easiest.

Running the Home Automation System

Let's run the actor host and the client to see the whole system in action:

1. First, navigate to the directory of the Home.ActorsHost project and start it. Make sure to check what port the application listens on by inspecting launchSettings.json:

```
dapr run --app-id actorhost --app-port 3000 --dapr-http-port
3500 -- dotnet run
```

2. Then open another terminal, navigate to the directory of the Home.Person project, and start it:

```
dapr run --app-id actorclient --dapr-http-port 3600 -- dotnet run
```

3. The logs outputted by the actor client will look like the following:

```
== APP == The current room temperature is 23.1. The AC is turned on and
set to Cool mode. It is currently idle as the target temperature of 24
degrees Celsius has been reached. The lights in the room are: On.
```

Summary

The Actor model is a simple yet powerful model. In this chapter, you learned what the Actor model is, what problems it aims to solve, in what cases it can be used, and some common pitfalls that you may fall into when using actors. After that, you learned how the virtual Actor model treats actors as perpetual objects whose lifetime is not tied to their in-memory representation at the current moment. When we covered everything in theory, it was time to make use of it. I walked you through the capabilities of the Actors building block of Dapr, how it works, and how you can use it via the HTTP or gRPC API. Then, we ran through the hands-on implementation of a simple home automation system based on the .NET SDK of Dapr.

In the next chapter, you will learn how to leverage the Secrets building block to gain easy access to various secret stores.

CHAPTER 11

Secrets

Sooner than later, a service will have to use one or more secrets to access other systems – whether it is an API key, a password, or something sensitive. In this chapter, you will learn what challenges the secrets impose on your applications and what are the bad practices that you have to stay away from. After a short introduction about what secret managers are and what benefits they bring to the table, you will learn how Dapr simplifies the retrieval of secrets with the Secrets building block. Next, you will learn what secret stores are supported and how you can access them by either referencing secrets right in the Dapr component manifests or by calling the Secrets API from your services. Later, you will see how easy it is to use Kubernetes Secrets and how to use Azure Key Vault if you want to back away from using solely relying on Kubernetes. To wrap up the chapter, I will show you how you can control the access of Dapr applications to secrets.

The Challenges of Secrets Management

A secret is an object you want to protect from leaking to public knowledge because it is something that one party provides to another in order to authenticate and establish some trust. Sometimes a secret has some additional information attached to it besides the identity of the caller – it can even contain what privileges it gives the secret holder. Secrets come in many forms – a password, an SSH key, a short-lived token (e.g., RSA or OAuth tokens), a private key, or a passphrase for a private key. Secrets can be used by various parties – users, services, applications, scripts, SaaS products, and so on.

The usage of secrets typically has two sides – a client provides a secret to gain access to a system, and then the system knows how to verify its validity and either accepts or rejects the client's request. A leak of a single user's password is not that severe incident as the public breach of the whole database of a big website that stores passwords in plain text. There are a lot of best practices when it comes to issuing and storing secrets;

© Radoslav Gatev 2021
R. Gatev, *Introducing Distributed Application Runtime (Dapr)*, https://doi.org/10.1007/978-1-4842-6998-5_11

however, in this chapter, we are going to explore the first side of the problem – the usage of secrets. If a secret has leaked from either one of both involved sides, it is considered a breach as parties that gain access to the secret can act on the user's behalf and do malicious actions.

Besides the technical implementation of secrets generation, storage, and retrieval, there a lot of processes that can be established to achieve a better level of security. Some typical questions that arise are as follows: What secrets are available? Who has access to them? Who has accessed a particular secret and when? How are secrets secured at rest? How is the rotation being performed? What policies apply to different types of secrets? How to track versions? How to revoke a secret that has leaked? Who is responsible for any of the prior topics?

Application Challenges and Anti-patterns

Quite often an application needs to call some external service or system that is not meant to be available publicly and has some type of authentication in place. In order to do so, it must provide a secret. As it is with password-based security, the most common security threat for a system is the actual user. They must be informed enough not to reveal their password to anyone, to be able to recognize any phishing attempts, and not to use the same password across websites.

When it comes to applications accessing other applications or services, the client applications must have access to the secret. For example, secrets can be defined as environment variables, in configuration files, or in application code, or they can be retrieved at runtime. The easier the secret sharing is, the worse practice it proves to be. I bet you have seen passwords hardcoded in a raw form right in the source code. Then those passwords are stored in source control and can be accessed by any developer. Of course, once you check out the code, you are all set to begin development, debugging, and so on. Whenever you establish some bad practice (intentionally or not), it becomes the status quo for the whole application. For example, having the secrets in the source code is handy for development scenarios, but the case is that in production the application will still expect the secrets to be defined in the same place as they were in development. Storing passwords in plain text in the source code is like writing your username and password on a piece of paper and sticking it on your desk or keeping a small piece of paper in your wallet with the PIN of your debit card next to it. When you lose your wallet, you will have lost all factors of authentication the bank card has. To be fair, losing your card alone is a debacle in itself with contactless payments and magstripe payments.

Deciding where to store the secrets can bring an avalanche of problems. If you choose to keep secrets somewhere within the application or service, it makes it difficult to know what secrets are used by each application whenever you try to get the bigger picture. Furthermore, the rotation and revocation of secrets are far more difficult because you have to identify all the services that use a particular secret. After that, you need to know where the service stores the secret and how to update it. It's a lot of work because access to secrets most likely won't be uniform across services, especially if they are developed by different teams. Some may utilize environment variables, while others read secrets from a configuration file.

So far, you have learned how Dapr building blocks utilize component definitions. For example, when you want to interface with an external system in the Resource Bindings building block, you have to specify the connection information like URL, password, or token right in the component definition. As we already discussed, storing secrets in raw format inside source code is a very bad practice. So the approach we followed so far prevents you from being able to keep your components under source control. But when you use Dapr, component manifests are one of the main artifacts that you need. Not having the component manifests renders Dapr building blocks unusable. Later in this chapter, you will learn how not to store secrets inside components.

The Need for a Central Secret Store

You already know what the most common anti-patterns are. It's not a good idea to store secrets on the application side – whether it is in code, configuration, environment variables, and so on. Instead, secrets must be obtained by an application or a service on demand from a central secret manager, often called a secret store. Because the secret store is an additional layer, it introduces an important distinction between secret store users – on one side, some services and applications retrieve secrets depending on their privileges, while on the other, there are secret store operators that can see what secrets are stored and how they are used and can revoke or rotate them.

Some of the benefits of a secret store are the following:

- A central place to store all security information – secrets, keys, and certificates.

- Access is secured with proper authentication and authorization mechanisms.

- Encryption at rest using industry-standard algorithms and key lengths.

- Hardware protection using *Hardware Security Modules (HSMs)*.

- Access and usage are monitored.

The Secrets Building Block

Dapr provides a building block for working with secret stores. All you have to do is to identify which secret store works best for you and define the respective component type.

Supported Secret Stores

At the time of writing, Dapr supports the following secret stores:

- AWS Secrets Manager

- Azure Key Vault

- GCP Secret Manager

- HashiCorp Vault

- Kubernetes Secrets

- Local environment variables (for development only)

- Local JSON file (for development only)

As you can see, Dapr supports the secret managers of the most used public cloud platforms. Kubernetes Secrets come out of the box without requiring any configuration at all when Dapr runs in Kubernetes mode. The name of the Kubernetes Secrets–based secret store is simply kubernetes. This means that in Kubernetes, you take it for granted and just reference it without defining a component for it. For development purposes, when you don't want to use a real secret store, you can either retrieve secrets stored in either a JSON file or as environment variables.

For any secret stores other than Kubernetes, a component should be defined. For example, the configuration of the state component that uses a local JSON file to retrieve secrets from looks like this:

```
apiVersion: dapr.io/v1alpha1
kind: Component
metadata:
  name: mysecretstore
  namespace: default
spec:
  type: secretstores.local.file
  version: v1
  metadata:
  - name: secretsFile
    value: <PATH-TO-JSON-FILE>
  - name: nestedSeparator
    value: ":"
```

As usual, you have to specify the name of the component and the namespace where it will be accessible. Then, you have to choose the particular type of component, which in the preceding case is `secretstores.local.file`. Depending on the type you choose, it will expect specific metadata. In this case, it is a path to the JSON file that stores the secret values in plain text, and the `nestedSeparator` specifies how you will reference the names of nested objects when retrieving the secrets. As you already know, the metadata typically contains the connection information if you are using a cloud secret store.

Once you define the manifest for the secret store, there are two ways you can utilize the Secrets building block.

Reference Secrets from Components

So far, you have seen component definitions containing access keys and connection strings in plain text. As I already explained, this is a very bad practice that prevents you from keeping those manifests under source control. Now let's see how the secret store component can be utilized from within other components.

If you recall from Chapter 9: Resource Bindings, we defined two binding components – one for Azure Blob Storage and another for Azure Queue Storage. Their metadata was almost identical, except that one references a queue, while the other references a storage account. Once you have defined a secret store component, you can rework the binding component to reference the access key of the storage account from a secret store. In my case, the secret store is named `mysecretstore` and contains a secret named `storageAccessKey` that holds the access key of the storage account:

```
apiVersion: dapr.io/v1alpha1
kind: Component
metadata:
  name: azblob
  namespace: default
spec:
  type: bindings.azure.blobstorage
  version: v1
  metadata:
  - name: storageAccount
    value: imgdetectstor
  - name: storageAccessKey
    secretKeyRef:
      name: storageAccessKey
  - name: "container"
    value: "images"
  - name: decodeBase64
    value: "true"
auth:
  secretStore: mysecretstore
```

As you can notice, the `auth.secretStore` section references the secret store by name. If this is omitted, Dapr assumes you are trying to use the default Kubernetes Secrets store, although it is not available in Self-hosted mode for obvious reasons. Then each secret you want to retrieve from the secret store can be referenced by introducing the `secretKeyRef` element, which has the properties `name` and `key`. In this case, only `name` is used because I am using a secret store that reads from a local JSON file. Other secret stores like Kubernetes can contain multiple keys inside a single secret; that's why you can reference the particular key by name. You can use the secret references in the `spec.metadata` section of any Dapr component.

Retrieve a Secret from the API

Like other Dapr building blocks, the Secrets building block provides an API that you can obtain secrets with. It's not reasonable to expect that you will communicate with external systems only via the Dapr building blocks as Dapr groups the similarities and the usage patterns of external systems into building blocks and handles them in one uniform way. For example, you will most likely need to establish a database connection by using some specific connection library in order to utilize 100% of the provided capabilities of the database. In order to connect to a database, you will need a connection string that you can retrieve from a secret store. The same example can be given to any other external system that you will want to fully leverage.

The Secrets API contains a GET endpoint that is used for retrieving a secret, as shown in Figure 11-1. The secret and the secret store in which it is stored are specified in the URL. In case the secret store supports storing multiple keys under a secret, the response contains the values of all keys in this secret. Otherwise, the payload contains just the name of the secret as a field and the secret content as a value, as shown in Figure 11-1.

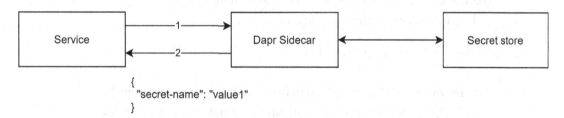

Figure 11-1. *Retrieving a secret via the API*

You can optionally specify metadata such as the version ID of the secret, in case the secret store supports secrets versioning. However, have in mind that specifying any metadata will most likely make your usage of a secret store tied to the specifics of a particular secret store. For example, not all secret stores support retrieving a specific version of a secret.

Retrieve All Secrets in the Store

We just explored how to get a particular secret from a secret store. But the Secrets building block provides a way to retrieve all secrets that are present in a secret store instead of performing individual requests and collecting secrets one by one. In order to do so, just issue a GET request to the bulk endpoint:

```
http://localhost:<daprPort>/v1.0/secrets/<secret-store-name>/bulk.
```

Using a Secret Store

I already mentioned a couple of times that the Kubernetes Secrets store comes out of the box if you are using Dapr in Kubernetes mode. You don't have to define a component for it. But let me show you how to access Azure Key Vault from the Secrets building block.

First, let's create the Azure Key Vault resource and create a *service principal* that can access the secrets in it. You can either use Azure CLI locally with a bash shell or open Azure Cloud Shell at shell.azure.com. Let's begin:

1. Log in to Azure. This is not needed if you are using Azure Cloud Shell:

```
az login
```

2. Set the default subscription. You can see all available subscriptions by running az account list:

```
az account set -s <subscription id>
```

3. Set the variables that are going to be used for further commands. This is the reason why you need bash. Although Azure CLI works on any platform, certain features vary across different shells as is the case with variable assignment:

```
LOCATION=<location>
RESOURCE_GROUP=<your-resource-group>
KEY_VAULT_NAME=<your-keyvault-name>
SPN_NAME=<your-spn-name>
```

4. Create the resource group that will hold the key vault:

```
az group create --location $LOCATION --resource-group
$RESOURCE_GROUP
```

5. Create the key vault in the specified resource group and location:

```
az keyvault create --location $LOCATION --name $KEY_VAULT_NAME
--resource-group $RESOURCE_GROUP
```

6. Create a service principal that will be used by Dapr to access secrets. The following command will also create a certificate for this service principal and will store it in the key vault you just created. It will eventually query the Application ID and assign its value to a variable named appId, which will be referenced later:

```
appId=$(az ad sp create-for-rbac --name $SPN_NAME --create-cert
--cert 'SpnCert' --keyvault $KEY_VAULT_NAME --skip-assignment
--query 'appId' -o tsv)
```

7. Get the objectId of the service principal by using the variable appId you set with the previous command:

```
objectId=$(az ad sp show --id $appId --query
'objectId' -o tsv)
```

8. Next, grant the service principal permissions to read secrets from the key vault. To reference the service principal, you will have to specify the objectId you just gathered from the previous command:

```
az keyvault set-policy --name $KEY_VAULT_NAME --object-id
$objectId --secret-permissions get
```

9. Make sure to copy the Tenant ID of your Azure Active Directory and the Application ID as you will later need them when we define the secret component:

```
az ad sp show --id $appId --query 'appOwnerTenantId' -o tsv
echo $appId
```

10.   And finally, let's save the certificate in a PFX format:

```
az keyvault secret download --vault-name $KEY_VAULT_NAME --name 'SpnCert'
--encoding base64 --file spn_cert.pfx
```

11.   If you use Azure Cloud Shell, you have to run one additional
command to download the file to your computer:

```
download spn_cert.pfx
```

Now that you have Azure Key Vault created and a service principal that can read
secrets from it, it's time to define the secret store component named myazurekeyvault:

```
apiVersion: dapr.io/v1alpha1
kind: Component
metadata:
  name: myazurekeyvault
  namespace: default
spec:
  type: secretstores.azure.keyvault
  version: v1
  metadata:
  - name: vaultName
    value: <your-keyvault-name>
  - name: spnTenantId
    value: "<your-tenant-id>"
  - name: spnClientId
    value: "<your-service-principal-appId>"
  - name: spnCertificateFile
    value : "<local-path-to-the-certificate.pfx>"
```

Make sure to substitute the placeholders in brackets. You should have saved the
Tenant ID and the App ID from step 9.

Note   When you specify the path to the PFX certificate on Windows, make sure to escape the backslashes, for example, "C:\\folder1\\spn_cert.pfx". On Linux, you can use single slashes, for example, "/folder1/spn_cert.pfx".

Next, save the component in the default components folder (or alternatively specify the `--components-path` flag). Then open a terminal and start a Dapr sidecar that will be used for calling the Secrets API:

```
dapr run --dapr-http-port 3500 --app-id secrettests
```

Make sure to inspect the logs and verify the secret store component has been loaded successfully and leave the terminal session open. Let's go to the Azure Portal to create a secret that we are going to retrieve from the API. Find the key vault in the resource group you created and select Secrets on the left side of the blade. Then click the Generate/Import button, provide values for the fields Name and Value, and click Create, as shown in Figure 11-2.

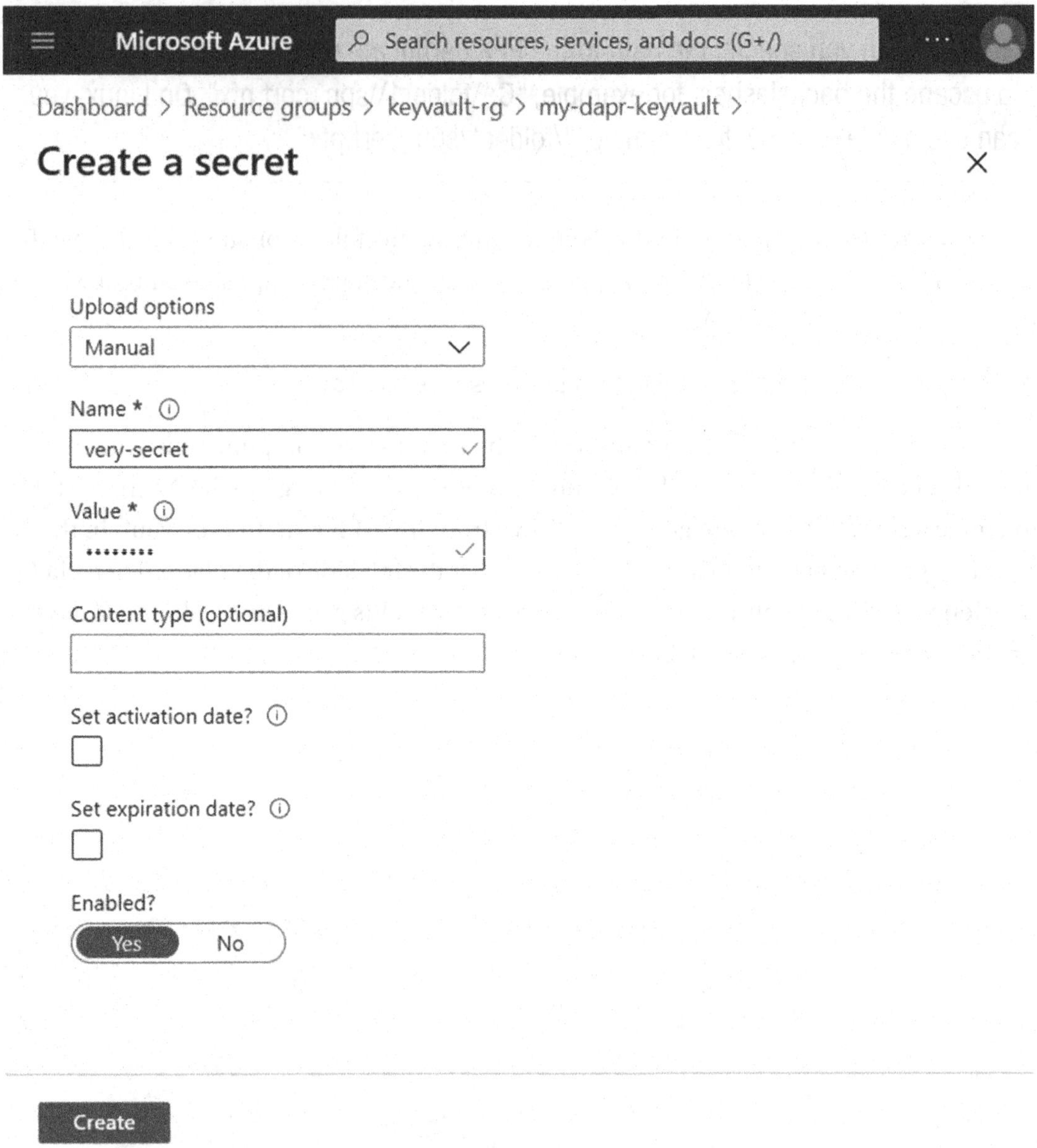

Figure 11-2. *Creating a secret in Azure Key Vault*

Once the secret is saved, you can open your browser and go to http://localhost:3500/v1.0/ secrets/myazurekeyvault/very-secret. If everything is configured properly, it should return {"very-secret":"VALUE"} as a response.

Now you should realize why it is an especially bad idea to expose Dapr externally when you have configured a secret store. This effectively makes it possible for everyone to dump the secrets in your secret store by using the bulk endpoint of the Secrets API. This could be somewhat alleviated by enabling the authentication on every request coming to Dapr sidecars.

Using a Secret Store in Kubernetes

We initially explored the idea of using a secret store to remove any plaintext credentials from components, but if you think about what we just did, the component of the secret store has a reference to a local path that contains the certificate with the private key with which you access Azure Key Vault. That ain't a smaller security risk either. But you still need a way to authenticate to Azure Key Vault by providing credentials.

Fortunately, you will most likely deploy applications in production to Kubernetes. As I mentioned, Dapr supports reading from Kubernetes Secrets out of the box. This means that you can upload the certificate file to a Kubernetes Secret and then use it as a reference in the key vault component manifest. Let's first create a secret in Kubernetes. Make sure you have a valid kubectl context:

```
kubectl create secret generic spn-cert --from-file="<local-path-to-
certificate.pfx"
```

Next, the component manifest that references the secret you just created looks like this:

```
apiVersion: dapr.io/v1alpha1
kind: Component
metadata:
  name: myazurekeyvault
  namespace: default
spec:
  type: secretstores.azure.keyvault
  metadata:
  - name: vaultName
    value: <your-keyvault-name>
  - name: spnTenantId
    value: "<your-tenant-id>"
```

```
  - name: spnClientId
    value: "<your-service-principal-appId>"
  - name: spnCertificate
    secretKeyRef:
      name: spn-cert
      key: spn_cert.pfx
auth:
  secretstore: kubernetes
```

You can keep the previous values that you used locally, except the changes in
spnCertificate and the auth section that was added to specify that referenced
secrets come from the Kubernetes Secrets store. Note the name of the metadata item
is spnCertificateFile when you specify a local file, but when you reference it from a
secret store, it is spnCertificate.

Let's apply this component manifest by running

```
kubectl apply -f keyvault-secretstore-k8s.yaml
```

At this point, the Azure Key Vault secret store has been deployed and can be
used by Dapr applications and components. To verify it works, let's deploy a Dapr
application in order to use its Dapr sidecar. Let's use the busybox container image
although this actually doesn't matter because you just need a Pod with the dapr.io
annotations applied:

```
kubectl apply -f busybox.yaml
```

Then find the container that starts with busybox-* from the output of kubectl get
pods. After that, let's set up port forwarding from the local 3500 port to the same port that
the Dapr sidecar container listens on inside the pod:

```
kubectl port-forward busybox-544bb85cd7-fzq6n 3500:3500
```

Now you can open http://localhost:3500/v1.0/secrets/myazurekeyvault/
very-secret in a browser to validate it successfully returns the value of the secret.

A Few Remarks on Kubernetes Secrets

You may ask why secret stores other than Kubernetes are supported at all since you can effortlessly store every secret as a Kubernetes Secret. While this is true, you have to remember that Kubernetes Secrets are a thing inside your K8s cluster and obviously you cannot use them as a central place to store all secrets. Maybe the cluster running all your Dapr applications is just a small part of the whole platform you are developing.

Furthermore, Kubernetes Secrets don't provide all features of the normal secret managers. For example, they don't offer HSM encryption. As a matter of fact, Kubernetes Secrets by default are stored in plain text inside etcd. It really depends on the type of cluster that you are using because, for example, Azure Kubernetes Service comes with secret encryption at rest enabled. If secrets are not encrypted at rest, this means that if an attacker gains access to etcd or kubeapi-server, all secret values will be exposed. That's why it's very important to configure the encryption of the secrets data at rest. You can either manage the encryption keys or configure a *Key Management Service (KMS)* provider. The KMS providers offer better security when compared to self-managed encryption keys. There is a Kubernetes KMS plugin for Azure Key Vault that enables you to encrypt the secrets data in etcd. And now we are back at where we started – Azure Key Vault.

There is actually an easier way to use the Azure Key Vault secret store if you use Azure Kubernetes Service. Azure Kubernetes Service supports *managed identities,* which are a wrapper around service principals so that you don't have to deal with the service principal credentials or their rotation as it happens automatically. There is a project that enables assigning managed identities to individual pods inside AKS. So whenever an application pod wants to access an Azure resource, the components that facilitate AAD Pod identities will gather a token on the Pod's identity. Then the application pod can extend a request to the particular Azure resource using the token. The secret store component for the key vault supports AAD Pod identity authentication to Azure Key Vault, but the installation of AAD Pod identity components is beyond the scope of this chapter. You can find out more about the project on GitHub: `https://github.com/Azure/aad-pod-identity`.

Controlling Access to Secrets

At this point, you understand how the Secrets building block is used for Dapr components and Dapr applications. The control of what secrets are used inside component manifests is in the hands of the developer who writes the manifest and in the operator who deploys it. After the component manifests are deployed, the secret references are evaluated.

But if you think from a Dapr application perspective, by using the Secrets API, you can dump all secrets present in a secret store. And it doesn't need to be intentionally implemented by the application as there can be some malicious code coming from some library that can do this silently. Therefore, it's a good idea to specify the set of secrets that a Dapr application is allowed to retrieve from a secret store. In this way, operators can validate the list of secrets before deploying the manifests. This can be done with Dapr configurations. For each Dapr application, you can specify a Configuration CRD that holds its configuration data. And there is a standalone secrets section in it for controlling access to secrets:

```
secrets:
  scopes:
    - storeName: kubernetes
      defaultAccess: deny
      allowedSecrets: ["secret1"]
    - storeName: localstore
      defaultAccess: allow
      deniedSecrets: ["secret1"]
```

In the preceding fragment, you can see that the secrets are enlisted per secret store. For each secret store, you can specify the following properties:

- defaultAccess – The default access modifier – allow/deny

- allowedSecrets – The list of secrets that can be accessed (no matter what the defaultAccess is)

- deniedSecrets – The list of secrets that cannot be accessed (no matter what the defaultAccess is)

The lists of allowed and denied secrets always take precedence over the value of defaultAccess. The value of defaultAccess is applicable when no specific lists are defined, jointly or separately. In the preceding fragment, for the kubernetes secret store only secret1 can be accessed and for the localstore all secrets except secret1 can be accessed. Although the secrets access lists offer a quite flexible configuration, I encourage you to deny access to all secrets by default by setting defaultAccess to deny and whitelist all secrets that can be accessed by the particular application in allowedSecrets.

Summary

Secrets must be handled with special care. That's why Dapr provides a Secrets building block that allows you to get all secrets from a central place for storing all security information – a secret store. Dapr supports the secret managers of the major public cloud providers and also Kubernetes Secrets for Dapr in K8s mode. The building block can be used in two ways – when other Dapr components need to reference secrets in their manifests and by calling the Secrets API. The Secrets API is useful when applications need runtime access to some secrets – a good example is a database connection string. Later on, you learned how to set up Azure Key Vault to be used as a secret store for both Self-hosted and Kubernetes modes. You also learned how Kubernetes Secrets can play a supplementary role when Azure Key Vault is used as the main secret store. Although Kubernetes Secrets come in handy without any configuration on the Dapr side, I outlined what are the trade-offs and what you can do to secure it further. Finally, we explored how access to secrets can be controlled by specifying the specific secrets that a Dapr application can access from each secret store.

In the next chapter, you are going to learn why observability is important and how you can monitor Dapr applications.

CHAPTER 12

Observability: Logs, Metrics, and Traces

Knowing what happens inside a system while it is running is beneficial for debugging, maintenance, and analysis purposes. In this chapter, we will explore the three pillars of observability – logs, metrics, and traces. You will learn what they are, how they are used, and what are the differences between them. After that, we will explore how Dapr allows you to put the telemetry data into practice by mostly leveraging the open standards such as the OpenTelemetry project. Then you will understand how to use various monitoring systems to collect, analyze, and visualize the information coming from Dapr and your applications.

The Three Pillars of Observability

The telemetry coming from your apps can be usually split into three categories: logs, metrics, and traces. Ideally, you should be working toward having a single pane of glass that can show all three categories so that you can navigate across them. For example, you may want to see the logs for a request at a given time that you identified to be slower than usual.

Logs

Logs are likely the simplest of the three. Simply put, they represent some insight about an event that happened at a given time; therefore, they carry a timestamp and some payload. There is support for logging in most of the frameworks and libraries that you will ever use. Sometimes it's as simple as outputting a line of text. Logs generally come in three forms:

© Radoslav Gatev 2021
R. Gatev, *Introducing Distributed Application Runtime (Dapr)*, https://doi.org/10.1007/978-1-4842-6998-5_12

- Plain text – The most common form you will likely see emitted from any running process.

- Structured – Logs are in structured formats like JSON, which makes it easy for further processing.

- Binary – Logs are stored in binary format. It's not likely for your application to have binary logs. An example of such type is the logs of some RDBMS, for example, MySQL. Binary logs are generally useful only for the system that is generating them.

What is the value of logs? Logs can give you some contextual information from a particular request that has been handled by a service. Depending on the granularity of your logs, you may be able to identify the root cause of some performance issues or to debug a problem without attaching any debugger whatsoever. This may sound like you should log each and every individual action your services happen to perform. However, you should think about the performance implications of this as logs are typically stored on disk. This means that depending on the logging system you use, generating too many logs can also degrade the performance of your services. Apart from that, too many logs can incur a huge operational cost for your whole application because logs are typically sourced to external systems in order to be consolidated, stored, and further analyzed.

Dapr Logs

So far, you should have already seen some logs coming from the Dapr system services and sidecars. Whether you run Dapr in Self-hosted mode or in Kubernetes mode, its system services emit logs that are as verbose as the log level you choose. These are levels of log verbosity:

- debug

- info

- warn

- error

The error level reports only errors, while debug is the most verbose level. By default, it uses the info level. Besides that, you can also specify the log format to be used – plain text or JSON. If you are planning to collect the logs into an external system for further analysis, you should configure Dapr to emit logs in JSON format; otherwise, the default is plain text.

For Self-hosted mode, you can specify the verbosity level by setting the `--log-level` flag whenever you start any system service or a Dapr sidecar (daprd). When starting Dapr applications with a sidecar, the flag is specified in the following way:

```
dapr run --log-level debug -- dotnet run
```

If you want to change the logging format in Self-hosted mode, you have to directly start the daprd binary as you cannot set the format with Dapr CLI, at the time of writing the book.

In Kubernetes mode, it's crucial what you select when you install Dapr. For example, here is how to specify both the verbosity level of each Dapr system service and the format of the Dapr system services when installing the Helm package:

```
helm install dapr dapr/dapr --namespace dapr-system --set global.
logAsJson=true --set dapr_operator.logLevel=debug --set dapr_placement.
logLevel=debug --set dapr_sentry.logLevel=debug --set dapr_sidecar_
injector.logLevel=debug
```

Then for each Dapr application, you control the logging behavior by specifying the following annotations:

```
dapr.io/log-as-json: "true"
dapr.io/log-level: "debug"
```

As you already know, the good practice is to have structured logs that allow you to better navigate between the properties. Here is an example of a log item in JSON format emitted by a Dapr sidecar:

```
{"app_id":"hello-service","instance":"hello-deployment-7bd95f6647-kh
q69","level":"info","msg":"internal gRPC server is running on port
50002","scope":"dapr.runtime","time":"2021-03-28T13:41:33.317200855Z","type
":"log","ver":"1.0.1"}
```

While logs can give you a lot of details about all events that happened in a system, you will hardly be able to notice a problem in a distributed system by solely inspecting the logs of every service. That's why you need a higher-level view – metrics and traces can be viewed as generalized derivatives of logs.

Metrics

Metrics are time-phased numeric information measured over time. Since it is a numeric representation, it is very convenient for any type of aggregation, summarization, and correlation that you will typically see in dashboards where you can explore some historical trends about your application. Metrics are accompanied by a set of key-value pairs called labels that provide details about where the particular metric was measured. Such a label in Dapr is the Dapr Application ID and the name of a component, to name a few. Labels give a *multidimensional* view of the metrics.

Time-series databases are well suited to collect metrics. The performance overhead is constant for the metric-emitting side. Unlike logs, the amount of metrics does not depend on how many operations the service is performing. Since metrics describe some state of a system, alerts can be triggered when a metric reaches a particular value. Metrics can also drive additional capabilities like auto-scaling in a Kubernetes cluster.

Dapr Metrics

Metrics are enabled by default in Dapr. Examples of metrics include the number of sidecar injection failures, the number of successfully loaded components, and latency of calls between Dapr sidecars and applications to name a few. Dapr metrics are exposed by a Prometheus endpoint that by default listens on port 9090 on both Dapr system services and application sidecars. Prometheus, apart from being the name of a Titan god from Greek mythology, is the de facto standard for a monitoring system in the cloud-native world. Prometheus collects metrics by scraping a metrics endpoint at regular intervals. At the time of writing, Dapr leverages the OpenCensus Stats exporter for the Prometheus endpoint. OpenCensus is a set of libraries for various languages that help you for collecting metrics and distributed tracing. OpenCensus and OpenTracing have merged to form OpenTelemetry, which aims to deal with the full set of telemetry data – logs, metrics, and traces. At some point, when OpenTelemetry reaches maturity, Dapr will fully leverage its capabilities.

There are different ways to scrape metrics data from this endpoint. However, to make it possible for all scrapers to know where to find the Prometheus metrics endpoint, you must specify the following Prometheus annotations on each Pod:

```
prometheus.io/scrape: "true"
prometheus.io/port: "9090"
prometheus.io/path: "/"
```

The `prometheus.io/scrape` annotation specifies whether the Pod should be scraped by metric collectors. The `prometheus.io/port` and `prometheus.io/path` annotations specify the port and the path of the metrics endpoint. Those annotations are automatically defined for all the Pods of the Dapr system services.

Metrics give you a general overview of how your system behaves. You can look for any outliers like failures in some operations, unusual CPU or memory usage, or performance degradation. But still, a distributed system is a set of small moving parts. A request to a single service can end up causing a vortex of subsequent requests hitting various services.

Tracing

Traces are the representation of the communication flow between services and other dependencies in a distributed system. It's also called distributed tracing because it captures trace information spanning across processes, nodes, networks, and security boundaries. If properly set up, a trace provides visibility over which services were involved from the start to the end of a request and how long it took for each of them to finish. You can also easily pinpoint where errors are happening.

The unit of work in distributed tracing is *a span* that represents the work done by a single service as part of the end-to-end workflow. A span constitutes a single operation happening in the service, for example, a request to another service or a database query. A span contains metadata information about the operation such as the operation name, the start and the end timestamps, and some attributes. A trace is a tree of spans united by a *root span* that encompasses the lifetime of all child spans. By inspecting the root span, you can tell how long the duration of the whole operation took. Child spans are united by a context that they have to provide. The W3C Trace Context specification defines how the context is populated in HTTP by different systems by leveraging Trace ID and the mechanism for sharing this context in a vendor-agnostic way.

Dapr Distributed Tracing

The distributed tracing support in Dapr is mostly useful for the Service Invocation and Pub/Sub building blocks as it can result in having a complex chain of requests that are otherwise difficult to be understood. Dapr leverages the standard headers defined by the W3C specification. Namely, the HTTP headers are `traceparent` and `tracestate`. The `traceparent` header contains the Trace ID that is the identifier of the whole trace and the identifier of the span in a vendor-neutral format. The `tracestate` header may contain some vendor-specific information, which can be set and incrementally augmented by all parties involved in a trace. For gRPC, the header is `grpc-trace-bin`, which is the binary equivalent of `traceparent`, albeit not being a part of the W3C spec. Those headers are all generated and propagated by Dapr. It's very handy that the whole communication flows through the system of Dapr sidecars.

By default, if Dapr detects that the trace context is present, it will simply propagate it to any further service calls. In case there isn't any trace context, Dapr will generate one and will propagate it further. Keep in mind that trace context might be missing if this is at the beginning of the request flow, and Dapr will generate a new one in this case.

Configuring Tracing

It's very important to have tracing data in production. But the volume of the tracing data can grow exponentially for an application that receives many requests as is the case with logs. However, in most cases, you would want to have at hand all generated logs because logs point to specific events that happened at a given time. Instead, you can benefit from traces even if you don't collect 100% of them. Of course, you will likely miss collecting some of the outliers; however, the general patterns that are applicable for the majority of requests will be captured. In this case, you can save some space and processing costs.

The ability to not persist each span is called *sampling*. The term sampling comes from statistics, where sampling is the process of taking a subset of individual observations from a statistical population in order to make a conclusion about the whole population by using extrapolation. The default sampling rate in Dapr is *0.0001*, which means that 1 out of every 10,000 spans is sampled. You can specify the sampling rate in the configuration file of Dapr in Self-hosted mode or by applying a Configuration CRD in Kubernetes mode. It is a number between 0 and 1, where 0 means tracing is disabled and 1 means that every span is sampled:

```
apiVersion: dapr.io/v1alpha1
kind: Configuration
metadata:
  name: daprConfig
spec:
  tracing:
    samplingRate: "1"
    zipkin:
      endpointAddress: http://localhost:9411/api/v2/spans
```

Now that traces are sampled at a given ratio, you need to export them to a tracing system to be able to realize any benefit from having them – trace collection, visualizations, analytics, and so on. By default in Self-hosted mode, Dapr sends the trace data to Zipkin, which is a distributed tracing system with a simplistic yet powerful UI. In Self-hosted mode, Dapr spins up a container running Zipkin, whereas in Kubernetes mode you have to deal with deploying it.

As you can see from the preceding code snippet, the address of the HTTP endpoint of Zipkin that collects spans is specified. Because Dapr is in Self-hosted mode, Zipkin runs in a container. In the case of Kubernetes, you have to change the address of the Zipkin collector endpoint to point to the FQDN of the Service that stays in front of the Zipkin Pod. Alternatively, you can use an OpenTelemetry collector to send the traces to various systems. More on that is covered later in this chapter.

Preserving the Trace Context

There might be certain cases where you want to take control over how the trace context is generated. For example, when the request chain starts outside Dapr, say you have some legacy web service that calls into a Dapr sidecar. This appears to be the first piece of the request chain, so you better provide some trace context to Dapr so that it propagates it further instead of generating a brand-new one. To generate the trace headers, you are better off using the OpenCensus SDKs to generate the context and pass it as the respective headers. Another option is to use some other vendor-specific monitoring SDKs that support W3C trace headers, or you can even implement the specification on your own.

Another challenge you can face is when a Dapr application calls multiple other applications via the Service Invocation building block. Dapr generates a new trace context when no such is provided for a given service invocation request. For example, if you have the following request chain – *Service A -> Service B -> Service C* – the trace context will be generated in Service A and propagated to Service B and then to Service C and so on. That's the case with a chain of requests.

To illustrate it further, let's assume we have the following topology of requests originating from Service A:

```
Service A -> Service B
... Service A executes some logic...
Service A -> Service C
... Service A executes some logic...
Service A -> Service C
```

In the preceding case, when Service A calls Service B, a context will be generated. Then along with its response, Service B will return the context as response headers back to the code of Service A. However, in this case, it is the responsibility of the caller to further propagate the returned context. If you don't do it, Dapr will generate a new context for each sequential service invocation. You have to explicitly instruct Dapr to link those calls in a single trace tree.

Let's revisit the distributed Hello World application that we implemented in Chapter 2: Introduction to Dapr once again. There were three services – Greeting, Hello, and World. The Greeting service is what produced the "Hello world" output by sequentially invoking the Hello service and World service and combining their responses.

Now, follow the same steps as outlined in Chapter 2: Introduction to Dapr to run the three services, and make a couple of requests to the Greeting service. Then open Zipkin UI, at `http://localhost:9411/zipkin/`. It has two pages – Find a trace and Dependencies. The first page enables you to see the recent traces and execute some *queries* against all the available traces. For example, you can filter by service name, duration, or timeframe. The Dependencies tab displays a graphical simulation of how requests flow logically from one service to others. Let's focus on the Find a trace page that displays the recent requests issued by the Greeting service as shown in Figure 12-1.

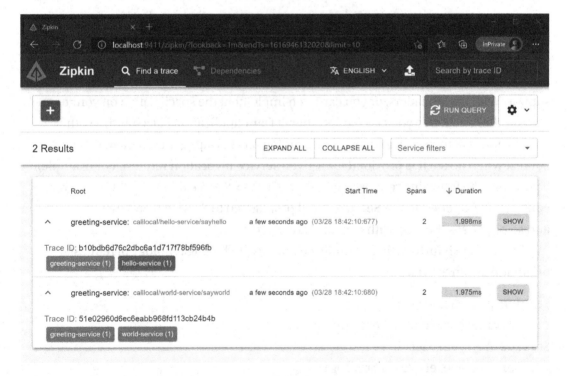

Figure 12-1. *Greeting service traces in Zipkin*

Did you notice anything? If you click each individual result, you will be able to explore more info about the particular trace. The problem with this is that the Greeting service seems to be invoking the other two services somewhat separately although you know this happens during the lifetime of a single request in the Greeting Service. Let's revisit the code that invokes the two requests:

```
app.get('/greet', async (_, res) => {
    hello = await fetch(invokeHello);
    world = await fetch(invokeWorld);
    const greeting = await hello.text() + ' ' + await world.text();

    res.send(greeting);
});
```

Do you see any trace of the traceparent header? In this case, Dapr thinks the request to the World service has nothing to do with the request to the Hello service and generates a trace context for both. Now, let's make sure we propagate the context to the World service appropriately by retrieving and propagating the headers on any consecutive calls:

```
app.get('/greet', async (_, res) => {
    hello = await fetch(invokeHello);
    const traceparentValue = hello.headers.get('traceparent');
    let tracestateValue = '';
    if (hello.headers.has('tracestate')) {
        tracestateValue = hello.headers.get('tracestate');
    }

    world = await fetch(invokeWorld, {
        headers: {
            'traceparent': traceparentValue,
            'tracestate': tracestateValue
        }
    });
    const greeting = await hello.text() + ' ' + await world.text();

    res.send(greeting);
});
```

After saving the new version of the Greeting service, stop the `dapr run` command by pressing Ctrl+C and rerun it so that it picks up the new changes. Then, do some requests to the Greeting service endpoint and refresh the Zipkin UI discover page. By observing the results, it should be clear that the Greeting service now invokes two other services in the lifetime of a single request; and by clicking one of the results, it will display the timeline of the request as shown in Figure 12-2.

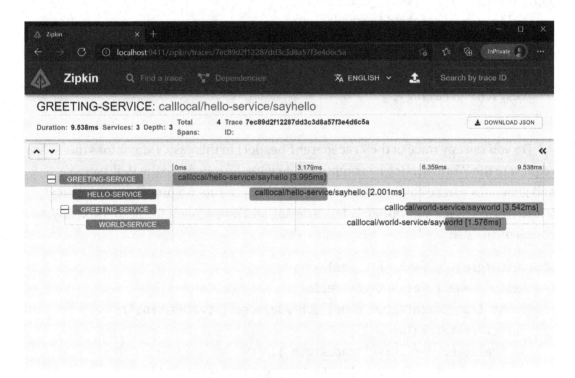

Figure 12-2. *Exploring the timeline of a request*

By now, you have learned what the capabilities of Dapr are when it comes to observability. With its system of sidecars, Dapr collects all the telemetry information. You don't have to make decisions about how to collect and where to store telemetry data per service, which otherwise may lead to having different practices across the services. Instead, all comes out of the box. However, Dapr doesn't provide any options to call, for example, a tracing middleware for any custom tracing needs.

To get the job done, Dapr relies on industry-standard projects like OpenCensus, OpenTracing, and OpenTelemetry. OpenCensus and OpenTracing were merged into OpenTelemetry, but at the time of writing, the underlying code still leverages OpenCensus. From another perspective, OpenTelemetry can also be seen as the next major version of both of the aforementioned projects. With time OpenTelemetry will become the de facto cloud-native telemetry standard covering all three aspects of observability – tracing, metrics, and logs. Be prepared for some changes around Dapr observability until OpenTelemetry becomes stable and fully adopted.

So far, I have shown you how to export tracing data in Zipkin, which comes by default for Dapr in Self-hosted mode. In the next paragraphs, you are going to learn how to export all the telemetry data to various monitoring tools and systems. Because what is the value of telemetry if you are not able to see, analyze, and react?

Azure Monitor

Azure Monitor is a comprehensive solution in Microsoft Azure that allows you to collect, store, analyze, and react on telemetry data coming from the cloud and from on-premises environments. When it comes to collecting telemetry from Kubernetes and any applications running on it, there are several approaches for collecting the data. The easiest is if you use Azure Kubernetes Service, as most of the things come out of the box.

Metrics and Logs from AKS

Collecting metrics and logs in Azure Kubernetes Service is easy-peasy. Let me show you how to configure AKS to leverage Azure Monitor for containers:

1. Firstly, you will need to have an Azure Log Analytics workspace that will store the monitoring data, so open Azure Portal and create an Azure Log Analytics workspace if you don't already have one.

2. Then create an AKS cluster if you don't have one. The AKS cluster should have Azure Monitor for containers (Container Insights) enabled. You can do it at the time of the creation of the cluster by checking the checkbox or later using Azure CLI. To find the different methods to enable it on existing AKS clusters, consult the Microsoft Docs: `https://docs.microsoft.com/en-us/azure/azure-monitor/containers/container-insights-enable-existing-clusters`.

3. Lastly, open a terminal, make sure kubectl connects to your
   AKS, and verify that the Log Analytics agent is up and running by
   executing the following commands:

```
kubectl get ds omsagent -n=kube-system
kubectl get deployment omsagent-rs -n=kube-system
```

After you verified the resources of the agent are present and healthy, you should
be able to see the health and resource utilization of your AKS cluster by opening the
Insights tab in your AKS blade in Azure Portal. The container logs are also going to be
available.

However, this setup won't collect any deep telemetry that is application-specific like
the one available from the Prometheus metrics endpoint of Dapr. To collect them, you
will usually need to have a Prometheus server with a store. But by using Azure Monitor
for Kubernetes, you don't need a server because it's capable of collecting metrics by
itself. Let's configure the Log Analytics agents to scrape Prometheus metrics:

1. Firstly, download the ConfigMap YAML from `https://aka.ms/`
   `container-azm-ms-agentconfig`.

2. Find the `prometheus_data_collection_settings.cluster`
   section and update it as follows:

```
prometheus-data-collection-settings: |-
  [prometheus_data_collection_settings.cluster]
     interval = "1m"
     monitor_kubernetes_pods = true
     monitor_kubernetes_pods_namespaces = ["dapr-system", "default"]
```

3. Then save and apply the ConfigMap:

```
kubectl apply -f .\container-azm-ms-agentconfig.yaml
```

4. Next, you have to annotate your Dapr application pods so that the
   Log Analytics agents can find the Prometheus metrics endpoint.
   You can do so right in the manifests of the distributed Hello World
   application we defined in Chapter 4: Running Dapr in Kubernetes
   Mode. And don't forget to instruct Dapr to log in JSON format:

```
dapr.io/log-as-json: "true"
prometheus.io/scrape: "true"
prometheus.io/port: "9090"
prometheus.io/path: "/"
```

5. Lastly, apply the updated application manifests.

If you have gone through those configuration steps, your applications will leverage the maximum support of Azure Monitor for containers. Then you can start running queries in Log Analytics or incorporate the collected data into Azure Monitor Workbooks, which provide visual reports and a lot of opportunities for customizations.

Queries against Azure Log Analytics are being written in *Kusto Query Language (KQL)*. Using KQL, there is a sample query that retrieves the Dapr logs:

```
ContainerLog
| extend parsed=parse_json(LogEntry)
| project Time=todatetime(parsed['time']), app_id=parsed['app_id'],
scope=parsed['scope'],level=parsed['level'], msg=parsed['msg'],
type=parsed['type'], ver=parsed['ver'], instance=parsed['instance']
| where level != ""
| sort by Time desc
```

The query displays a chart showing the change of used memory of both Dapr system services and Dapr sidecars, as you can see from Figure 12-3:

```
InsightsMetrics
| where Namespace == "prometheus" and Name == "process_resident_memory_bytes"
| extend tags=parse_json(Tags)
| project TimeGenerated, Name, Val, app=tostring(tags['app'])
| summarize memInBytes=percentile(Val, 99) by bin(TimeGenerated, 1m), app
| render timechart
```

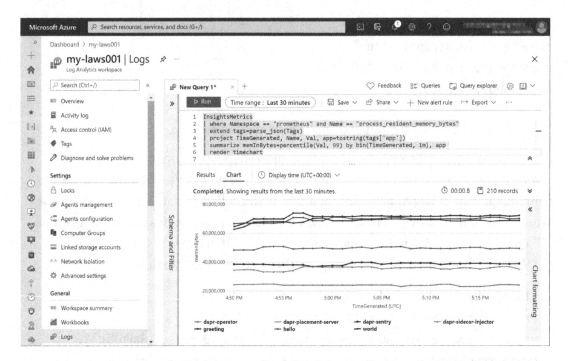

Figure 12-3. *Running a Kusto query that displays used memory by Dapr system services and Dapr applications*

Metrics and Logs from Any K8s

Azure Monitor for containers comes out of the box in AKS with a simple flip switch. However, if you have Kubernetes clusters running on-premises, you will have to do some manual configuration in order to enable them to integrate with Azure Monitor:

1. First, you have to deploy the Container Insights solution for your Azure Log Analytics workspace.

2. Then, install the Helm Chart of the Log Analytics agent.

I won't guide you through those steps because they are out of scope for this chapter. You can find more info in the Azure Monitor for containers documentation at Microsoft Docs: `https://docs.microsoft.com/en-us/azure/azure-monitor/containers/container-insights-hybrid-setup`.

Another alternative just for the logs is to use Fluentd for collecting them, and then you can utilize an output plugin for Fluentd to transfer them to Azure Log Analytics.

Traces from Any K8s

There are several options to collect traces. We have already explored how to do it locally with Zipkin. Now you are going to learn how to leverage the OpenTelemetry collector that is configured to use the Zipkin endpoint to collect the traces. Then those traces can be exported to multiple monitoring solutions like Azure Monitor (Application Insights), Datadog, Instana, Jaeger, Kafka, and many others. The OpenTelemetry collector is deployed as a Pod in the K8s cluster. Let me show you how to send traces to Application Insights by levering it:

1. Firstly, create an Application Insights via the Azure Portal.

2. After it is created, make sure to copy the Instrumentation Key that you can find from the Overview tab of the Application Insights resource blade.

3. Open the `open-telemetry-collector.yaml` file that you can find in the source code of the book. It defines all resources needed by the OpenTelemetry collector. The most important one among them is the ConfigMap that configures how the collector works. Inside it, you configure pipelines that collect data from receivers, process it, and send it to exporters. In this case, the receiver will be the service exposed by this same manifest to which Dapr will send the traces in Zipkin format. The exporters in the current case are two – `azuremonitor` and `logging`. The `logging` exporter comes in handy when you want to make sure the collector receives any data.

4. Find the `otel-collector-conf` ConfigMap, navigate to `exporters.azuremonitor.instrumentation_key`, and substitute the `<INSTRUMENTATION-KEY>` placeholder with the Instrumentation Key that you just copied. Next, apply this manifest:

```
kubectl apply -f open-telemetry-collector.yaml
```

5.   Then, you have to enable tracing for your Dapr applications. Create a Configuration CRD, if you haven't done so. This component not only configures the `samplingRate` of tracing but also configures what is the endpoint that the traces should be sent to. In this case, it is the service exposed by the OpenTelemetry collector that understands traces sent in Zipkin format:

```
apiVersion: dapr.io/v1alpha1
kind: Configuration
metadata:
  name: appconfig
  namespace: default
spec:
  tracing:
    samplingRate: "1"
    zipkin:
      endpointAddress: http://otel-collector.default.svc.cluster.
      local:9411/api/v2/spans
```

6.   All your Dapr applications must use the configuration you just created. Add the following Dapr annotation that references the previously created configuration to their manifests and apply it:

```
dapr.io/config: "appconfig"
```

7.   Make sure to make a good amount of requests to the Greeting service so that some data is sent to Application Insights.

After all those steps, opening the Application Map of your Application Insights instance should display the collected information about the interdependencies of the services in your application as shown in Figure 12-4.

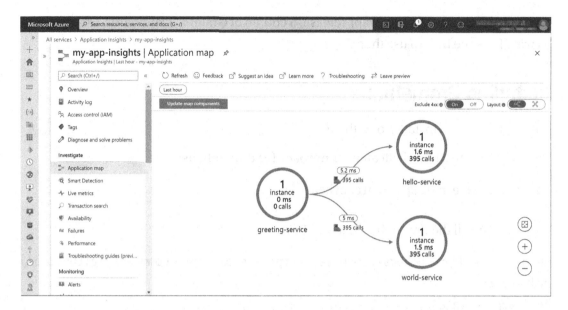

Figure 12-4. *Application Insights – Application Map*

In case nothing appears in the Application Map, validate you have supplied a correct Instrumentation Key and consult the logs of the OpenTelemetry collector. Find out what is the name of the OpenTelemetry pod and run `kubectl logs otel-collector-556c98b76b-nrwrq`. If it receives anything, you should be able to see the spans as they come.

Note   At the time of writing, Zipkin is the preferred format for traces. However, at some point in time when OpenTelemetry becomes more stable, it will also be supported. When this happens, most likely Zipkin will become deprecated as Zipkin is just one of the many supported receivers by the OpenTelemetry collector.

Grafana

Grafana is a very popular open source data analysis and visualization solution. It is capable of integrating with a large number of data sources – Prometheus, InfluxDB, Elasticsearch, Azure Monitor, and many others. Although Azure Monitor is supported, in a typical stack that uses Grafana, you will most likely use the Prometheus server to collect metrics, instead of *Azure Monitor for containers*.

Furthermore, with every Dapr release, a couple of Grafana dashboards are shipped as well. Let's see how to use them.

Installing Prometheus

Follow the steps to install Prometheus:

1. Create a new dedicated namespace for Prometheus:

```
kubectl create namespace prometheus
```

2. Install the Prometheus Helm Chart:

```
helm repo add prometheus-community https://prometheus-community.github.io/
helm-charts
helm repo update
helm install prometheus prometheus-community/prometheus -n prometheus
```

3. Make sure your Dapr applications have the Prometheus annotations so that Prometheus discovers the metrics endpoints to scrape.

Setting Up Grafana

Now let's deploy and set up Grafana:

1. Create a new namespace for Grafana:

```
kubectl create namespace grafana
```

2. Install the Grafana Helm Chart:

```
helm repo add grafana https://grafana.github.io/helm-charts
helm repo update
helm install grafana grafana/grafana -n grafana
```

3. Get the Grafana admin password:

```
kubectl get secret --namespace grafana grafana -o jsonpath="{.data.admin-
password}"
```

4. Decode it from base64 using an appropriate tool for your machine. On Linux and macOS, you can use `base64` or `certutil` on Windows. Alternatively, you can use some website to decode the password.

5. Set up port forwarding to the Grafana service:

```
kubectl port-forward svc/grafana 8080:80 -n grafana
```

6. Open `http://localhost:8080` in a browser and enter the admin for username and the password you just decoded.

7. Next, let's add Prometheus as a data source. Find Data Sources under Configuration in the menu on the left-hand side.

8. Find the name of the Prometheus server service, which ends on `prometheus-server` in the output of

```
kubectl get svc -n prometheus
```

9. Add Prometheus as a data source by specifying the IP you just copied. The URL should be `<service-name>.prometheus.svc.cluster.local`; in my case it is `prometheus-server.prometheus.svc.cluster.local`.

10. Click Save & Test to save your Prometheus data source.

Importing the Dapr Dashboards

With each release Dapr ships a few useful Grafana dashboard templates – for visualizing the state of system services, sidecars, and actors. Let me show you how to install them:

1. You can find the dashboards at `https://github.com/dapr/dapr/releases/`.

2. Click the + icon from the left menu and then Import.

3. Import the dashboard templates.

Having those dashboards gives you a lot of insights about what happens with Dapr as shown in Figure 12-5.

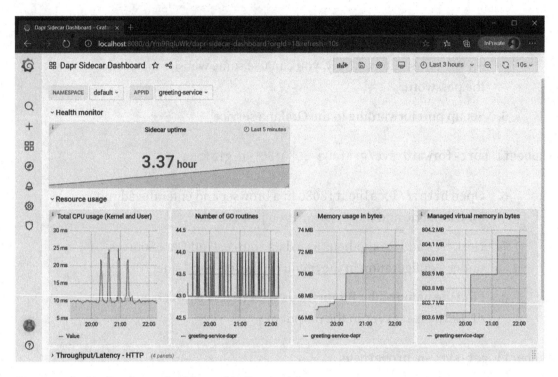

Figure 12-5. *Grafana dashboard – Dapr sidecar*

Summary

Being able to tell what is going on inside a given system while looking from the outside is crucial. By collecting, storing, and analyzing the three pillars of observability – logs, metrics, and traces – you can very productively spot any issues or investigate some corner case scenarios. In this chapter, you learned how Dapr supports each one of those telemetry types. Then you learned how to ship that information to various monitoring systems like Azure Monitor and Grafana and do further analysis.

This was the last chapter of Part 2, which covers all Dapr building blocks. Part 3 aims to explore how Dapr can integrate and work side by side with other technologies. In the next chapter, you are going to learn how to plug in middleware to execute additional actions during the request pipeline.

PART III

Integrations

CHAPTER 13

Plugging Middleware

Being able to change the behavior or to extend the functionality of a piece of software, without changing it from the inside, is pretty neat. In this chapter, you will learn how to plug middleware in the request pipeline of Dapr to deal with things like rate limiting, authentication, and authorization.

Middleware in Dapr

Using middleware is a very popular technique for request-based pipelines. It is essentially a system for chaining plugins that do some kind of processing on a request, one after another. Every middleware is a layer that performs a specific function.

Dapr is very much a request-based runtime, and that's why it is very handy to define a custom middleware pipeline as shown in Figure 13-1. As a matter of fact, Dapr internally utilizes a built-in chain of middleware for certain functions. For example, there is a tracing middleware, a metrics middleware, and *a* Cross-Origin Resource Sharing (CORS) middleware. The distributed tracing and the Dapr metrics that were covered in Chapter 12: Observability: Logs, Metrics, and Traces rely heavily on the tracing and the metrics middleware. The CORS middleware is what enables you to whitelist the URLs that will be allowed to access the sidecar by the browser. The URLs can be configured by specifying the `allowed-origins` flag on the sidecar.

© Radoslav Gatev 2021
R. Gatev, *Introducing Distributed Application Runtime (Dapr)*, https://doi.org/10.1007/978-1-4842-6998-5_13

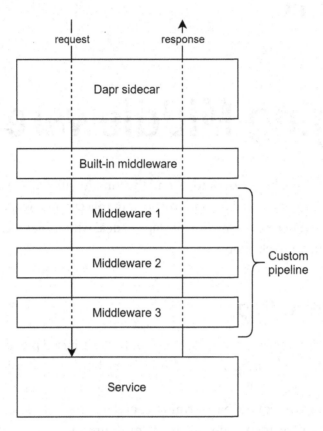

Figure 13-1. Middleware pipeline

Every request that comes into a Dapr sidecar gets processed sequentially by each middleware until it reaches the endpoint of a service, which returns some payload as a response, which is then processed by the same middleware but in reverse order. It is up to the implementation of the middleware to choose whether to implement its logic on the ingress, the egress, or both sides.

At the time of writing, Dapr only supports HTTP-based middleware. However, keep in mind that the middleware is not only applicable to service invocation but also publish and subscribe, state management, resource bindings, actors, and pretty much anything that hits an endpoint of the Dapr API.

Configuring and Using Middleware

In Figure 13-1, middleware 1–3 constitute a custom pipeline. But before you can define the pipeline of middleware, you have to create a component for each middleware you want to use. One exception to this is the `middleware.http.uppercase`, which is a preregistered component that changes the text in the request body to uppercase. It's useful for local development purposes in order to test whether the middleware pipeline is properly configured and thus functioning.

Let me show you how to define a rate-limiting middleware that allows you to limit the number of requests per second. All components that we are going to explore are going to be created in a folder named components, which you can find in the source code of the book. The component manifest of the rate-limiting middleware looks like this:

```
apiVersion: dapr.io/v1alpha1
kind: Component
metadata:
  name: ratelimit
spec:
  type: middleware.http.ratelimit
  version: v1
  metadata:
  - name: maxRequestsPerSecond
    value: 2
```

The way it is configured in the preceding, the rate-limiting middleware will make sure that no more than five requests are processed per second. Whenever the limit is reached, it will respond with status code 429: Too Many Requests. Don't get rate limiting confused with the `max-concurrency` flag for Dapr in Self-hosted mode and the `dapr.io/app-max-concurrency` annotation in Kubernetes mode. The rate limiting counts and limits the requests per second, while the concurrency setting makes sure that no more than the configured number of requests is being executed at any single point of time.

Now that you have defined all the middleware components you are about to include in a pipeline, let me show you how to configure it. The pipeline is defined in the `httpPipeline` section of a Dapr configuration. It is up to you to configure the number of middleware and their order. In this example, I am going to define a pipeline that consists of two middleware – the `uppercase` and the `ratelimit` – in a file named `pipelineconfig.yaml`:

```yaml
apiVersion: dapr.io/v1alpha1
kind: Configuration
metadata:
  name: pipelineconfig
  namespace: default
spec:
  httpPipeline:
    handlers:
    - name: ratelimit
      type: middleware.http.ratelimit
    - name: uppercase
      type: middleware.http.uppercase
```

Before running this example, let me show you a simple web service based on ASP.
NET Core that I have built that will serve for debugging all requests in this chapter. It
has a single endpoint that returns all information about the HTTP request – the HTTP
method, the query string, the HTTP headers, and the body:

```csharp
[Route("/test")]
[HttpGet, HttpPut, HttpPost, HttpDelete]
public async Task<string> Test()
{
        var response = $"HTTP Method: {Request.Method}\n" +
                $"Query: {Request.QueryString} \n" +
                "Headers\n";
        foreach (var header in Request.Headers)
        {
                response += $"\t{header.Key}: {header.Value}\n";
        }

        using var reader = new StreamReader(Request.Body);
        response += $"Body: {await reader.ReadToEndAsync()}";

        return response;
}
```

Now, it is time to run and test our pipeline with Dapr in Self-hosted mode:

1. Open a terminal and navigate to the project folder of the ASP.NET Core service in the source code of the book.

2. Run the application by specifying the path where components are located and also the path to the configuration file. If you are on Linux or macOS, make sure to replace the backward slashes with forward slashes:

```
dapr run --app-id tester --dapr-http-port 3500 --app-port 5000
--config ..\pipelineconfig.yaml --components-path ..\components
-- dotnet run
```

3. Issue a POST request. You can use your favorite tool for making HTTP requests. I will use cURL:

```
curl -X POST http://localhost:3500/v1.0/invoke/tester/method/
test -d 'the body'
```

4. Examine the casing of the returned body. If everything was correctly set up, it should be in ALL CAPS.

5. Issuing more than the specified number of requests per second will return HTTP status code 429: Too Many Requests. You can easily test that by opening a browser at the same address from step 3 and doing a couple of fast refreshes.

Utilizing the OAuth 2.0 Middleware

OAuth 2.0 is a very widely used protocol for authorization. OAuth 2.0 defines four roles – Resource Owner, Resource Server, Authorization Server, and Client. Resource Owner is the user who gives their consent to an application to access their resources (any user data) on their behalf. Resource Server is a system that contains the user's data. Authorization Server is the central point where users are prompted to approve or deny any requests for permissions. After a request is approved, the Authorization Server issues a token to the application demanding access to the user's data. This means that the typical implementation of the OAuth 2.0 server will have at least two endpoints – one for authorizing the consent and another for issuing an access token. Client is the application that is requesting access to some portion of the user's data. Once the Client obtains an access token, it can perform operations in the Resource Server on behalf of the Resource Owner (the user). The general flow of the protocol is shown in Figure 13-2.

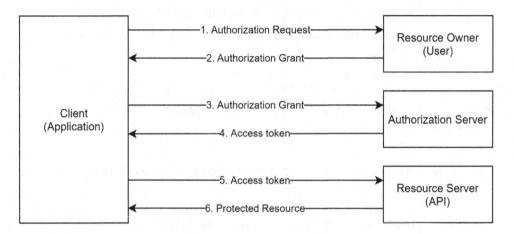

Figure 13-2. *OAuth 2.0 protocol flow*

But depending on the way the client application obtains the access token, there are several different *grant types* that can be used. Two of the most widely used authorization grants are the Authorization Code grant and the Client Credentials grant. They both obtain an access token in the end; however, they serve different user types. In the Authorization Code grant, the user is being redirected to the Authorization Server by the client application. After the user enters their credentials, the Authorization Server redirects the user back to the client application along with the Authorization Code. Once the client application receives the Authorization Code, it is exchanged for an access token by making a call to the token endpoint of the Authorization Server. In contrast, the Client Credentials grant is applicable whenever a system wants to access its own data by exchanging its own credentials to obtain an access token. In this case, it means that the Resource Owner and the Client are basically the same thing – an application. This is enough for you to have a basic understanding, and it's beyond the scope of this chapter to discuss the OAuth 2.0 protocol in further detail.

To see how widely used the OAuth 2.0 protocol is, here are some of the most popular technologies that can be used as an Authorization Server. Some of them are pure *Identity and Access Management (IAM)* solutions, while others are social networks. Most of them follow the SaaS model, while others like IdentityServer provide a good room for customization and various hosting options:

- Azure Active Directory

- Facebook

- Google APIs

- Twitter

- Okta

- IdentityServer

Dapr provides out-of-the-box middleware for both the Authorization Code grant and the Client Credentials grant. I will show you how to use them with Azure Active Directory (AAD). However, they work with any server that supports OAuth 2.0. The main difference will be in the way that you register a client application using the respective user interface.

For some reason, you may need to publicly expose the Dapr sidecars to the Internet. This will require you to make sure that only authenticated users are allowed to use the Dapr API. Dapr supports out-of-the-box API token–based authentication, although the token for all clients is the same. In Self-hosted mode, the token is in the `DAPR_API_TOKEN` environment variable, whereas in Kubernetes mode it must be stored as a Kubernetes Secret and then referenced by name with the `dapr.io/api-token-secret` annotation. You will be responsible for rotating the secret frequently. However, in production you will most likely use some kind of an Identity Provider and a protocol like the OAuth 2.0 authorization grant or OpenID Connect, depending on whether the client is a user or another application.

Authorization Code Grant Middleware

As you already learned, when using the Authorization Code grant, the Resource Owner is a user, and the Client is an application. In the context of Azure Active Directory, this means that the user should already be a part of the directory. The client application should also be registered within the Azure Active Directory so that it knows what is this application that calls into it. The process of registering such an application is the following:

1. Navigate to Azure Active Directory in Azure Portal.

2. Click App Registrations, which is a tab of the AAD blade.

3. Click the + New registration button.

4. Enter the name of your application and click the Register button.

5. From the Overview tab of the newly created application, copy the values of Application (client) ID and Directory (tenant) ID, as you are going to need them when defining the middleware component.

6. Go to the Certificates & secrets and create a new secret by clicking + New client secret. Make sure to copy the value of the secret as you won't be able to see it after you close the page.

7. Go to the Authentication tab and click + Add a platform, select Web as a platform type, and specify `http://localhost:3500/v1.0/invoke/tester/method/test` as a Redirect URI. This is the URI that will receive the access token.

After you have done all the preceding steps, it is time to define the component. Make sure you replace all the placeholders with the values that you have copied from the previous steps:

```
apiVersion: dapr.io/v1alpha1
kind: Component
metadata:
  name: oauth2
  namespace: default
spec:
  type: middleware.http.oauth2
  version: v1
  metadata:
  - name: clientId
    value: "<Client-ID>"
  - name: clientSecret
    value: "<Client-Secret>"
  - name: scopes
    value: "User.Read"
  - name: authURL
    value: "https://login.microsoftonline.com/<Tenant-ID>/oauth2/v2.0/
    authorize"
```

```
- name: tokenURL
  value: "https://login.microsoftonline.com/<Tenant-ID>/oauth2/v2.0/token"
- name: redirectURL
  value: "http://localhost:3500/v1.0/invoke/tester/method/test"
- name: authHeaderName
  value: "Dapr-Access-Code"
- name: forceHTTPS
  value: "false"
```

After you have defined the component, you have to reference it in the `httpPipeline` section of the Dapr configuration. Then this configuration should be referenced by the Tester application that you already have upon calling `dapr run`. If you are still unsure how to do those steps, please revisit the previous paragraphs that explain them. If you still have the previous middleware in the pipeline, it is a good idea to remove them.

Now, after you started the application with a Dapr sidecar, you can open `http://localhost:3500/v1.0/invoke/tester/method/test` in your browser, and you will be redirected to Azure Active Directory that will prompt for your consent to logging into this application that you just created. Once you give your consent, you will be redirected back to `http://localhost:3500/v1.0/invoke/tester/method/test`, which will output the access token that is received as a value of the `Dapr-Access-Code` header.

This means that all further requests that your service receives will carry the access token via the header you specified. Of course, the service must use a Dapr configuration that incorporates the middleware. Depending on the permissions you choose in the application settings in AAD, the application will be able to call various APIs on the user's behalf using the provided token. By default, the application will only have the `User.Read` permission, which grants privileges to read the profile of the signed-in user and some basic company information.

Client Credentials Grant Middleware

The Client Credentials grant is designed to be used by any daemons, services, and applications. The user that is being authorized is an application, which means that there isn't a third party to get the consent of (no real user interaction). This simplifies the process flow as the credentials of the client (Client ID and Client Secret) are directly exchanged with the Authorization Server for an access token.

Let me show how you can use the Client Credentials flow in order to enable your Dapr applications to easily obtain an access token, which then can be used for calling any other APIs, for example, getting all Azure AD users from the Microsoft Graph API:

1. Firstly, although you can use the same application that you created for the Authorization Code grant, I encourage you to register a new one as this is the best practice for different applications. Note that for the Client Credentials grant, you don't have to configure a platform, as there won't be any redirects happening before you receive the token.

2. Since you will query the Microsoft Graph API to get all users, appropriate permissions must be granted to the Azure AD application. Go to API Permissions, click Microsoft Graph to display all available permissions, select Application permissions as these permissions will be applicable for the Dapr application itself, and add User.Read.All.

3. After you added the User.Read.All permission, you have to grant an admin consent, since such applications typically access all the data. You can do so by clicking Grant admin consent.

4. Optionally, you can remove the default delegated User.Read permission that is created when you register an application in Azure AD. When you are done configuring the API permissions, the configuration should be as shown in Figure 13-3.

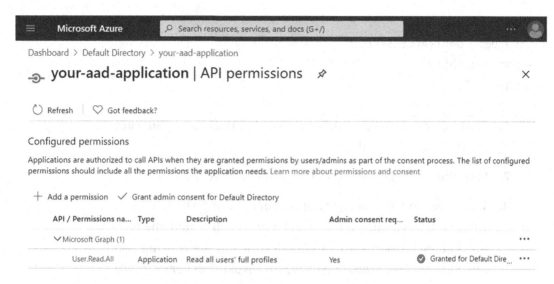

Figure 13-3. *API permissions configuration*

5. Define the middleware component and substitute the
    placeholders with the values of your Azure AD application:

```
apiVersion: dapr.io/v1alpha1
kind: Component
metadata:
  name: oauth2clientcreds
  namespace: default
spec:
  type: middleware.http.oauth2clientcredentials
  version: v1
  metadata:
  - name: clientId
    value: "<Client-ID>"
  - name: clientSecret
    value: "<Client-Secret>"
  - name: scopes
    value: "https://graph.microsoft.com/.default"
  - name: tokenURL
    value: "https://login.microsoftonline.com/
    <Tenant-ID>/oauth2/v2.0/token"
```

```
- name: headerName
  value: "Dapr-Access-Code"
- name: authStyle
  value: "1"
```

6. Next, reference the component created in the last step in your Dapr configuration file.

7. Start the Tester application in the same way we did earlier.

8. Whenever you invoke any endpoint of the Dapr API, it will check whether it has a cached token and if not it will obtain one before proceeding further. Since this application has just one method, open `http://localhost:3500/v1.0/invoke/tester/method/test`, and you should be able to see the access token that was passed in the `Dapr-Access-Code` header. Copy the value of the token as you will need it for calling the Microsoft Graph API.

Now, to verify the token that Dapr got for you can be used, let's get all users by calling the `/users` endpoint of the Microsoft Graph API. You can use a tool like Postman or cURL according to your preference. The request with cURL looks like this – of course, the access token is truncated:

```
curl -X GET https://graph.microsoft.com/v1.0/users -H 'authorization:
Bearer eyJ0e...' -H 'content-type: application/json'
```

Utilizing the OpenID Connect Middleware

OpenID Connect is a standard for federated authentication that is built on top of OAuth 2.0. It uses an additional token called ID token which is a JSON Web Token (JWT) that is given to the client application along with the OAuth 2.0 access token. If you have used, for example, Google authentication to log into third-party websites, you have most likely leveraged OpenID Connect for Single Sign-On.

The bearer middleware helps you to make the Dapr API a protected resource where all clients should provide a bearer token in the Authorization header of the request. Then before further processing the request, Dapr will check with the Identity Provider whether this bearer token is valid.

Before I show you how to utilize this middleware, let me make a few important points on the Azure AD application configuration. But of course, you can use just about any other Identity Provider that supports OpenID Connect:

- The Redirect URI should be `http://localhost:5000/test` so that you work around the Dapr sidecar. This is used because you already have a handy Tester application that shows everything about an incoming HTTP request. In reality, the client application will obtain a token by itself, and then it will provide it via the Authorization header when calling the Dapr APIs.

- The option for issuing ID tokens must be enabled for the AAD application

If you have properly configured it, it should look exactly as shown in Figure 13-4.

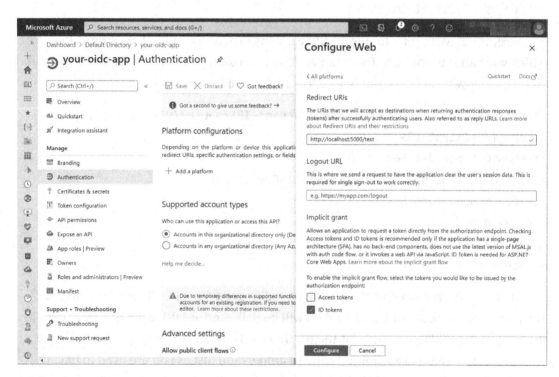

Figure 13-4. Configuring an Azure AD app for OpenID Connect

Now, let's configure the middleware component by replacing the Client ID of the application and the Tenant ID in the respective placeholders:

```
apiVersion: dapr.io/v1alpha1
kind: Component
metadata:
  name: bearer
spec:
  type: middleware.http.bearer
  version: v1
  metadata:
  - name: issuerURL
    value: "https://login.microsoftonline.com/<Tenant-ID>/v2.0"
  - name: clientID
    value: "<Client-ID>"
```

Next, you have to refer to this middleware inside your Dapr configuration, after which you can start the app. To obtain an OpenID token, you have to open a browser and go to the following address, but before that make sure to replace the placeholders:

```
https://login.microsoftonline.com/<Tenant-ID>/oauth2/v2.0/authorize?
client_id=<Client-ID>
&response_type=id_token
&redirect_uri=http%3A%2F%2Flocalhost:5000%2Ftest
&response_mode=form_post
&scope=openid
&state=12345
&nonce=678910
```

After you log in successfully, you will be redirected with a POST request to `http://localhost:5000/test`, and the ID token will be delivered as URL-encoded form data in the body of the HTTP request. This means that the ID token and some other fields are encoded as key-value tuples joined with an ampersand just as you are used to having any GET parameters in the URL. Make sure to copy only the value of the `id_token` key.

If you try accessing an endpoint of the Dapr API without a valid bearer token in the Authorization header, Dapr will reject the request and return HTTP status code 401 Unauthorized. Now open your favorite application for issuing HTTP requests and make the following request, but make sure to include the full value of the ID token that you obtained because I have trimmed it here:

```
curl -X GET http://localhost:3500/v1.0/invoke/tester/method/test -H
'authorization: Bearer eyJOeX...'
```

Open Policy Agent Middleware

The Open Policy Agent (OPA) middleware is one of the latest additions to the collection of Dapr middleware. OPA provides a unified way for enforcing policies across the whole stack of your cloud-native applications. It successfully integrates with container orchestrators, proxies, API Gateways, web frameworks, build systems, databases, and many more. The policies are being defined declaratively by using the Rego language. The policy decision making and policy enforcement are decoupled and happen in the following flow:

1. A service or system where the policy must be enforced consults OPA by supplying data in a structured format (JSON). This is typically triggered by any request received by the service or any event that triggers the service.

2. OPA evaluates the Rego policies on the input data that was received. Then OPA sends the final decision to the calling service or system. The output is in a structured format (JSON).

3. The service receives the output from OPA and enforces the decision.

By using the OPA middleware in Dapr, you can apply some conditions to the incoming requests to the Dapr API. When you define the OPA policy for Dapr, the end result will be whether or not to allow the request, what HTTP status code to return, and what additional headers to inject. All those policies can be described in the Rego language. Dapr provides the properties of the incoming HTTP requests as an input to OPA. Such properties are the HTTP method, the request path, the query string, HTTP headers, and so on. You can learn more about Open Policy Agent in the official documentation: www.openpolicyagent.org/docs/latest/.

Summary

Injecting a middleware is a great idea for request-based workloads. Multiple middleware can be chained together to control the ins and outs of a request to Dapr. In this chapter, you learned about the OAuth 2.0 middleware for Authorization Code grant and Client Credentials grant. You also learned how to verify incoming OpenID Connect tokens using the bearer middleware. Lastly, we touched on what Open Policy Agent is and how the OPA middleware can be used.

In the next chapter, you are going to learn about how the Dapr .NET SDK makes ASP. NET Core development with Dapr simpler.

CHAPTER 14

Using Dapr in ASP.NET Core

In this chapter, you will learn about the integration between Dapr and ASP.NET Core. If you made it so far in the book, you have already seen a lot of examples implemented in ASP.NET. Dapr does not need really anything special to be used with any web framework. However, when it comes to ASP.NET Core, Dapr has some syntactic sugar that makes it even easier. There is support for using the State Management and the Publish and Subscribe building blocks natively inside a controller. There is also a way to expose a secret store as an ASP.NET Core configuration. Furthermore, implementing a gRPC service doesn't mean that you have to import the Protobuf files of Dapr in order to call its gRPC API. It comes pre-packaged inside the support for ASP.NET Core.

Overview

A lot of the examples in the book were based on .NET Core, and in some of them I even used the Dapr .NET SDK. You might be wondering what else you can see for Dapr in the context of .NET Core given that I have covered all in terms of the Dapr functionality. The Dapr .NET SDK covers a somewhat broad area of use cases. It is split into a couple of NuGet packages, some of which you have already seen:

- `Dapr.Actors` – The actor runtime.

- `Dapr.Actors.AspNetCore` – Provides methods for registering the actor runtime within ASP.NET Core, maps the routes of the Actors API, and implements the actor activation.

271

© Radoslav Gatev 2021
R. Gatev, *Introducing Distributed Application Runtime (Dapr)*, https://doi.org/10.1007/978-1-4842-6998-5_14

- `Dapr.AspNetCore` – Delivers native support for Dapr inside ASP.NET Core. This is the main NuGet package that I am going to use in this chapter.

- `Dapr.Client` – The Dapr client that allows you to call operations on the Dapr API. `Dapr.AspNetCore` uses `Dapr.Client` behind the scenes.

- `Dapr.Extensions.Configuration` – A configuration provider that utilizes the Dapr Secrets building block.

Support for ASP.NET Controllers

Before I show you how you can leverage the Dapr syntactic sugar for ASP.NET Core controllers, let me outline the process for setting up the Dapr support inside an ASP.NET Core project:

1. Firstly, install the latest version of the `Dapr.AspNetCore` NuGet package.

2. Then in the `ConfigureServices` method of the `Startup` class of your ASP.NET Core project, add the following line to register Dapr within controllers, add an instance of the `DaprClient`, and configure some model binders. Optionally, you can set an additional configuration for the Dapr client by using the builder pattern inside `AddDapr`:

```
public void ConfigureServices(IServiceCollection services)
{
        services.AddControllers().AddDapr();
}
```

3. Next, in the `Configure` method of the `Startup` class, register a middleware that automatically unwraps the CloudEvents data that is by default sent to every subscriber of a topic. In this way, the subscribing action method doesn't even know that the payload has been received in CloudEvents format:

```
app.UseCloudEvents();
```

4. In the same Configure method using the endpoint route builder, register an endpoint that will output all subscribers at /dapr/ subscribe. If you recall from Chapter 7: Publish and Subscribe, there are two ways for subscribing to a topic – programmatic and declarative. Behind the scenes, this is the programmatic way, except you don't have to do anything but apply the TopicAttribute on your action methods that will handle the subscription:

```
app.UseEndpoints(endpoints =>
{
        endpoints.MapSubscribeHandler();
        endpoints.MapControllers();
});
```

The last two steps are only required if you use the Publish and Subscribe building block and you want to leverage the support for ASP.NET controllers that comes with the Dapr .NET SDK.

To further demonstrate the capabilities inside a controller, I will implement a very made-up application (yet simple) that has one endpoint that processes incoming messages in a topic and saves them into a state store. There is also another endpoint that gathers the information about a given key by taking it from the state store. You can find this project in the source code of the book; it is named ControllersExample. There is a DummyData class that contains just two properties – an Id property of type string and a Data property of type string. It is located in a Common project that is referenced by all example projects in this chapter. There is also a Constants class that keeps the names of the state component, the pubsub component, and the topic in it. Having such a class is not a good practice; however, it simplifies a lot the examples we are going to explore.

Subscribing to a Topic

Subscribing to a topic is as easy as applying the TopicAttribute and providing the name of the pubsub component and the name of the topic:

```
[Topic(Constants.PubSubName, Constants.TopicName)]
[HttpPost(Constants.TopicName)]
```

```
public async Task<ActionResult> ReceiveMessageFromTopic(DummyData newData,
[FromServices] DaprClient daprClient)
{
        await daprClient.SaveStateAsync<DummyData>(Constants.
        StateStoreName, newData.Id, newData);

        return Ok();
}
```

DummyData is received as a POCO object, although before the middleware processes it, it is in the CloudEvents format. You can notice that the DaprClient instance that was earlier registered is also being injected as a parameter. Once the message is received by this action method, it saves it into the state manager by using the Id property as a key of the state item. The processing of the Pub/Sub message is being acknowledged by calling the Ok method, which returns HTTP status code 200 back to Dapr.

Retrieving an Item from a State Store

The obvious way to gather an item from a state store is by either using DaprClient or directly calling the State API. But there is an easier way to work with state inside ASP. NET Core controllers. You can bind the value of a state item directly to a parameter of an action method:

```
[HttpGet("/data/{id}")]
public ActionResult<DummyData> GetDataFromStateStore([FromState(Constants.
StateStoreName, "id")] StateEntry<DummyData> data)
{
        if (data.Value is null)
        {
                return this.NotFound();
        }

        return data.Value;
}
```

In the preceding code, the key of the state entry is provided in the URL as you can see from the route template /data/{id}. Then the name of the route parameter is specified in the FromStateAttribute. Then the state entry is obtained from the state store, and you can even call some methods that change it, for example, DeleteAsync and SaveAsync.

You can test this example locally. You can publish a message by calling the /publish/<pubsub-name>/<topic> endpoint of the Dapr sidecar. Then you can retrieve the state item by calling http://localhost:<app-port>/data/<state-item-key>.

Note   DaprClient needs to know the ports of both the HTTP and gRPC APIs of Dapr. It expects the port numbers to be defined as the environment variables DAPR_HTTP_PORT and DAPR_GRPC_PORT; otherwise, it uses port numbers 3500 for HTTP and 50001 for gRPC by default. When you use the dapr run command of Dapr CLI, to start your application with a command like dotnet run, it automatically injects the environment variables into your application.

Support for ASP.NET Core Endpoint Routing

There might be a case where you don't want to leverage ASP.NET Core controllers. If that is the case, you will most likely directly register your endpoints to respond to specific routes and define some functions that accept an instance of HttpContext. As it comes to the initial configuration, it is almost the same as when using controllers, except you don't have to add the Dapr support for controllers by calling services.AddControllers(). AddDapr().

Since you don't have any controllers, you cannot simply apply the attribute for subscribing to a topic or directly obtaining some state items from a state store. There is a special extension method coming from the Dapr SDK, called WithTopic. Let's rebuild the same example as with controllers, but this time let's use endpoint routing. This is how you register the endpoints for the two methods:

```
app.UseEndpoints(endpoints =>
{
        endpoints.MapSubscribeHandler();
```

```
    endpoints.MapGet("/data/{id}", GetDataFromStateStore);
    endpoints.MapPost(Constants.TopicName, ReceiveMessageFromTopic).
    WithTopic(Constants.PubSubName, Constants.TopicName);
});
```

The implementation of the endpoints resides in two local functions –
GetDataFromStateStore and ReceiveMessageFromTopic. Each of them obtains the
instance of the DaprClient that was added as part of the initial configuration. The
implementation of ReceiveMessageFromTopic is as follows:

```
async Task ReceiveMessageFromTopic(HttpContext context)
{
        var client = context.RequestServices.GetRequiredService<DaprClient>();

        var newData = await JsonSerializer.DeserializeAsync<DummyData>(cont
        ext.Request.Body, serializerOptions);
        await client.SaveStateAsync<DummyData>(Constants.StateStoreName,
        newData.Id, newData);

        context.Response.StatusCode = 200;
}
```

As you notice, it simply retrieves the body of the request that contains the payload
and deserializes it to an instance of the DummyData class. Then it persists the object in
the state store by using the instance of the DaprClient and later acknowledges that the
message was successfully processed by returning HTTP status code 200. That was a lot of
work that otherwise you take for granted in ASP.NET controllers.

Implementing a gRPC Service

Most of the services that I showed you in this book were HTTP-based. If you want to
implement a gRPC service to run side by side with Dapr, you have to implement the
AppCallback interface. In Chapter 6: Service Invocation, I showed you how to import
the Protobuf files and utilize the Protobuf code generation so that it materializes to a C#
class. The good news is that by using the Dapr .NET SDK, the base class for gRPC comes
pre-packaged.

Let's build the same made-up example with `DummyData`, this time with a gRPC service. The base class `AppCallback.AppCallbackBase` that your gRPC service must extend has three methods that you have to override – `OnInvoke`, `ListTopicSubscriptions`, and `OnTopicEvent`. Let's take a look at each of them.

Firstly, the `OnInvoke` method gets called whenever a method has been invoked via the Service Invocation building block. In contrast with HTTP-based services, there is a single method that accepts all method invocations. You will typically have a switch-case statement for each of the methods your service supports:

```
public override async Task<InvokeResponse> OnInvoke(InvokeRequest request,
ServerCallContext context)
{
        var response = new InvokeResponse();
        switch (request.Method)
        {
                case "GetData":
                        var input = JsonSerializer.Deserialize<GetDataI
                        nput>(request.Data.Value.ToByteArray(), this._
                        jsonOptions);
                        var output = await _daprClient.GetStateAsync<DummyD
                        ata>(Constants.StateStoreName, input.Id);
                        response.Data = new Any
                        {
                                Value = ByteString.CopyFrom(JsonSerializer.
                                SerializeToUtf8Bytes<DummyData>(output,
                                this._jsonOptions)),
                        };
                        break;
                default:
                        break;
        }
        return response;
}
```

Then, let's override the `ListTopicSubscriptions` method that returns all topic subscriptions:

```
public override Task<ListTopicSubscriptionsResponse>
ListTopicSubscriptions(Empty request, ServerCallContext context)
{
    var result = new ListTopicSubscriptionsResponse();
    result.Subscriptions.Add(new TopicSubscription
    {
        PubsubName = Constants.PubSubName,
        Topic = Constants.TopicName
    });
    return Task.FromResult(result);
}
```

And finally, let's override the OnTopicEvent method that processes all incoming messages:

```
public override async Task<TopicEventResponse>
OnTopicEvent(TopicEventRequest request, ServerCallContext context)
{
        if (request.PubsubName == Constants.PubSubName)
        {
                var transaction = JsonSerializer.Deserialize<DummyData>
                (request.Data.ToStringUtf8(), this._jsonOptions);
                if (request.Topic == Constants.TopicName)
                {
                        await _daprClient.SaveStateAsync<DummyData>
                        (Constants.StateStoreName, transaction.Id,
                        transaction);
                }
        }

        return await Task.FromResult(new TopicEventResponse()
        {
                Status = TopicEventResponse.Types.TopicEventResponseStatus.
                Success
        });
}
```

Note   When running the gRPC service, don't forget to specify to Dapr that the protocol of the application is gRPC along with the port it listens on. The Dapr CLI accepts the `--app-protocol` flag for this purpose. In Kubernetes mode, the annotation is `dapr.io/app-protocol`.

Retrieving Secrets

Secrets can be retrieved by calling the Dapr API or using the `DaprClient` class in .NET, for example. But if you want a more elegant solution, the Dapr SDK for .NET ships also a configuration provider that loads the secrets your application will need. Then by registering the `IConfiguration` instance in the dependency injection container, you can use it even inside controllers.

The Dapr configuration provider comes from the `Dapr.Extensions.Configuration` NuGet package. Once you have installed the latest version of it, go to the `Program.cs` in your ASP.NET Core project to configure the provider:

```
public static IHostBuilder CreateHostBuilder(string[] args)
{
        var client = new DaprClientBuilder().Build();

        return Host.CreateDefaultBuilder(args)
                .ConfigureServices((services) =>
                {
                        services.AddSingleton<DaprClient>(client);
                })
                .ConfigureAppConfiguration((configBuilder) =>
                {
                        var secretDescriptors = new DaprSecretDescriptor[]
                        {
                                new DaprSecretDescriptor("very-secret")
                        };

                        configBuilder.AddDaprSecretStore("mysecrets",
                        secretDescriptors, client);
                })
```

```
        .ConfigureWebHostDefaults(webBuilder =>
        {
                webBuilder.UseStartup<Startup>();
        });
}
```

In the preceding code, an instance of the DaprClient is created at first. It is later registered in the dependency injection container. After this, the Dapr Secrets configuration provider is registered inside the ConfigureAppConfiguration extension method. This is the place where each secret is enumerated as an instance of the DaprSecretDescriptor class.

Now secrets are loaded into the application configuration. You can retrieve any of them by calling the indexer of the IConfiguration instance:

```
var secretValue = Configuration["very-secret"];
```

To validate that it works, after you run the Dapr application with dapr run, open http://localhost:5000/secret, and it should return the value of the secret coming right from the JSON file.

Note   Keep in mind that this example requires you to have a secret store component. I have included one that keeps all secrets in a JSON file as it is useful for local testing purposes. It is very important to consider that the location of the JSON file is addressed depending on the local directory where you have called dapr run. Make sure to call dapr run --app-id secrets --components-path components -- dotnet run in the project directory; otherwise, it won't be able to locate the secrets file.

Summary

In this chapter, you learned what goodies the .NET SDK for Dapr brings. You can leverage certain attributes to subscribe to topics and to retrieve items from a state store. The support for those two operations is also available when you don't want to use ASP.NET Core controllers for some reason but routing endpoints, instead. You also learned how to implement a gRPC service by overriding the methods of the `AppCallback.AppCallbackBase` base class provided by the Dapr .NET SDK. Then you learned how to leverage the Dapr Secrets configuration provider in order to load secrets into the application configuration.

In the next chapter, you will learn how Dapr integrates with Azure Functions.

CHAPTER 15

Using Dapr with Azure Functions

Functions are a powerful programming model for event-driven applications. In this chapter, you will learn what Azure Functions are and what hosting models they support. Later on, you will get introduced to the capabilities of the integration between Azure Functions and Dapr. To put all knowledge into practice, I will walk you through building a simple function-based application that leverages several of the Dapr building blocks – Service Invocation, Publish and Subscribe, and State Management.

Azure Functions Overview

Azure Functions provide an opinionated programming model that is very suitable for event-driven applications. The unit of work is *a function* that gets triggered upon some event.

Each function has exactly one trigger that makes it execute. For example, it can be an incoming HTTP request in case you are implementing a function-based API. Or the trigger can be a new message in a message queue or a change that occurred in a database. Besides the function activation, triggers also carry the input payload of the initiating operation so that the function code can directly consume it. Additionally, a function may have one or more bindings declared as parameters of it. Bindings provide a way to integrate a function with another resource. As in the Dapr Resource Bindings building block, the bindings in Azure Functions also have a direction. For example, there is an input binding for Azure Blob Storage that reads a blob and provides it as an argument to a function that then can process the blob. On the other way around, there is an output binding that enables you to modify or delete a blob. To make the example complete, there is also a trigger for any changes inside an Azure Blob Storage container.

© Radoslav Gatev 2021
R. Gatev, *Introducing Distributed Application Runtime (Dapr)*, https://doi.org/10.1007/978-1-4842-6998-5_15

By default, the Functions runtime includes only HTTP and timer triggers. If you want to use any of the number of supported triggers and bindings, you have to install the respective NuGet package. Those packages are called *extensions*. For example, the extension for Azure Blob Storage is `Microsoft.Azure.WebJobs.Extensions.Storage`. Likewise, the Dapr APIs are wrapped as triggers and bindings inside the `Dapr.AzureFunctions.Extension` NuGet package. Extensions are implemented in .NET but can be used by any of the supported languages inside Azure Functions – C#, F#, Java, JavaScript, TypeScript, Python, PowerShell, and Go.

Functions are one of the enablers of *serverless* computing. The popular cloud computing model *Function as a Service (FaaS)* is powered by those small and modular pieces of code – the functions. Because of the fact that the underlying infrastructure is abstracted away, FaaS in theory provides limitless scaling of function-based applications. FaaS also has an intrinsically simpler cost model that is based on the number of executions, duration of execution, and memory consumption. Keep in mind that the limitless nature of scaling of FaaS also carries limitless charges. It might make sense to introduce some throttling of client requests or allocate a dedicated capacity to safeguard against a huge cloud bill.

There are several hosting plans for Azure Functions inside Microsoft Azure. First, the Consumption plan starts at the lowest cost possible (almost zero), and as the demand for function executions changes, it dynamically adds or removes Azure Functions host instances on the fly. Second, the Premium plan builds upon the Consumption plan by adding some advanced features like perpetually warm instances, VNET connectivity, unlimited duration of execution, and others. The third hosting plan is to reuse a Dedicated App Service plan to host your Functions-based application alongside any web applications that might be running. That's a great option when you have some spare capacity left in the App Service Plan that you otherwise pay for. This is also helpful if you want to avoid any unexpected charges incurred by the otherwise limitless scalability.

However, at the time of writing the book, the integration between Dapr and Azure Functions provided by the extension does not support any of the cloud-based Azure Functions hosting plans. Fortunately, the Azure Functions runtime is open source and can be deployed to any Self-hosted environment, for example, Kubernetes and IoT Edge.

Dapr Triggers and Bindings

Before putting all this into practice, let me walk you through what triggers and bindings are supported when it comes to integration with the Dapr API. As I already explained, all the Dapr-related functionality comes from the extension, installed as a NuGet package.

First of all, a trigger is needed so that a function is started. The following trigger types are supported at the time of writing the book:

- `DaprBindingTrigger` – Triggered by a Dapr input binding.

- `DaprServiceInvocationTrigger` – Triggered by an incoming service invocation. This trigger allows you to implement the methods of your service with Azure Functions instead of relying on any web framework in order to build your API.

- `DaprTopicTrigger` – Triggered by an incoming message on Pub/Sub topic subscription.

Once triggered, a function can do a number of actions and optionally integrate with some external resources by leveraging bindings. Note that the binding types we are about to explore represent Azure Functions bindings and not the Dapr Bindings building block. Input bindings supply input payload to your functions by gathering data from various places. The following are the supported input binding types:

- `DaprSecret` – Retrieves the value of a secret

- `DaprState` – Retrieves the value of a state

During execution, a function may output data to zero or more external services by leveraging output bindings. At the time of writing, the following output binding types are supported:

- `DaprBinding` – Invokes a Dapr output binding

- `DaprInvoke` – Invokes a method of another Dapr application

- `DaprPublish` – Publishes a message to a Dapr Pub/Sub topic

- `DaprState` – Persists some value in a state store

Azure Functions Development

Developing Azure Functions can happen in plenty of ways. First of all, there are many languages that you can choose to implement your functions. In order to access the Dapr goodies, at first, you must install the extension `Dapr.AzureFunctions.Extension`. For .NET Functions projects, this is installed just like any other NuGet package. However, for other languages, you have to install the extension using the Azure Functions Core Tools, which is a CLI for working with Azure Functions. It has commands for initializing projects using the ready-made templates, installing extensions, and running and deploying functions, among other commands. You can find more in Microsoft Docs: `https://docs.microsoft.com/en-us/azure/azure-functions/functions-run-local?tabs=windows%2Ccsharp%2Cbash#install-a-specific-extension`.

When it comes to using IDEs, there is good support for Azure Functions both in Visual Studio 2019 and in Visual Studio Code. To make your life easier when developing functions in Visual Studio Code, you have to install the Azure Functions extension.

Note   The latest version of the Azure Functions runtime that is generally available for production usage is version 3.x, which supports .NET Core 3.1. There is a preview of .NET 5 support for Azure Functions.

Ports of Dapr and Azure Functions

At times having too many ports can be confusing. Let's get this sorted out before I show you how to get started implementing any Azure Functions applications. As you might expect, each Azure Functions host runs alongside a companion Dapr sidecar.

The Azure Functions host exposes port 7071 locally and port 80 when running in a container. This is a standard endpoint that listens for HTTP triggers, for example, if you are implementing a function-based API.

The Dapr extension for Azure Functions that contains the implementations of Dapr triggers and bindings exposes port 3001. This is a special port where the Azure Functions runtime listens on in order for Dapr to call into your functions when you have one or more Dapr triggers defined. From Dapr's perspective, this is the port of the Dapr application. That's why you have to point Dapr to port 3001 by either defining the `dapr.io/app-port` annotation in Kubernetes or the `--app-port` flag in Dapr CLI. Make sure to only define the application port when you have at least one Dapr trigger in your functions. Otherwise, the extension will not expose it, and it may cause issues during the initialization phase of the Dapr sidecar.

In order for the function application to reach out to Dapr, it needs to know the port on which the Dapr sidecar listens for HTTP. To achieve this, the value of DAPR_HTTP_PORT is inspected; and in case it is empty, the function application uses port 3500 by default. If you start the function application by invoking dapr run, it will automatically set the HTTP port of the Dapr sidecar as an environment variable. In any case, when you want to debug a function, you may start just the Dapr sidecar, but don't forget to explicitly set the port to 3500 by specifying the --dapr-http-port flag. Otherwise, the Functions runtime won't be able to access the Dapr sidecar.

Implementing an Application

Let's build a simple application to put all this knowledge into practice. There will be four functions. The first function is triggered by the Dapr Service Invocation building block and pushes a message to a Pub/Sub topic. This results in a message-based workflow of functions. The next function will be triggered by the incoming message from one topic and will output the same message to another topic. Then the message in the other topic will trigger another function that will persist the message in a state store. And to verify that the data is persisted in a state store, there is one function that provides an HTTP endpoint to retrieve the data from the state store. All that is achieved by only using Dapr triggers and bindings that come from the Dapr extension for Azure Functions. You don't have to deal with HTTP requests, web frameworks, or any clients.

To get this started, open your favorite code editor or IDE. Visual Studio Code with the Azure Functions extension and Visual Studio 2019 can guide you through the project creation. Make sure to create a Functions project based on .NET with functions implemented in C#. Then install the latest version of the Dapr.AzureFunctions. Extension NuGet package. You are all set for writing the code of the functions!

The first function that is triggered by Dapr service invocation looks like this:

```
[FunctionName("Ingest")]
public static void Run(
        [DaprServiceInvocationTrigger] JObject payload,
```

```
        [DaprPublish(PubSubName = "%PubSubName%", Topic =
        "%SourceTopicName%")] out object outputEvent,
        ILogger log)
{

        log.LogInformation("C# function was invoked by Dapr with the
        following payload: " + payload);
        log.LogInformation("Sending the payload to a topic.");

        outputEvent = payload;
}
```

The Ingest function has two important parameters with some attributes applied. As you can notice, the DaprServiceInvocationTrigger attribute is applied to the payload parameter, which contains the input data. This has the same effect as implementing an endpoint with our favorite web framework to be called by the Dapr Service Invocation building block. As the name of the other parameter outputEvent suggests, it is used for pushing messages into a topic by leveraging the Publish and Subscribe building block. In the function body, the value of the payload parameter is assigned to the binding parameter that accepts the outgoing messages. The name of the pubsub component and the topic can be specified directly in code, or you can reference an application setting. In the preceding case, the percentage notation is used to represent a key in app settings so that values are retrieved from the local.settings.json.

When the message is pushed to a topic, another function takes it from there and sends it to another topic in the same underlying messaging system as configured by the pubsub component. It uses a topic trigger and a Pub/Sub output binding:

```
[FunctionName("ChainTopic")]
public static void Run(
        [DaprTopicTrigger("%PubSubName%", Topic = "%SourceTopicName%")]
        CloudEvent inputEvent,
        [DaprPublish(PubSubName = "%PubSubName%", Topic =
        "%TargetTopicName%")] out object outputEvent,
        ILogger log)
{

        log.LogInformation("C# function received an event by a topic
        trigger from " + "Dapr with payload: " + inputEvent.Data);
```

```
        log.LogInformation($"Sending the event to another topic.");
        outputEvent = inputEvent.Data;
}
```

Once received by the target topic, another function is triggered to persist the incoming message into a state store by using a key that is specified in application settings as well. Multiple incoming messages will result in replacing the value that is stored in the state store:

```
[FunctionName("PersistState")]
public static void Run(
        [DaprTopicTrigger("%PubSubName%", Topic = "%TargetTopicName%")]
        CloudEvent inputEvent,
        [DaprState("%StateStoreName%", Key = "%StateItemKey%")] out object
        state, ILogger log)
{

        log.LogInformation("C# function received an event by a topic
        trigger from" + " Dapr Runtime with payload: " + inputEvent.Data);
        log.LogInformation($"Persisting the payload into a state store");

        state = inputEvent.Data;
}
```

And let's see the last function that exposes an endpoint that you can use to retrieve the latest version of the data stored in the state store. It is accessible at http://localhost:7071/api/state/<key> where the key is a placeholder for the key of the state item:

```
[FunctionName("GetState")]
public static async Task<IActionResult> Run(
        [HttpTrigger(AuthorizationLevel.Anonymous, "get", Route = "state/
        {key}")] HttpRequest req,
        [DaprState("%StateStoreName%", Key = "{key}")] string state,
        ILogger log)
```

```
{
        log.LogInformation("C# HTTP trigger function processed a
        request.");

        return new OkObjectResult(state);
}
```

It's time to see it in action. Navigate to the directory of the project and execute the following command:

```
dapr run --app-id functionapp --app-port 3001 --dapr-http-port 3500 -- func
host start
```

If you want to debug the Functions app, with say Visual Studio 2019, you can omit the `func host start` in order to start just a Dapr sidecar. When you have both the Functions app and the Dapr sidecar up and running, you can issue a POST request to `http://localhost:3500/v1.0/invoke/functionapp/method/ingest` using, for example, Postman or cURL. Make sure to send some payload in the body of the HTTP request. Then a chain of functions will be triggered that will finish with persisting the payload from the initial request into the state store. To check whether this payload made it into the state store, open `http://localhost:7071/api/state/stateitem1`; and if everything is good, it will return the payload back to you.

Summary

In this chapter, you learned how to unleash the power of Azure Functions and use them alongside Dapr. Firstly, we touched upon the basics of Azure Functions, its hosting models in the cloud, and how you can you can host it yourself. I also covered what features the Dapr extension for Azure Functions provides and showed you how to leverage them in a simple function-based application.

In the next chapter, you are going to learn about the integration between Dapr and the low-code development experience provided by Azure Logic Apps.

CHAPTER 16

Using Dapr with the Azure Logic Apps Runtime

In this chapter, you are going to learn how you can utilize Dapr building blocks from Azure Logic Apps with its low-code experience for defining business workflows. First of all, we will go through the basics of Azure Logic Apps, and then you will learn how to build a simple workflow.

Azure Logic Apps Overview

Azure Logic Apps is a service from Microsoft Azure that enables you to schedule, automate, and orchestrate tasks by using its low-code or no-code experience. It is very common to use mainly its designer to define business processes as workflows, although it is entirely possible to directly write the whole JSON definition by hand.

Both Azure Functions and Azure Logic Apps are enablers for having serverless workloads. You can implement complex orchestrations with both technologies; they can even call each other. To develop orchestrations inside Azure Functions, you have to use the Durable Functions extension, which is very popular. However, to compare one with the other, Azure Functions are implemented with snippets of code, whereas you design Azure Logic Apps via a designer or optionally by writing JSON.

Let's build the Azure Logic Apps lingo. Business processes are represented as a series of steps in a workflow. Triggers are what activates the workflow. Then the steps defined in the workflow are called actions, and they are provided by managed connectors or custom connectors. There is another set of actions and triggers that are often referred to as built-in. They are native for Azure Logic Apps and allow you to achieve the basic tasks like running on schedule, having conditions and loops, *calling* Azure Functions, calling APIs, and so on. Managed connectors are another group of triggers and actions

291

© Radoslav Gatev 2021
R. Gatev, *Introducing Distributed Application Runtime (Dapr)*, https://doi.org/10.1007/978-1-4842-6998-5_16

that are deployed and managed by Microsoft and that are used to access cloud services or on-premises systems. For example, by using them, you can access data in SQL Server, Office 365, Salesforce, and others. Of course, to access any on-premises services, you will need to have the on-premises data gateway installed. It establishes a secure communication channel between the cloud and on-premises.

Like Azure Functions, Azure Logic Apps is no longer a cloud-only offering. Azure Logic Apps started shipping a set of NuGet packages that enable you to deploy and use Logic Apps–based workflows in any environment you have – on-premises, in any cloud, or in Kubernetes or not. This means that the engine behind Azure Logic Apps does not lock you to a specific vendor. The release at the time of writing the book is a preview, and one of its restrictions is that managed connectors cannot be used at this point. However, you can use the built-in triggers and actions. Another limitation is that you will still have to provide the credentials to an Azure Storage Account where the state of the workflows will be saved.

Integration Between Dapr and Logic Apps

The fact that Logic Apps can be executed anywhere overlaps with the goal of Dapr to be cloud-, platform-, and language-agnostic. This creates a unique opportunity to integrate them both and use Logic Apps as a workflow execution engine that accesses various resources in a microservices environment. It's entirely possible to have a standalone service that is implemented with the single purpose of being able to orchestrate and execute a workflow of tasks. It can call other services or send some payload to a Dapr output binding, for example. If you think about it, the code itself can be categorized as a boilerplate. The fact that you have implemented it as code does not necessarily add a lot of value. Instead, you can create it visually (or declaratively) by leveraging the Logic Apps designer.

The current integration between Dapr and Logic Apps is rather in an early but functional stage. To trigger a workflow, you can either invoke it directly by using the Service Invocation building block, or it can be triggered by an incoming event from an input binding. The Logic Apps host is a Dapr-enabled application as shown in Figure 16-1. It starts a gRPC server that implements the AppCallback interface that is required for any gRPC services that are onboarded on Dapr. Of course, there is a companion Dapr sidecar that relays all incoming requests and serves outgoing requests from the workflow. The name of the workflow is the name of the JSON file that contains its definition. To trigger a workflow by using Dapr service invocation, you have to specify the workflow filename as a method of the service:

```
http://localhost:3500/v1.0/invoke/<app-name>/method/<workflow-name>
```

Workflows can also be triggered by Dapr input bindings. The name of the binding component should be the same as the name of the workflow that should be triggered by it.

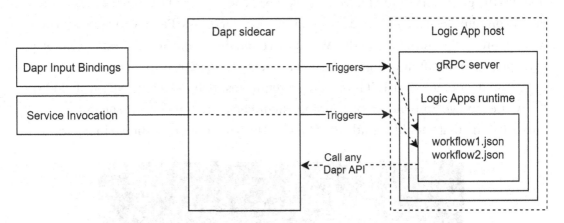

Figure 16-1. *Integration between Dapr and Logic Apps*

You can call the entire Dapr API inside a workflow. It is just a simple HTTP action. Have in mind that at the time of writing, there isn't any custom connector for Dapr that provides Dapr-specific triggers and actions. The triggers are possible because of the gRPC service that implements the `AppCallback` interface needed for communication with Dapr and by raw HTTP requests.

Designing a Workflow

Let me show you how to build a very simple workflow that gets triggered by Dapr service invocation and persists the HTTP body of the request into a state store.

First of all, I should mention the tooling that you can use. Both Visual Studio Code and Visual Studio 2019 have an extension for Azure Logic Apps that makes it easy to visually design a workflow or declaratively edit its JSON definition. Keep in mind that there are slight differences in the support in both places. For example, Visual Studio 2019 expects you to have a fully fledged ARM template containing the Logic Apps workflow in order to be able to open it in the designer. However, for this example, I am going to use the Azure Logic Apps extension for Visual Studio Code, which is currently in preview.

Two projects are required for running workflows with Dapr. You can find them in the source code of the book. The Dapr.Workflows project represents the Logic Apps host that has the gRPC server and loads all workflows. The other project is named Workflows, and it contains the actual JSON definitions of your workflows. Each workflow is placed in a folder under the workflows folder. When you open the Visual Studio Code Explorer, you can open each workflow using the designer that is provided by the extension. Consult the extension documentation as it has a few prerequisites such as having .NET installed and the Azure Storage Emulator to be running. Right-clicking a workflow.json file opens a context menu that should include the Open in Designer option as shown in Figure 16-2.

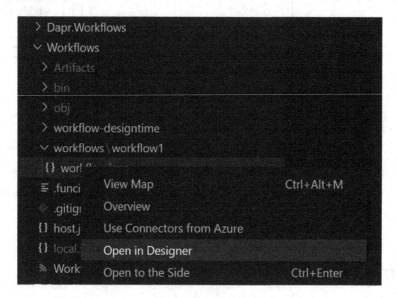

Figure 16-2. *Opening a workflow in the designer*

The workflow itself is very simple. It contains a single HTTP trigger that is actually triggered by the Dapr AppCallback implementation of the Logic Apps host. Once this workflow is triggered, it persists the body of the HTTP request in a state store under the key workflow-state. Opened in the designer, the request to the State API is depicted in Figure 16-3. Then, as a response, the workflow just returns the body that was received by the trigger.

It's time to see this in action. But before starting the project, make sure to update the values of the environment variables that point to an Azure Storage Account for the Dapr.Workflows project. Those environment variables are defined in launchSettings. json. This is currently needed because the state of the workflow is saved in an Azure

Storage Account. This dependency will likely be removed in future versions of the Logic Apps NuGet packages. Note that it won't be possible to use the Azure Storage Emulator; instead, use a real Azure Storage Account.

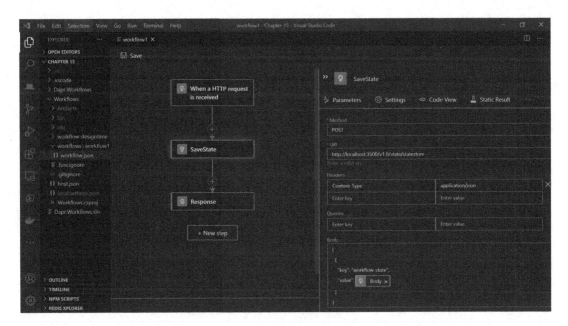

Figure 16-3. *Saving state in Dapr as HTTP action*

You have to make sure that there is a state store component named statestore in the components folder. Now that everything is ready, let's start the Logic Apps host alongside a Dapr sidecar. Make sure the local storage emulator is running and also the environment variables inside launchSettings.json point to a real Azure Storage Account. Open a terminal and navigate to the Dapr.Workflows project directory and run the following command that also includes a flag that points to the folder where the JSON definitions of the workflows can be found and loaded from:

```
dapr run --app-id workflows --app-protocol grpc --dapr-http-port 3500
--app-port 50003 -- dotnet run --workflows-path ..\Workflows\workflows
```

Next, you can trigger the workflow via the Service Invocation building block. You can use your favorite tool for issuing HTTP requests like Postman or cURL. With cURL the request that also passes some JSON content in the HTTP body looks like this:

```
curl -X POST http://localhost:3500/v1.0/invoke/workflows/method/workflow1
-H 'content-type: application/json' -d '{"test": "1234"}'
```

It will return HTTP status code 200 if everything ran properly and the body of the HTTP request was persisted in the state store. To verify this, open your browser at `http://localhost:3500/v1.0/state/statestore/workflow-state` and you will find out.

Summary

Azure Logic Apps offers a powerful way to develop complex workflows that automate business processes. In this chapter, you learned how Dapr and Logic Apps can work together in any environment, except in the cloud as the integration is still in preview. The integration with Dapr makes it possible to define workflows that are triggered by Dapr building blocks such as Service Invocation and Resource Bindings. Additionally, you can call just about any endpoint of the Dapr API. You also learned how to design workflows by using the Logic Apps extension for Visual Studio Code.

Index

© Radoslav Gatev 2021
R. Gatev, *Introducing Distributed Application Runtime (Dapr)*, https://doi.org/10.1007/978-1-4842-6998-5

Printed in the United States
by Baker & Taylor Publisher Services